For Lisa + Josh —
With gratitue
and hope be
the ways you
made this dialogue
deeper and ever
more significant.

Rabbi Jacob
Hanukah 2017

The *Fragile* Dialogue
New Voices of Liberal Zionism

The *Fragile* Dialogue

NEW VOICES OF LIBERAL ZIONISM

Rabbi Stanley M. Davids

& Rabbi Lawrence A. Englander, DHL

EDITORS

CENTRAL CONFERENCE OF AMERICAN RABBIS

RJP, a division of CCAR Press
355 Lexington Avenue, New York, NY 10017
(212) 972-3636
www.ccarpress.org

LIBRARY OF CONGRESS CATALOGING-IN-PUBLICATION DATA
Names: Davids, Stanley M., editor. | Englander, Lawrence A., editor.
Title: The fragile dialogue : new voices of liberal Zionism / Rabbi Stanley
    M. Davids & Rabbi Lawrence A. Englander, DHL, editors.
Description: New York, NY : Central Conference of American Rabbis, [2017] |
    Includes bibliographical references.
Identifiers: LCCN 2017041324 (print) | LCCN 2017042210 (ebook) | ISBN
    9780881233100 | ISBN 9780881233056 (pbk. : alk. paper)
Subjects: LCSH: Zionism. | Israel. | Reform Judaism.
Classification: LCC DS149 (ebook) | LCC DS149 .F67 2018 (print) | DDC
    320.54095694--dc23
LC record available at https://lccn.loc.gov/2017041324

Text design and composition by Scott-Martin Kosofsky
at The Philidor Company, Rhinebeck, NY

Printed in the United States of America.
10 9 8 7 6 5 4 3 2 1

Contents

In the Classroom and on Campus

Conversations across Generations and Continents

Zionism, Liturgy, and Theology

Zionism and *Tikkun*

EDITORS' NOTE

In soliciting the essays for this collection, our goal was to truly create a dialogue. In pursuit of this goal, we cast a wide net within the world of progressive Zionist ideas. As a result, there may be some views expressed within these chapters that you disagree with, or that are troubling. Yet our goal is to demonstrate in as public a way as possible both the need and the possibility of creating a broad tent beneath which liberal Zionists can debate and discuss our differences, and find areas of agreement. We wanted to open up conversation, not shut it down. Not all views represented in this volume are the views of the editors, the editorial advisory group, or the Central Conference of American Rabbis. But we opted for inclusiveness in the strong belief that excluding voices that profoundly trouble us will not be helpful in bringing our world to a better place.

Foreword

RABBI RICK JACOBS

President, Union for Reform Judaism

T HE FRAGILE DIALOGUE: *New Voices of Liberal Zionism* is making its appearance between two significant anniversaries for Zionism and the Jewish people: fifty years since the Six-Day War in 1967 and seventy years since the establishment of the modern State of Israel in 1948. Our tradition teaches that each generation has its unique interpreters; our time—with its blessing and its challenges—demands that we share renewed thinking from the liberal perspective.

While the essays in this powerful book contextualize locations where the dialogue with the Zionist idea seems fragile—for example, on the college campus (Rabbi Leah Cohen), in responding to the tense relationship between Jews and Arabs (Yoav Schaefer), or in how we prioritize our Jewish commitments when Israel is downplayed by some of our movement's most committed young people (Max Chaiken and Eric Rosenstein)—we must remember that Reform Judaism's capacity to effect change in matters related to Israel is much stronger today than it was seventy years ago and even fifty years ago.

What does that strength look like? A few examples: in 2017, Hebrew Union College–Jewish Institute of Religion in Jerusalem has ordained its one hundredth rabbi, the Israel Movement for Reform and Progressive Judaism's more than fifty *k'hilot* have become part of the Israeli mainstream from "Dan to Beersheva," and the population of Reform Jews around the world is growing. Today's Reform Judaism draws strength from being pluralistic and open.

Israel, too, was founded on those values. The diverse collection of voices in this book, in a sense, returns us to the Jewish state's fundamental principles and offers ways to withstand the most significant challenges to Israel's future coming from fundamentalist and hardened ideologies.

Now more than ever, our movement's core values of social justice, inclusion, and openness to Jewish renewal are critical to make real the democratic promise upon which Israel was founded. In June 2017, when the Israeli government reversed its commitment to open an egalitarian prayer space at the Kotel (Western Wall), we saw our activism on behalf of religious pluralism in Israel gain allies from across the Jewish world. Is this not a crucial tipping point for ensuring a vibrant and meaningful Zionism for generations to come? There are so many issues in Israeli society today where our values are needed. As we write this, the debate about gay parental adoption is alive in Israel, with our movement taking the lead against those who use fundamentalist and anti-democratic Judaism as a societal wedge. Racism and overriding questions about Israel's future are urgent—and our rabbis leading Reform Judaism in Israel, most of them now Israeli born and educated, are there to guide and lead our movement.

Cheshbon hanefesh—holding ourselves as Jews accountable to our highest values—is central to the way Judaism understands its relationship with the Divine. If we take *cheshbon hanefesh* seriously, we will always strive to do better; we will constantly redraw the road map that brings truth to what the siddur (prayer book) says about the Torah, that "all its paths are peace." *Cheshbon hanefesh* is, of course, mostly associated with Yom Kippur. Jubilee, *Yoveil*, is marked according to the Torah on Yom Kippur at the end of a fifty-year period. In this fiftieth year since 1967, *The Fragile Dialogue* challenges readers to reflect and to participate in *cheshbon hanefesh* on the peoplehood level. To mark this *Yoveil*, it is fitting then that most essays raise the ongoing challenges of the unresolved Israeli-Palestinian conflict.

Soon after the Six-Day War, the great Israeli poet Yehuda Amichai published a series of poems called "Jerusalem 1967." In poem

5, whose setting is Yom Kippur a few months after Israel's capture of the Old City, East Jerusalem, and the West Bank, Amichai reveals his typical prescience about the significance of historical events and their far-reaching implications. By situating the poem in the late afternoon during *N'ilah* of that Yom Kippur, Amichai suggests that this new relationship between Jew and Arab is going to require *cheshbon hanefesh*:

> On Yom Kippur 5728 I put on
> dark holiday clothing and I walked to the Old City in Jerusalem.
> I stood a long time before a crypt-like shop of an Arab,
> not far from Damascus Gate, a shop of
> buttons and zippers and spools of thread
> in every color, and snaps and buckles.
> A light of splendor and many colors, like an open Holy Ark.
> I said to him in my heart that my father also had
> a shop like this of thread and buttons.
> I explained to him in my heart about all tens of years
> and the factors and events, that I am now here
> and that my father's shop is burned-down there and he is buried here.
> When I finished it was the hour of *N'ilah.*
> He too lowered the shutters and locked the gate
> and I returned home with all the worshipers.
>
> —Yehuda Amichai, "Jerusalem 1967"
> (in *Now in the Storm* [1968], trans. Reuven Greenvald)

It isn't too difficult to imagine that today is the day after Amichai's Yom Kippur, the morning after those gates were shuttered. Inspired by *The Fragile Dialogue*, we call upon Reform Judaism to lead a collective *cheshbon hanefesh* for the Jewish people. Let's begin this new day so that fifty years from now, a book about liberal Zionism will be a book that is truly about triumph and celebration.

Preface

Rabbi Janet Liss

Chair, CCAR Israel Committee

אם תרצו, אין זו אגדה.
If you will it, it is not a dream.
—Theodor Herzl

WHEN THEODOR HERZL wrote these words, he could not have had any idea what the Zionist enterprise would look like over a hundred years later. What is the "it" in today's context? Who is the "you"? Is the envisioned "it" the Israel of today, and if not, how can we help the "it" that we yearn for become reality and not just a dream? Are we, Jews of the Diaspora, included in the "you," or does the "you" just refer to Israelis and those who have made *aliyah*? Throughout the essays presented in *The Fragile Dialogue: New Voices of Liberal Zionism*, you will hear from those who wrestle with Zionism in a postmodern world. This timely and current work grapples with the challenges of our relationship with Israel today in all of its manifestations.

Are we partners with Israel in trying to influence political decisions made in the Knesset that often run counter to our understanding of democracy and Jewish values? Can we publicly voice our dissatisfactions with and criticisms of Israel? How do we understand the concept of "unconditional love" as it relates to Israel? How do we utilize our rich Jewish sources to guide us in our understanding of Israel today? How do we change the old-school Israel narrative that has alienated large swaths of Diaspora Jewry who do not accept Prime Minister Netanyahu's policy of maintaining the status quo? Where are the ideals and aspirations of Israel's Declaration of Independence in Israeli politics? How can we as Reform Jews partner with the Israel Movement for Reform and Progressive Judaism to help bring about the types of changes that are needed in order to reengage with the myriads of Diaspora liberal Jews who have been turned off by decades-old policies of inequality for Israeli Arabs and Palestinians? Where is social justice in Israel's policies and practices? How do we achieve a seat of respect at the powerbroker table in Israel?

How do we talk to our teenagers about Israel? How do we prepare our college-bound students and how do we support our college students as they confront the challenges of powerful oppositional voices on campuses today? How do we engage respectfully with members of our community who do not share our views and encourage open dialogue?

More than ever, reports from the Pew Research Center tell us that Israel is becoming irrelevant for many American Jews. It is imperative that we do not turn our backs on Israel because of its current leadership and policies. It is incumbent upon us to take this challenge on through study, through honest and open dialogue. We need to actively reach out and influence as many people as possible to go to Israel, meet Israelis, and feel the magic of the miracle of our Homeland even as we call Israel to task to achieve its highest aspirations of full equality and democracy for all its inhabitants.

This collection of essays will provide us with an excellent text to open up these discussions, as each essay articulates a different aspect and layer of the conversation. This book will enable us to have meaningful dialogues that hopefully can lead to more engagement with Israel on multiple levels.

The biblical verse "And the old shall dream dreams and the youth shall see visions" (Joel 3:1) reflects our reality today. We are grateful for the early pioneers who believed in the Zionist dream and made Israel a reality, but it is time to move in a direction where younger voices can help us articulate a new vision that will bring Israel back into our conversations. We need a new vision that not only will allow for disparate opinions but will welcome a true partnership between those of us who live in Israel and those who live outside of Israel, recognizing that we all have a stake in both a Jewish democratic state and homeland and the survival of Judaism.

With great pride as a lover of Israel, I commend each of the authors featured in this work and look forward to sharing it, engaging with it, and reaping the benefits of the conversations that it will inspire.

"Without a Vision, a People Will Perish"

RABBI STANLEY M. DAVIDS

> What I tend to see happening more and more is people retreat-
> ing into their own corners. People seem scared to get things
> wrong or be shouted at so they form villages in which they agree
> with every other member, and maybe they go out and shout at
> the people in the next village for fun, but there's no interchange
> of ideas going on. I think we have to encourage the idea that
> you're allowed to think things. I have thought a great many stu-
> pid things over the years, and I can tell you that there's not one
> stupid thing that I have ever thought where I changed my mind
> because someone shouted at me or threatened to kill me.[1]

THIS MAY BE the first time that one of my all-time favorite
science fiction and fantasy writers has ever been quoted in a
volume dedicated to an exploration of twenty-first-century Progressive Religious Zionism. But very few of the default scholars of North
American Jewish life have better described the current situation of
internal discourse regarding our relationships with and our commitment to the State of Israel, even if Neil Gaiman did not at all have
Zionism in mind.

Far too often we do in fact shout at each other. We delegitimize
each other. We scorn each other. We exclude our ideological others
from those public platforms that, one way or another, we happen
to control. Or we retreat to our own little villages, preferring not to
get engaged with what has become a conversation as fraught as it is
important.

Losing the Ability to Speak Comfortably with Each Other
In February 2016, Frank Luntz, a specialist in market research, a
highly regarded national pollster, and a consultant to the Republican

Party, was invited to address a large gathering of student leaders of the Alpha Epsilon Pi Fraternity. Luntz had the assigned task of helping to guide these passionately committed Jewish young men in their campus battles against the BDS (Boycott, Divestment, Sanctions) movement. One of his strongest suggestions to our future communal leaders that day was that they stop using "Zionism" in their debates. The word is too confusing; it is too little understood. It carries too much negative baggage. It calls to mind descriptives such as radicalism and extremism. Should the students talk about Jews? Yes. Should they talk about Israel? Yes. But please don't mention Zionism!

In the 1990s, when I was serving as national chair of the Association of Reform Zionists of America (ARZA), we hired a marketing consultant to help us better promote the ARZA brand among Reform congregations. The consultant came back with a variety of suggestions, a few of which we even found useful. But one suggestion in particular deeply troubled us. We were advised to stop breaking the acronym ARZA down into its constituent words in our marketing materials. Why? Because when people see the word "Zionists" they get turned off. We refused the expensive advice, but the message still rankled. Had we truly come to a point in our people's history when the very mention of the word most commonly associated with the rebirth of Jewish sovereignty not only has lost its attraction, but has become a trigger for negative response among Jews?

Zionism, most especially the socialist expression of Zionism, was born out of endless dialogue and debate. Disagreements and public debate in Judaism in fact date back to Hillel and Shammai, if not earlier. And those disagreements sometimes focused on matters of life and death. But famously, the members of the schools of Hillel and Shammai met with each other in the *beit midrash* (study house) to conduct those debates. They spoke with and to each other. And despite profound ideological differences, in practice the families of those scholars were often connected through marriage. Their debates were characterized as *l'shem shamayim*—for the sake of heaven. And very often they were summarized under the rubric of *eilu v'eilu divrei Elohim chayim*: no matter the depth of their disagreement, both sides are expressing divine intentions.[2]

We have traveled great distances since that time. At various moments in our history we have even chosen to manipulate the foreign powers, under whose governance and through whose tolerance we were allowed to maintain our communities, to take sides in our internal disputes. The battles between the Orthodoxy of the eighteenth century and rising Chasidism were often decided by one side or another having recourse to secular authorities. The birth of Reform Judaism in the nineteenth century was similarly scarred by our ideological opponents seeking to make our undertakings illegal under secular law, so that they might then be banned under threat of criminal penalties.

In the twenty-first century, though the means we choose are different, we seem increasingly to be turning our backs on *eilu v'eilu* in favor of tone-deaf confrontation when matters of Israel and of Zionism are being considered. And not just confrontation, but exclusion as well. Should we allow J Street to be considered a Zionist organization or not? Should it be admitted into membership of the Conference of Presidents of Major American Jewish Organizations, or is J Street as bad as Israel's current permanent delegate to the United Nations, Danny Danon, has claimed?[3] Is the right-wing Zionist Organization of America, once a profoundly respected voice of Zionism, still to be considered mainstream enough to be included in public debates? Should individual campus Hillel organizations have the right to invite speakers to their forums who are supportive of BDS?

Even more complicated is the reality that BDS itself comes in many different forms. Can one be an actively committed supporter of the existence of a Jewish democratic state and yet also support one form or another of BDS? And on the flip side, can one still be welcomed within the community of Liberal Religious Zionists while supporting a future somewhere in between a one-state and a two-state solution?

Should an Israeli member of the Knesset (MK) who is a strong supporter of settlement expansion in the Occupied Territories be treated respectfully and be warmly welcomed when she visits our North American communities? What about embracing an MK who voted to deny entry into Israel by anyone who is on record as supporting BDS? Do we need to listen to voices that would lay out a scenario in which not all of Israel's actions in the War of Independence were above severe reproach?[4] Were there really times when the Arab inhabitants of Palestine were invisible to the eyes of the Zionist pioneers? Is that still true today? I suspect it is.

The disagreements, the epic and bitter and at times hate-filled intra-Jewish arguments over the Obama administration's agreement (known formally as the Joint Comprehensive Plan of Action) that sought to limit Iran's capacity for nuclear proliferation, only brought new reasons for Jews to set aside the need for respectful and potentially productive dialogue. These disagreements helped shape the choices of some during the 2016 presidential election. They also opened yet deeper fissures within the "organized" Jewish community.

Dr. Micah Goodman, a research fellow at the Shalom Hartman Institute in Jerusalem, was sadly correct when he noted in a lecture in Los Angeles in February 2017 that "the last great moment of unity of the Jewish people was immediately before the beginning of the Six-Day War." Dr. Kenneth Stein of Emory University has often referred to that war as a "legacy moment" in Jewish history.

Do We Need Safe Spaces?

It was during the Iran debates that conversations about the need to find safe spaces[5] within which reasoned and respectful discussions and debates could be carried out began to proliferate. A safe space in this context is understood to be a setting within which people can come together with widely divergent thoughts, feelings, and perspectives regarding Israel and Zionism and participants can know that there are others who, though they may differ dramatically, will still be willing to listen, to think, and to thoughtfully respond. Within such safe spaces, be they Jewish community forums, synagogue discussion groups, or salon-like gatherings in private homes, personal attacks are set aside, and the grip over rigidly held positions is loosened enough for both hearing and listening to be possible.[6]

It is reasonable to dream, to be *aserai tikvah*, "prisoners of hope," that through the productive use of such safe spaces the North American Jewish community can begin to model the rebirth of civility and the rebuilding of internal dialogue out of which the richness of Jewish life once emerged and upon which our very future might depend.

Those responsible for this volume, its editors and its authors, believe that such a fragile dialogue is vitally necessary. We have come together to try to be of assistance to all of those willing to try.

Genesis

There is no need to review here the well-known Pew surveys of American Jewish life that have brought uncomfortable clarity as to how Jews practice, what their domestic political proclivities might be, how they understand the very nature of their Jewish identity, the role (or lack of same) of denominational differences, attitudes toward marriages between Jews and non-Jews—and to what extent, if any, Israel and Zionism should help define the nature of Jewish identity in the twenty-first century. Those Pew studies, especially as they relate to millennials and the State of Israel, have given the North American Jewish community new data, new images, new metaphors—and new reasons to worry.

Responses to the Pew research, layered over by the bitterness and divisiveness that now accompany our diverse perspectives as to how Israel is responding to a daunting array of domestic and foreign challenges, have helped stimulate the spread of hardened, dogmatic attitudes as to who is to blame, how matters can be improved, how we should balance our ethnic in-groupness with the demands of our universalistic prophetic tradition, and why we should even bother to care.

Some North American Jews may battle alongside Women of the Wall; others may not understand why such a struggle even matters. Some may vigorously work to disestablish the Israeli chief rabbinate and its vast array of often corrupt intrusions into the rights of Israeli citizens to marry as they choose, divorce as they choose, convert as they choose, or simply not be involved as they choose; others may find the entire subject so medieval and repugnant that they want nothing to do with the Jewish state. Some American Jews might choose to apply a cost-benefit analysis to holding on to nationalism in what they view as a post-nationalist world. For them, Zionism is out of step with the world as we know it.

In both the General Assembly and in various committees, member nations of the UN regularly condemn the Israeli Occupation of the West Bank (or Judea and Samaria), spicing their relentless critique with a bitter and dangerous anti-Semitism masked as anti-Zionism. Can anyone be surprised that for too many of us the default response to such abuse would be to try to distance ourselves from Israel?

Is it even appropriate for Jewish non-Israeli citizens to criticize actions of the Israeli government? Aren't Israelis the only ones who must live with decisions about one state or two states, about whether Palestinians ought to have a right of return or not, about whether to repeat on the West Bank the high-minded but ultimately very controversial unilateral Israeli Gaza withdrawal—which led to thousands of rockets raining upon Israel?

In 2017 it has become accepted doctrine in many quarters that acts of violent anti-Semitism, anti-Zionism, and the more usual noxious blend of both have increased in the United States and across Europe. Along with all of our confusion about contemporary Jewish identity, we are again being reminded that it is still dangerous to be a Jew. Wouldn't we be better off setting aside all of that which Zionism seems to represent, all of its dividing of both our larger world and our smaller world into us-versus-them categories so that we can fit more easily, invisibly, safely, into the comfortable stereotypes as to what being a part of North American culture is alleged to mean?

This requires some very serious conversation.

How Did We Get to This Point?

The first official definition of Zionist commitment for American Reform Jews is embodied in the original ARZA platform.[7] In that platform, ARZA described itself as "a religious Zionist body" and declared that ARZA "was created out of the recognition that in our tradition there is no division between the religious domain and the polity of the Jewish people."[8]

In June 1989, the Central Conference of American Rabbis (CCAR) adopted a resolution calling for the creation of a Reform[9] Zionist think tank. The first gathering of that think tank was held at the Harrison Conference Center in Glen Cove, New York. The co-chairs were Rabbi Leon Jick, z"l, Constance Kreshtool, and myself, with the professional guidance of ARZA's executive director, Rabbi Ammiel Hirsch. The rich and highly productive papers from that gathering were published in the *Journal of Reform Zionism*,[10] which was accompanied by a study guide.[11] Following the second gathering of the Reform Zionist Think Tank at the Hotel Thayer at West Point, volume 2 of the *Journal of Reform Zionism* was published.[12]

As a direct result of the think tanks and of the journals, the CCAR adopted its historic platform on Reform Zionism (see p. 271).[13] Among the most significant statements in that platform was a declaration that *aliyah* (establishing a home in Israel) is a Reform mitzvah (a religious obligation) and that the serious study of the Hebrew language is a vital aspect of Zionist commitment.

Sadly, platforms alone did not suffice to greatly alter the nature of Reform Zionist commitment. At the end of the day, very little actually changed on the ground. In similar fashion, the much-ballyhooed agreement[14] between Israeli prime minister David Ben-Gurion and American Jewish Committee president Jacob Blaustein that sought to permanently resolve who speaks on behalf of world Jewry failed to achieve its stated purposes. In the real world, words and platforms and declarations are simply not enough.

We are therefore being challenged time and again to drill down to what it really means—in deeds, not just in statements—to be a Zionist in a world within which the Zionist dream was supposedly fulfilled with the establishment of the State of Israel in 1948.

The stage was thus set for the publication of my article entitled "A Proposed Taxonomy for a Twenty-First-Century Theology of Reform Zionism."[15] That article tried to assemble and to clarify the most challenging questions that Reform Jewish Zionists must confront in the evolving reality of the modern Jewish state. Those questions included the following:

- What does it mean to long for something that already exists?
- Can Jewish nationalism thrive in an America increasingly committed to a celebration of the individual?
- Can a Reform Zionism raise *aliyah* to the category of mitzvah?
- To what extent is the Hebrew language a necessary part of the Reform Jewish theological encounter with the Land?
- Is there a geographical center to Jewish life?
- Where, then, are God and *k'dushah* (holiness) in our twenty-first-century Reform Zionist theology?

And now, a decade later, feeling the extraordinary pressure of rapidly changing geopolitical, psychosociological, and demographic facts on the ground, Rabbi Lawrence A. Englander[16] and I, under the inspired guidance of Rabbi Hara Person of the CCAR Press, have brought together a creative and diverse group of scholars, students, educators, and political activists to address these and other questions.

What Do We Hope to Achieve?

1. In the face of increasingly angry voices, calling out their truths with no intention whatsoever of actually engaging with others in thoughtful, productive, and meaningful conversation, we mean this book to model how liberal Jewish religious Zionists with dramatically differing perspectives can speak with each other safely, with no fear of intimidation, with no effort to judge or to exclude.

2. Rabbi Dr. Donniel Hartman of the Shalom Hartman
   Institute was among the first to begin speaking seriously
   about the increasing manner in which the Jewish people
   is afflicted by tribalism: Those Jews for whom Israel is a
   significant part of their identities and those for whom it is
   not. *Separate tribes.* Those for whom a national identity is
   felt to bring great personal benefit and those for whom it
   does not. *Separate tribes.* Those who bear personal responsibility for the meaningful survival of the Jewish people
   and those who do not. *Separate tribes.* Diaspora Jews and
   Israeli Jews. *Separate tribes.*

     It is our hope that readers of this book will feel called
   upon to examine just what it would really mean if their
   particular threads were removed from the tapestry of
   Jewish life. What impact would such separation have
   both upon the individual and upon the collective? What
   significant value might be derived from lowering the level
   of our rhetoric and simultaneously enhancing our desire
   to rediscover the dreams of Jewish unity? And why should
   anyone care? We would like to point the reader's way
   toward caring.

3. The year 2017 represents an interesting array of special
   dates. In 1897, 120 years ago, the First World Zionist Congress was convened in Basel, Switzerland. On November
   2, 1917, one hundred years ago, the Balfour Declaration
   was issued. On November 29, 1947, seventy years ago, the
   UN Partition Plan was approved. On June 5, 1967, fifty
   years ago, the Six-Day War began. It is our hope that such
   a confluence of significant dates will provide an additional
   impetus, now and into the future, for significant conversations about the meaning of Reform Religious Zionism
   to be undertaken at the interpersonal as well as on the
   communal level, among undergrads, Gen Xers, millennials, baby boomers, and everyone else. We intend this book
   to serve as a solid foundation for those conversations.

What This Book Is and Is Not

- This book *is not* intended to subtly guide the reader to the "correct" conclusions.
- It *is* intended to guide the perplexed.[17]

There is a certain order to the various chapters. Some of our authors discuss the theories and the philosophies of Zionism. In those chapters the reader will discover mythos and hard historical reality, combining to help us grapple with Reform Zionism as a system (albeit a somewhat chaotic system) of thought. From where do Zionist dreams emerge? Have we fulfilled those dreams or have we abused them into unrecognizable forms?

It seems obvious to all that our day schools, afternoon schools, youth groups, and adult education classes have, in the main, failed in their efforts not just to teach the facts about Israel, but to drill far more deeply into why it is that any of us should care. Students of all ages complain that our Israel-oriented education lacks nuance, far too often opting for a black-and-white presentation of the issues at hand: There are good folks and bad folks, and it is always easy to differentiate between the two. The War of Independence and the Six-Day War were occasions of messianic fulfillment—even if the "other side" views those same occurrences as a profound disaster or cataclysm (Nakba). Or not.

It is often that lack of nuance in how we teach that leaves our college-age students totally unprepared for what they encounter on their campuses. Loading our students up with more *hasbarah* (propaganda materials) will not make them better communicators.

Can we bring nuance and ambiguity into our educational processes, or does any perceived "softening" of our approach give succor to those who still hold that Reform Jews cannot truly be Zionists?

Reform Zionism is far more than a political undertaking. It is far more than a religious undertaking. It is far more than rectifying the past or building walls of protection against an unknown future.

Reform Zionism can and should be one of the primary means for the Jewish people to become engaged in *tikkun*, in perfecting our world. From the time of the prophets to our own day, we Jews have proclaimed our desire to become *l'or goyim*, "a light unto the nations" (Isaiah 42:6, 49:6). Can and should our Zionism embrace social justice, economic justice, racial and gender justice, educational justice? Should protection of the physical environment of M'dinat Yisrael (the State of Israel) be a religious mandate or just another token bow to liberal values? Is actively seeking peace a Reform Zionist mandate or just another means of attacking Israelis for having (in the eyes of some) trampled upon Palestinians' human dignity?

Reform Judaism has a sometimes dizzying array of theologies and philosophies, seeking to inspire, to guide, to explain the sources of meaning in our lives. If God is indifferent to our individual and/or collective lives, is there any meaning at all to mitzvah—let alone a mitzvah that would bind us together in passionate support of the Jewish state? If we are in covenant with God, does that covenant truly enhance our peoplehood as well as our humanity? Can that covenant make demands upon us? Can it guide us to new understandings of freedom? Is peoplehood less a matter of religious and national commitment than it is a component of our psychological well-being?

Our Reform Judaism, our institutions and our programs, have not served well in igniting the passions of peoplehood in our midst. Indeed, some rabbis no longer actively involve themselves in matters connected to Israel because they see their time better dedicated to "more significant" issues (please note Chaiken and Rosenstein, p. 105), or else they shy away from the topic because it has become a third rail. Most of us understand true caring as an active caring, not just a set of well-intentioned emojis that claim to express feelings that are often less than skin-deep. Why have we not done better? Or are we already doing more than we should?

And finally, is there a shared path to the future, and will Israeli Jews and American Jews, liberal Jews and conservative Jews, angry Jews and satisfied Jews, disinterested Jews and passionately committed Jews find a way toward the future that we might all want to walk together?

All of those topics will be addressed. But what the reader will not find here is a set of answers. Not because the world is not awash with answers, not because the editors and authors don't have their own answers, but far more important than *our* answers will be the process of open and respectful, thoughtful and nondogmatic conversations conducted by individuals, by organizations, and by communities that provide safe places within which the full diversity of Jewish thought and opinion regarding Reform Religious Zionism will be welcomed and rationally debated.

Tzei ul'mad. Go forth and study. Let the conversations begin.

◎ ◎ ◎

HaRav Kook, the first Ashkenazi chief rabbi of British Mandatory Palestine, is said to have taught that the Land of Israel does not *belong* to the Jewish people, but rather it is an *organic part* of who we are. We believe that to be the case.

Proverbs 29:18 poignantly reminds us that without a vision, a people will perish. We believe that to be the case.

We welcome our readers and those whose lives they touch to this fragile dialogue.

Notes

1. Neil Gaiman, interview by Tyler Malone, "Neil Gaiman on Making Art, Mistakes and His 'View from the Cheap Seats,'" *Los Angeles Times*, June 24, 2016, http://www.latimes.com/books/jacketcopy/la-ca-jc-neil-gaiman-20160616-snap-story.html.
2. BT *Eiruvin* 13b.
3. I attended a Knesset committee meeting chaired by Danon while he served as chair of the Diaspora Affairs Committee, during which he condemned J Street as an anti-Israel, anti-Zionist organization.
4. I strongly recommend reading *My Promised Land*, by Ari Shavit. Personal matters regarding the author aside, the text is solidly constructed. It would also be useful to then read Yossi Klein Halevi's *Like Dreamers*.
5. The term "safe spaces" currently conveys two very different notions. On college campuses, the demand for a safe space is often a plea that campuses should *not* be places where students are forced to confront ideas with which

they are not comfortable. In our use, a safe space is meant to indicate a setting that welcomes open, honest sharing of divergent viewpoints.

6. I strongly recommend exploration of what is called a "Jeffersonian Dinner
   Discussion" as one possible model. The concept emerged out of dinners
   originally held by President Thomas Jefferson at Monticello. Today, such
   dinners are being widely promoted.

7. Adopted by ARZA's First National Assembly in Washington, DC, September 16, 1978.

8. Ibid.

9. Across the world, "Reform" Zionism, "Progressive" Zionism, and "Liberal"
   Zionism are basically synonymous. The Israeli Reform Movement has now
   renamed itself the Israel Movement for Reform and Progressive Judaism.
   In North America, we overwhelmingly opt for "Reform," as in the Union
   for Reform Judaism (URJ). We want to emphasize this point so that our colleagues and partners across the globe will fully understand that we intend to
   embrace them in this project. We are one family.

10. *Journal of Reform Zionism*, March 1993; New York; Naomi Patz, editor.

11. *Journal of Reform Zionism*, September 1993; New York; Mindy Davids and
    Rabbi Ronn Davids, authors.

12. *Journal of Reform Zionism*, March 1995; New York; Naomi Patz, editor.

13. June 24, 1997; Miami, http://ccarnet.org/rabbis-speak/platforms/reform-
    judaism-zionism-centenary-platform/.

14. More correctly, an exchange of statements made on August 23, 1950.

15. Rabbi Stanley M. Davids, "A Proposed Taxonomy for a Twenty-First-
    Century Theology of Reform Zionism," *CCAR Journal* (Spring 2007): 27–41.

16. Besides being president of ARZENU and a distinguished scholar and con-
    gregational leader in his own right, Rabbi Englander has been my *chevruta*
    (study partner) at the Shalom Hartman Institute for many years.

17. With a myriad of apologies to Maimonides!

Acknowledgments

I T WAS RABBI LEON KRONISH, *z"l*, who many years ago brought me into the world of Zionist thought and Zionist action. Rabbi Richard Hirsch remains an inspiration and a source of strength. Rabbi Ammiel Hirsch and Rabbi Daniel Allen, who each served as ARZA's Executive Directors during my period of leadership, and Rabbi Gilad Kariv, Executive Director of the Israel Movement for Reform and Progressive Judaism, guided my practical education in the rough and tumble of Zionist politics. Yaron Shavit, former chair of the IMPJ, is one of the true giants of Reform religious Zionism in Israel. Rabbi Ira Youdovin, ARZA's first Executive Director and a precious friend, taught me the history of our undertakings and remains a constant goad when he feels that my love of Zion needs to be revitalized.

Two years ago Dr. Barry Silverman, a member of the Hevra Torah that I lead at University Synagogue in Los Angeles, had heard that I was dreaming of this book. He made a generous gift to help in marketing *The Fragile Dialogue* before any contracts were signed, before any words were written. His faith in me is deeply appreciated.

I have been in love with my people and with its dreams and aspirations in the State of Israel for as long as I can remember. But that passion would have lain fallow had I not discovered in my wife, Resa, not only someone who shared my dreams, someone who would be my partner in every undertaking—but someone whose own enormous skills in leadership expressed through the Women of Reform Judaism would make her a heroine of Zionism in her own right. The lives of our children, Rabbi Ronn Davids (and Nicole), Shoshana Dweck and Aviva Levin (and Jason), have been profoundly shaped by their many extended experiences in Israel, and they have each found meaningful pathways to their own forms of Zionist commitment.

This book is dedicated to those who will need it the most, my grandchildren: Elizabeth and Hannah Davids; James (J.J.), Joshua, and Gabriel Dweck; Zeke, Mya, and Cole Levin. I pray that the love of Zion, the love of the Jewish people, and the love of the Torah of Israel and of the God of Israel will flourish in their hearts and in their deeds.

It has been an incredibly rewarding experience to work with my friend and colleague Rabbi Lawrence Englander, on this volume. Ours was a partnership based upon mutual respect and a shared passion for Reform/Progressive religious Zionism. We both owe not only an extraordinary debt of gratitude to the scholars and teachers and activists and students who wrote the various chapters of *The Fragile Dialogue*, but we are in awe of their integrity and thoughtfulness. Their lives, their words, prove that carrying forward a fragile dialogue not only is absolutely necessary—but it is also possible.

—RABBI STANLEY M. DAVIDS

✳ ✳ ✳

Zionism was a consistent part of my upbringing. My parents, although they had not yet visited Israel, always spoke fondly about it and kept up with the news. In my third-grade Hebrew classroom at *talmud Torah*, I still remember the photograph of Yitzchak Ben-Tzvi that presided over us from his perch on the wall.

My own first visit to Israel came in 1970 as a first-year rabbinical student at Hebrew Union College. Michael Klein, *z"l*, the Assistant Dean, led *tiyulim* from stem to stern of the country and conveyed not only his thorough knowledge of the land but also his deep love for it.

The next quantum leap for me was when I joined ARZENU, the international Reform Zionist organization, through the persuasion of my friend and fellow Zionist Les Rothschild. My predecessor as Chair of ARZENU is Joan Garson, who served as my mentor in putting our Progressive Religious Zionist theory into practice in the

Israeli National Institutions. Her keen insight and her indefatigable energy continue to be an inspiration to me.

My wife Cheryl preceded me in organizational Zionist work in her role as Executive member of ARZA Canada. She and I have spent a total of close to three years in Israel; her love for the people has been a constant motivation for me in pursuing my work. My work with the ARZENU Executive and Board members has been extremely rewarding, and I thank each of them for their dedication and wisdom. In particular, our Executive Director, Dalya Levy, has been a one-person encyclopaedia of information and a bulwark of strength during challenging times—and even more, a dear friend.

During the past few years I have also become acquainted with an Israeli team, some holding professional positions and some serving as volunteers. These individuals are too numerous to mention, but each of them brings a unique blend of background and talent to our work; and all share a deep commitment to building a democratic and pluralistic Israel that will make us all proud. My gratitude to them goes beyond words.

I first got to know Rabbi Stanley Davids during our *chevruta* studies at the Hartman Institute. I encountered a man who could not only decipher complicated texts but could also apply their teachings to Israeli society today. His passion for a renewed Zionism has been the driving force behind this volume and I am deeply honored to be his sidekick.

—RABBI LAWRENCE A. ENGLANDER

And nothing would have been achieved without the superb professional guidance of Rabbi Hara Person, Publisher of the CCAR Press. Her wisdom and her commitment to this project are deeply appreciated. We thank Rabbi Hara Person, Rabbi Steve Fox, and the whole CCAR for their confidence in our endeavor. We are grateful to the staff of the Press, including Ortal Bensky, Debbie Smilow, Sasha Smith, Rabbi Dan Medwin, and Carly Linden, as well as copyeditor Debra Hirsch Corman and designer Scott-Martin Kosofsky. We extend our deepest gratitude to the advisory board who helped us develop this book and whose feedback was so important, as well all the authors who have contributed to this dialogue. Our best way to acknowledge them is to let their words jump off the pages into lively discussions among our readers. That privilege we now place into your hands.

Zionist Theory and Zionist Politics

Myths and Facts
Zionism and Reform Judaism

Rabbi Michael Marmur

SOME DECADES AGO, Israeli embassies around the world used to distribute a pamphlet entitled *Myths and Facts*. It set out all a young Israel activist needed to know in two columns, somewhat like the blessings and curses ranged against each other on two mountains described in the Book of Deuteronomy. On one side of the page were the "myths," libelous calumnies perpetrated and disseminated by Israel's enemies. The "facts" of the case were presented on the other side of the page. Here we were reminded that Israel is a peace-seeking beacon of democracy surrounded by bellicose adversaries. The booklet allowed no space for ambivalence or complexity. Rather, the power of facts was prescribed as an antidote to the poison of myth.

As the years have passed, my views about the meaning of myths and facts have changed. A myth is not a lie. It is usually a story, a way of marshaling experiences and memories and attitudes. Myths are not the opposite of facts, but rather the way in which we prioritize and deploy them, in order to serve a communal or personal need, to explain a mystery, or to bridge a gulf between what seems to be happening and what I believe must be the truth. It would be nice to believe that people who believe what I believe walk by the clear light of the truth, while those who believe something different are condemned to stumble around in the gloom. This is not my understanding of the way things actually are in the world.

I do not espouse a point of view according to which everything is simply a question of your point of view. We live in a period of history in which Big Lies have been disseminated with genocidal consequences. Lies should be exposed and resisted. But for every lie out there in the world, every gruesome fabrication designed to deceive, there are a hundred "facts," presentations of reality that have been squeezed into a myth in order to make sense of the world.

Is it a myth or a fact that Israelis and Palestinians are prepared to negotiate a two-state solution? Those in favor of such a solution point out that despite terrible circumstances, surveys suggest that a majority of people on both sides still express this preference. Those dead set against this eventuality insist that such "surveys" are part of an attempt to encourage appeasement and eventual destruction. Simply considering the facts of the case will not settle the debate, because it all depends on how you prioritize and consider those facts. On both sides of this debate, we are acutely aware of the myths perpetrated by the other, and usually we are oblivious to our own myths. The facts we consider to be incontrovertible live within myths, narrative frameworks. Is the story of the Binding of Isaac the tale of a delusional father on the verge of homicide or that of a hero of monotheism ultimately oriented to the ethical?

Rather than see everything in terms of an epic battle between truth and falsehood, we might do better to become more aware of the different stories we tell each other, the myths into which we pour our facts. To believe that my myth is the only true one on the market is improbable and arrogant. I reject the possibility that everyone who puts the world together differently than I do is a rogue or a fool. Truth may be rare (a Rabbinic tradition points out that the Hebrew word for truth, *emet*, is made up of letters of the alphabet as far away from each other as possible), but I strongly believe there is more than one myth capable of expressing it. This makes me a pluralist.

When myths clash, the result can be volatile. The State of Israel provides a classic example. Is 1948 the "flowering of redemption" or the "great disaster"? Is 1967 about reunification or occupation? Is Israel a symbol of repression of national rights or protection of national rights? In recent years the gulf between the different versions of the facts seems to be growing still wider, as can be witnessed on university campuses around the world. Which version of what is taking place in Israel/Palestine do you accept? The Tibi version (Ahmed Tibi is a Palestinian member of Israel's Knesset) or the Bibi version (named for Prime Minister Netanyahu)? Is your prism that of BA (B'nei Akiva, an Orthodox Zionist youth movement), or of the BBC, or of BDS?

While it has not been as bitter or as violent as that clash of narratives, the discourse between Reform Judaism and Zionism can be understood as a case of competing myths. Both movements rose to prominence in the nineteenth century, each striving to offer a response to the dizzying challenges of modernity. From the start, each tended to regard the other with a degree of suspicion and a marked lack of sympathy. For many classical Reformers, the idea of a rampant nationalism seemed the very antithesis of their most cherished values. In the Zionist camp, meanwhile, Reform was often portrayed as tepid assimilationism incapable of engendering deep Jewish commitment.

In 1916 an article appeared in the American *Jewish Chronicle*.[1] Its author, David Neumark, was a member of the faculty of the Hebrew Union College, having been brought to the faculty as an expert in Jewish philosophy. Before coming to America (he was born in Galicia and had been living in Germany), Neumark had been involved both in the Reform Movement and in the movement for Hebrew national revival. As part of these activities he had become acquainted with Asher Ginzberg, known by his pen name Achad HaAm, the leader of what was often known as cultural Zionism.

In his 1916 article, Neumark attempted to resolve and harmonize the apparent conflict beween Zionism and Reform Judaism. His proposed solution was startling: "In fact, all modern Zionists, except, perhaps, a very few who may not be religious at all, are good reform Jews."[2] It is perhaps not surprising that Neumark's essay was met by a stern rejoinder from Achad HaAm himself, who used a very similar form of logic to reach the opposite conclusion. Anyone inspecting the theological claims of the Reform Movement, he argued, would soon appreciate how flimsy and unconvincing they were. So there must be another reason to explain the commitment of these well-meaning if misguided Jews to the project of Jewish life. He proposed that the Reformers were in fact Jewish Nationalists, however much some of them attempted to deny the fact.

A century ago these Reform Jews and Zionists were attempting to squeeze the others' facts into their own myths. "You're really Reform; you just haven't realized it!" "You are a Zionist after all!" This is hardly an example of meaningful discourse. It is instead a kind of name-calling. Rather than insult the other, we accuse them of being something they did not wish to be. You may think you are someone, we say to the other, but in fact you are just like me—you just never knew it.

I am a Reform Jew who has chosen to make his life in Israel. As such, I am the product of two heady myths. Reform Judaism is predicated on the notion that modernity is a fact of life and that we Jews have to come up with a way of responding to it. We believe that if we hold up the finest of our Jewish tradition to the light of modernity, we will be able to examine, further, and refine a Judaism robust and relevant enough to be passed on to our children.

I live in Israel, a land of potent myths. Here, so the story goes, millennia of wandering have come to an end, and Hebrew culture can be embodied and enacted. Here the Jews can live as an *am olam*, a particular people with a strong universal orientation. Here the values of humanity and compassion can live alongside a vigorous nationalism. This, at least, was the vision on offer in *Exodus* (the Hollywood movie, rather than the book of the Bible), gleaming in Paul Newman's bright blue eyes.

In recent years, the myths of classical Reform and classical Zionism have been in decline. It is painful and uncomfortable to face up to this, and perhaps for that reason we sometimes greet examples of hatred from our opponents with something like relief. When someone crazy does something crazy to a worshiper at the Western Wall, when a university campus seethes with vitriol, when we encounter some old-fashioned anti-Semitism, when a nuclear neighbor calls for our destruction—in these and other cases we are excused from having to think in a nuanced way about our own narrative. The dictates of survival surpass the imperative of self-examination.

But such self-examination is in fact crucial. It is difficult to avoid two extreme aspects of ideological discourse. One is arm wrestling, as exemplified by the 1916 correspondence noted above. We show that our approach is in fact the dominant one, and even if we appease our adversaries, we are in fact attempting to defeat them. Another extreme response is breast-beating. We become hyperaware of the shortcomings and hypocrisies of our own side and reject previously held beliefs with the zeal of the convert.

There is a third way, however difficult it is to find, that runs between arm wrestling and breast-beating. It might be called soul-searching. It calls us to take a look at our own declarations and see how they hold up in reality. Here are just a couple of examples. Many Reform Jews still adhere to the notion of informed choice, according to which each autonomous individual attains a level of education on ritual and other matters and can make decisions on their own practice based on this erudition. In my view, an honest appraisal of this approach will compel us to look for an alternative currency for decision-making and commitment.

To maintain that what we should do, that what we in fact do, is send every possible mitzvah to the laboratory for forensic examination before deciding whether it is to be adopted is fanciful. For some, this means abandoning the project of non-Orthodox Judaism. For others such as me, this heralds its next chapter. In my example of the mitzvah laboratory, we should look to our communities as arenas for growth and experimentation based on our commitment to each other and the dynamism of Jewish tradition. Perhaps the next iteration of informed choice would involve communities—synagogues or small groups of individuals—agreeing to take on certain activities for a year, experiencing and learning together, and then discussing the long-term resonance and applicability of these mitzvot in the lives of each individual.

Tens of thousands of Israeli youngsters travel to Poland each year, where a certain version of the Jewish experience is presented to them. Wrapped in the Israeli flag, our children walk through the death camps (often accompanied by their Diaspora contemporaries) and are expected to return home motivated to defend the motherland. We have to find another story to tell our children, one that does not root a philosophy of life in a collective memory of death.

In Israel we rehearse our founding myths regularly, and they form part of the civil religion of the state. To proceed to Israel's next stage of maturity, it is necessary to acknowledge the dreams and narratives of our Palestinian neighbors and fellow citizens. What to do with all these conflicting myths, so many facts and truths all shouted out simultaneously? What we mark as Independence Day is seen by Palestinians as the Day of Disaster (Nakba). Some in Israeli government circles have proposed that any mention of this competing Nakba narrative be suppressed. A law passed in 2011 gives the finance minister the right to withhold funds to organizations that refuse to see Independence Day as a cause for unalloyed rejoicing. I believe that the strategy of denial is doomed. We will need to find ways of acknowledging that our neighbor's myths are as real as our own, even if they seem to be at odds with each other.

Each of us should be encouraged to confront the problematic elements of our own myths and to be attentive to the power of the myths of the other. Those of us enamored of the views currently dominating Israeli politics should ask ourselves if in fact we have no potential partner for negotiation; if in fact our army is the most ethical in the world; if there are in fact palatable alternatives to a two-state solution, and where settlement activity is actually leading. Left-leaning Zionists should ask themselves if the current state of the Middle East allows for the kind of peace process they dream of, if the idea that we can be both a military and an ethical superpower has any grounding in reality. And they might also wonder why the solutions they offer are not currently favored by the majority of Israeli citizens.

Reform Jews have some soul-searching to do as well. I have mentioned the axiom of informed choice, and there are others that also bear serious examination. We offer our adherents a Judaism of meaning—moments of transcendence and affirmation—but it is not clear that the worldview underpinning this approach can provide what the anthropologists called "thick" experience. When summer camp is over and everyday life resumes, is our Judaism engaging and fulfilling enough?

Classical secular Zionism and Reform Judaism have much in common, and an honest encounter between the two may yield important and creative results. Zionism's emphasis on Jewish peoplehood can influence and yet also be tempered by Reform's awareness of the dangers of chauvinism. Reform's openness to the spiritual and ritual domains can influence and yet also be tempered by Zionism's engagement with the gritty realities of building a functioning society. We need each other's myths to enrich our own.

The biblical Jacob, so the Book of Genesis recounts, struggled with a mysterious being at the Ford of Jabbok, and after this encounter he received an extra name: Israel. Many explanations have been offered for the identity of Jacob's nocturnal adversary. I want to suggest that his struggle that night, and our challenge every day, is with our myths. They are powerful—after all, they give us the energy we need to continue. But part of our narrative is that they have to be faced. Zionists, Reform Jews, and the others too—we have to be prepared to dismantle our grand stories if our grand story is to continue. We have to confront our myths and our facts in order to continue to become Israel.

NOTES

1. The article and Achad HaAm's response are both discussed by Michael A. Meyer in "American Reform Judaism and Zionism: Early Efforts at Ideological Rapprochement," *Judaism within Modernity: Essays on Jewish History and Religion* (Detroit: Wayne State University Press, 2001), 362–78, particularly 368–73. Neumark's essay in full can be found in David Neumark, *Essays in Jewish Philosophy* (Vienna: Central Conference of American Rabbis, 1929), 91–100.
2. Neumark, *Essays in Jewish Philosophy*, 98.

Peering into the Nationalist Mirror

DR. JOSHUA HOLO

For the Love of Zion

THE LIBERAL ZIONIST dialogue among American Jews feels fragile indeed—a fragile and fractious internal contest between its two components: liberalism and Zionism. On the face of it, the ideological tension in this debate need not pose a problem: Jews argue over the things that they care about. It's the underlying precariousness that troubles us. We sense that American Zionism, well beyond the confines of the liberal camp, is in the balance.

In fact, contemporary American Jewish Zionism faces stark challenges. To be sure, American Jews still, in their strong majority (69 percent according the 2013 Pew study "A Portrait of Jewish Americans"[1]), feel either somewhat or very attached to the State of Israel. Nevertheless, a more recent Pew poll on Israeli and American Judaism has articulated some key differences between our two populations.[2] And few, if any, doubt the fact that we can no longer count on the instinctive support for Israel that characterized generations past. That kind of reflexive loyalty is irretrievably lost.

In truth, this sea change is welcome. If "instinctive" support means unreflective, jingoistic Zionism, then good riddance. We can aim higher, for a mature, pondered American Jewish Zionism that is reliable and committed, by virtue of its legitimacy. And to achieve that kind of support for Israel among American Jews as a whole, Liberal Zionism in particular must participate in its formulation.

Overall, American Jews predominantly take what one might call "liberal" positions on basic Israel policy questions. We favor a two-state solution (60 percent) and widely view Israeli settlements as harmful to Israeli security (44 percent believe that settlements hurt,

17 percent believe they help, 29 percent believe they make no difference).[3] In American political terms, roughly 70 percent of Jews voted
for both Barack Obama and Hillary Clinton. In short, if we are to revitalize a compelling Jewish American Zionism writ large, it must be
one that speaks to the liberal sensibility so preponderant among us.

At the same time, it is the liberals who are feeling most torn about
Zionism, because persistent and articulate doubts about Israel from
our left flank—mostly from our *Jewish* left flank—have struck a particularly jarring chord. Those of us in our forties and older grew up
in world where Zionism and liberalism seemed synonymous, and we
celebrated them both with unburdened (and perhaps unexamined)
ease. Now, in many Jewish quarters, our warm, late-twentieth-
century associations of Zionism with kibbutzim, egalitarian army
service, and the rescue of Ethiopian Jews have given way to credible,
Jewish descriptions of certain aspects of Israeli politics as land grab-
bing, militaristic, and even racist. And that's even before tackling
the hardening attitudes among non-Jews. Simply put, times have
changed. Now, as Peter Beinart ruefully points out, when liberal
Jews are forced to confront a Zionism at odds with their liberalism,
they increasingly choose the latter.[4]

So liberal Zionists need to articulate an intellectually honest and
conceptually coherent platform that draws from both sides of our
political personality: our core *chibat Tzion*, or love of Israel, and our
equally committed liberal ideology. In so doing, we can and should
draw from various perspectives on Israel, authentically Zionist and
constructively critical, from across the political spectrum, including
the likes of Rabbi Rick Jacobs, Yossi Klein Halevi, Rabbi Donniel
Hartman, and even our sometime political adversaries like current
president Reuven Rivlin. But more than that, we need to forge an
American Jewish Zionist *argument*, an affirmation genuinely liberal
and Zionist, without which American Zionism as a whole cannot
flourish. Such an argument necessarily roots itself in how we frame
competing national claims: how we embrace Judaism's national
identity and rights while acknowledging and negotiating those of
our national counterpart, the Palestinians.

Framing the Difficulty: 1948 versus 1967

On a class trip to Israel in 2014, students from the Hebrew Union College–Jewish Institute of Religion met a delegation of Arab-Israeli women who offered their grievances. In solidarity, one Jewish student lamented the effects of the 1967 Six-Day War. Specifically, she commiserated with the women about the Israeli occupation of Arab-majority lands outside of Israel proper. One Arab woman sternly clarified: It was not 1967 that she mourned, but the foundation of the State of Israel in the first place.

This challenge blindsided the Jewish student. She expected a rejection of Israel's perceived injustices, but not of Israel's existence altogether. And therein lies the problem: the student's surprise—not the Arab woman's opinion—illustrates our failure to frame the situation accurately. Intending to adopt a clear-eyed, morally sustainable Zionist posture to the problem of occupation, the student ignored the real problem of Israel altogether. At root, she confused 1967 and 1948.[5]

We liberals live comfortably with—even unconsciously foment—that anodyne confusion, precisely because it numbs the deeper moral problems of 1948. By and large, liberal American Jews have no commitment to the Israeli occupation of the West Bank in the first place. If anything, it is safe to say that as a general matter, liberal Zionist Jews look forward to the day when Israel leaves the Occupied Territories and when Palestine becomes a functioning and neighborly state. (At the time of the Pew study in 2013, 50 percent of Reform Jews and 56 percent of Jewish Democrats believe the continued building of settlements hurts Israel's security; 58 percent of Reform Jews and 70 percent of Jewish Democrats think a two-state solution is feasible. Meanwhile, presumably reflecting, in part, distaste with the Occupation, only 38 percent of Reform Jews believe that Israel is making a sincere effort at peace.)[6] And among those who have no faith in such a scenario in light of Palestinian rejectionism, many liberals would still be content with a durable divorce: a two-state solution for the sake of Israel alone.

At its heart, the two-state solution to 1967 resolves any internal

ideological tension between liberalism and Zionism in one fell
swoop. A two-state solution is Zionist because it obviously seeks
to guarantee Israel's existence and its Jewish and democratic character. Additionally, the two-state solution satisfies our liberalism or
relative dovishness (insofar as liberalism and dovishness overlap).
If a Palestinian sympathizer or activist cries, "End occupation!" the
liberal Jew responds, "Please help me do so! Help end the cycle of
violence on your side, and I will take it upon myself to help end occupation on mine."

The 1967 conundrum of occupation hounds all Zionists, but
American Jewish Liberal Zionism has generally resolved it as an
ideological matter, by disavowing the West Bank. Consequently, neither our liberalism nor our Zionism is threatened by the challenges
that grow out of 1967, even if we are obviously beholden to those dif-
ficulties from a practical perspective. As a result, by focusing on our
moral indignation at the consequences of 1967, we spare ourselves
the hard introspection about 1948.

But we cannot avoid it, because the real difficulty lies precisely in
"1948," shorthand for the Zionist enterprise and its realization in
the founding of the State of Israel. When otherwise informed and
proud liberal Jewish students find themselves confounded and embarrassed in debates on college campuses, it is not 1967 that defeats
them. It is 1948 that poses a basic moral quandary between internally
competing, core values. Liberal Jewish Zionists find themselves
adrift and discomfited by critics of Israel because we have not fully
worked through the confrontation between our own liberal values
and Zionism itself.

At the outset, we can dispense, once and for all, with the contingent and pat rejoinders to the critics of Zionism: "Israel is the only
democracy in the Middle East"; "Israel is the only outpost of American values in the region"; "Israel is the convenient scapegoat for the
cynical tyrants of the Muslim world"; "Israel is the safest country
in the Middle East for Christians or, for that matter, for Muslims";
"While Muslim countries are busy repressing their people, Israel is
leading the world in science, medicine, etc."

Though true, these statements miss the point in addressing Zionism's fundamental challenges. Worse, their irrelevance makes these protestations appear tone-deaf, defensive, facile, and ultimately meaningless—no matter that they afford very compelling arguments in other contexts.

Liberal Zionism struggles internally with 1948 because the Jews' success meant the displacement and defeat of another population. As a consequence of this nation-building problem, Zionism and its product, the State of Israel, intrinsically challenge liberalism, which purports to recognize the other, and so to incline toward dovishness; to uphold democratic ideals; and in some measure to share prosperity. In light of displacement caused by 1948, Liberal Zionists basically recognize the Arab claim to Palestine as legitimate, even as they simultaneously adhere to their own, directly competing Zionist claim.

In this internal tension lies the fragility of Liberal Zionism, and because Liberal Zionism remains at the very center of American Zionism writ large, we must address it. One way to work through this struggle is through the concept of *irredentism*, a notion that impels the national movements of both the Palestinians and the Jews into a kind of mirrored relationship and, by extension, a grudgingly shared destiny.

The Irredentist Mirror

"Irredentism" comes from the Italian word for "unredeemed," and it refers to the pursuit of national reestablishment in one's homeland. Both Jewish and Palestinian nationalism emerged as irredentist movements, arguably in roughly the same period (the late nineteenth and early twentieth century) and in relation to one another, with designs on roughly the same patch of territory.[7] At the outset, in other words, they simultaneously mirror and confront one another.

Consider, by contrast, the (admittedly caricatured) case of the Native Americans and the European conquest: with very obvious "natives" and "colonists," they do not mirror each other at all. Unlike Israel and Palestine, which both claim priority, none doubts who was "here first" in the Americas. Ironically however, one sometimes hears hawkish Zionists cite the example of the Americas by way of analogy, to illustrate the implausibility of decisive withdrawal from the West Bank: "Should we allow the Native Americans to return to their lands?" Presumably, this rhetorical question compares the Palestinians with the Native Americans, but the analogy is utterly misplaced, so it breaks down off the bat. Are the Palestinians to be compared to the Native Americans? Or are the Jews? Mirrors belie such distinctions.

Ze'ev Jabotinsky (generally cast as the most illiberal of characters) put it best when he characterized the nature of the conflict in his signal 1923 essay "The Iron Wall": "Every native population . . . regards its lands as its national home, of which it is the sole master, and it wants to retain that mastery always; it will refuse to admit not only new masters but even new partners or collaborators."[8] Jabotinsky here refers to the Arabs when he says "native," but the simple logic of his own Zionism assumes a *prior* status as "native" for the Jewish people. It is the Jews who invoke their ancient claim to the Land of Israel as their origin and homeland, and it is the Zionists who exercise the characteristically "native" right of reclamation. In other words, the irredentist notion of being original and attached to the Land applies to both Jews and Arabs, and it defines their mirrored, contested settlement of a single region.

Our side of that conflict, our irredentist effort called Zionism, holds a distinctive place among such movements for at least two related reasons. First, it was a long time coming—the proverbial two thousand years since the destruction of the Temple by the Romans in 70 CE. Second, by the time Zionism finally did gain traction in the late nineteenth century, an overwhelming majority of different inhabitants had settled and dominated the Land.

The antiquity of the Zionist dream is a double-edged sword. Perceived positively, its antiquity evokes legitimacy: no other people living today has a prior historical connection to that particular land. From the negative point of view, antiquity gets cast as delay. It begs the impatience of those who would argue, in principle, that one's claim eventually lapses under the weight of some theoretical statute of limitations. Most of all, from a practical perspective, the delay is so long that other peoples have had ample time not merely to settle the land, but also to develop a fully mature and centuries-long history of their own.

But there is a twist: over the millennia, the Jews never quit their claim nor sold their birthright to the Land of Israel, nor, for that matter, have non-Jews meaningfully contested the historical underpinnings of that birthright. Even more trenchantly, Jews affirmatively persisted in their claim—and not merely spiritually or abstractly in their poems and messianic prayers, but also specifically, continuously, and pragmatically: in their legal structures, patterns of settlement, remittance of monies, pilgrimages, burials, and search for refuge.

Documents spanning tens of centuries attest to this tenacity. And our steadfastness itself echoes the very real, historical and even physical, archaeological proof of our origins in the Land. Jews evolved fully as a civilization, rooted in that specific land, more than a full millennium *before* the Romans destroyed the Temple and precipitated our irredentism in the first place. Subsequently, since the destruction of the Temple we have zealously prayed for God to "return us in joy to our land."[9] Rabbinic law, the basis of Jewish civilization in the wake of the Roman conquest, undertook to preserve the laws of Temple sacrifice in their granular detail and to offer prayerful substitutes for those sacrifices until such time as our return would permit us to rebuild the Temple. Well into the fifth century CE, Rabbinic academies still flourished in the Land of Israel and commanded the recognition of the Roman Empire as the Jewish people's official leadership—throughout the empire. As the Byzantines, Persians, and Muslims vied for Jerusalem and the Holy Land in the seventh century, the role of the Jewish population, though not decisive, notably mattered.[10] In 1267, the leading light of Spanish Jewry, Moses Nachmanides, emigrated to the Land of Israel and helped rebuild the Jerusalemite community ravaged by the Mongol invasion.[11] In the wake of the expulsion of the Jews from Spain in 1492, many Jews followed in his footsteps, reigniting the kabbalistic school of mysticism that would later take hold throughout the Jewish world.[12] Seventeenth-century Italian synagogues documented remittances to impoverished coreligionists in the Land of Israel.[13] And the evidence only mounts over time.

Ultimately, these examples represent merely a few dots on the timeline of history, but they connect to draw a coherent picture of far-flung Jewish populations in active, sustained relationship with both the Land of Israel and their coreligionists in it. In fact, modern Zionism merely reflects the fact that Jews and Judaism are tightly bound up with the Land of Israel.

All the while, Jews as a body politic have never renounced our claim to the Land. It is true that two catastrophic rebellions, in the first and second centuries CE, dissuaded us from pursuing political and military conquest thereafter; and early Reform Judaism, exceptionally among Jewish voices, abjured the Jewish national identity in an attempt to validate the European emancipation. But if anything, Jewish irredentism has remained explicitly at our center of gravity and the object of our pursuits—both religious and communal.

To be sure, one may coherently disagree with Zionism on a number of accounts. Some might reject irredentism in principle. Alternatively, one may disagree with the particular case of Zionism by arguing that our irredentist claims, even if construed as theoretically legitimate, have no right to trump the existing, real-life interests of the population whom the irredentism might unsettle. Or finally, one may invoke the abstract principle of a statute of limitations.

The strength of liberalism is that it does not deny the cogency of these arguments against Zionism; it merely insists that the coherence of the Zionist argument cannot be dismissed either. None can reasonably aver that the Jewish claim to the Land of Israel is fatuous. Jewish religion, Jewish history, and the Jewish people constitute a complex of coherent, overlapping, and mutually reinforcing elements, knowable and known from within and without, by Jews and non-Jews alike. And the Land of Israel is an enduring and inalienable part of that complex, demonstrably so. The Zionist claim derives its legitimacy from that fact, and as such, interlocutors of good faith cannot in fairness write it off, even if they may favor other arguments over it.

It is reasonable to point out the Jews' legal purchases of land throughout Palestine, in which Arabs freely sold their patrimony to the Zionists. It is fair play to query the novelty of Palestinian nationhood; to contextualize its politicization in relation to other Arab countries in the region—all of which emerged from twentieth-century imperialism; and to contrast it to Judaism's coherent national identity of millennia. And there is no reason to shy from the ways in which Zionists genuinely pioneered new areas for human settlement.

Meanwhile, frank liberalism peers into the irredentist mirror and insists that Zionism also confront a diametrically opposite Palestinian claim, also knowable and known. (And it bears recognizing that the pro-Palestinian camp is not intrinsically anti-Semitic, even though it not infrequently becomes a cipher for, or companion to, anti-Semitism.) As a matter of fact, 1948 displaced part of the Arab population in Palestine against their will, sometimes violently. Even when Jews bought land legally, they often did so from absentee landlords unconcerned with the welfare of the settled Arab population. And the idea of Palestinian nationalism also has coherent claims, as the 1936 Arab Revolt would at least intimate. Even if one were to argue that Palestinian nationalism emerges only in response to Jewish nationalism, that argument does not undermine it as a "fact on the ground," a functioning organizing principle and political motivator—acknowledged as such by early Zionists, no less.

In these ways, we can and should break down history's nuances. However, all the nuance in the world will not change the irrevocable fact of Palestinian collective identity and political interests; nor the fact that not only liberals, but also those on the right, have long acknowledged them; nor the fact that they generated and still animate Zionism's irredentist mirror-image: Palestinian nationalism.

It is not just that liberal Zionists are *willing* to acknowledge the legitimacy of both sides of our mirrored rivalry. Much more than that, our combined, interwoven liberalism-and-Zionism *demands* it. Confronting the irredentist mirror of Palestinian and Jewish nationalism frees Liberal Zionists to pursue their side of the dispute vigorously, without apology and without expectation of an Arab apology.

Liberal Zionists can say: Yes, Zionism displaced a local Arab contingent. But no less so, Zionism, even in its most mythologized form, reflects a basically true relationship between the people Israel and the Land of Israel. The Declaration of Independence points out that "the Land of Israel was the birthplace of the Jewish people. . . . After being forcibly exiled from their land, the people kept faith with it throughout their Dispersion and never ceased to pray and hope for their return to it and for the restoration in it of their political freedom." The pursuit of that irredentist truth is fundamentally reasonable in the course of human events and history, regardless of the fact that it is no less contentious for its reasonableness.

Liberal Zionism can find opportunity in this mirrored irredentism, because it frames both our Zionist claim and our liberal inclination to identify with our competitors. If anything, American Jewish Liberal Zionism feels fragile, because we are temperamentally attuned to hearing the arguments of the Palestinians, while we have neglected our own half of that dual story—our own irredentist narrative. Our empathy reflects well on us, because it grows out of decency and out of Leviticus's admonition that "the strangers who reside with you shall be to you as your citizens; you shall love each one as yourself, for you were strangers in the land of Egypt" (19:34). But it is worthwhile to shore up that fragility by vigorously teaching our side of the narrative; it, too, is very compelling. If we do so, we will land not far from Ze'ev Jabotinsky's capacity and willingness to see the other, despite his associations with the Zionist right wing.[14] We will stay true to the principle of the Jewish national dream, even as we recognize the reasonableness of the Palestinian one. The respect built into this perspective, both for ourselves and for the Palestinians, puts the conflict between us in stark, even inevitable, terms, but it can also color and modulate that conflict as we search for a compromise solution.

With an unflinching gaze into the irredentist mirror of 1948, liberalism and Zionism can coexist conceptually, with coherence and intellectual honesty, by acknowledging the legitimacy of the conflict and, from that point of departure, by pursuing the most dignified and durable negotiation of it.

Conclusion

Liberal Jewish Zionism has hobbled itself by dancing around a simple but profound challenge: we honor Jewish sacrifices and celebrate the stunning, long-awaited national success of 1948, but we shy away from the full force of its corollary, namely, the Palestinian national defeat.

The mirrored quality of the Palestinian-Israeli conflict offers at least one perspective on revitalizing our flagging Zionism with integrity. The irredentist mirror frames a moral appreciation of the fact that the competition between our national claims is irreducible and unavoidable, but also *legitimate*. From that point, we can proceed to argue energetically for compromise, not because it satisfies the Palestinians (it may not), but because it meets our own liberal-Zionist standards.

This perspective is not new; some key theorists embraced this strategy in Zionism's infancy. In 1905 Yitzchak Epstein, an impassioned Zionist of the *Yishuv*, addressed the Seventh Zionist Congress with a speech later published as "The Hidden Question." In it he admitted that "at the present time, there is no Arab national or political movement in Palestine. But this people has no real need of a movement: it is large and numerous and does not require a revival because it never ceased to exist for even a moment." But Epstein also warned, "Let us not tease a sleeping lion!"; he understood that Zionism would likely precipitate its doppelganger counterpart.[15] And though his proposed solution proved too utopian for the history that unfolded, his grasp of the situation was prophetic.

Our nationalisms reflect one another, and Liberal Zionism offers a bold, unapologetic, intellectually defensible, morally honest, and politically sustainable view of a long-term contest. We can reasonably confront the problem of irredentism without fracturing our political personality and the values that undergird it. By peering into the mirror, we discern the contours of this conflict more accurately, the better to tackle its sober and stubborn challenges. What is more, in the United States, no Zionism flourishes without Liberal Zionism. We owe it to ourselves, to Israel, to our fellow Jews, to our neighbors, and to the advancement of peace to hone the argument and articulate it with clarity and conviction, in the spirit of the Prayer for the State of Israel, which pleads for "peace in the Land and everlasting happiness for its inhabitants."

NOTES

1. Pew Research Center's Religion & Public Life Project, *A Portrait of Jewish Americans* (Washington, DC: Pew Research Center, 2013), http://www.pewforum.org/2013/10/01/jewish-american-beliefs-attitudes-culture-survey/.
2. Pew Research Center, *Religion and Public Life, American and Israeli Jews: Twin Portraits from Pew Research Center Surveys*, Sept. 27, 2016, http://pewrsr.ch/2jn2IAs
3. Pew Research Center, *A Portrait of Jewish Americans*.
4. Peter Beinart, "The Failure of the American Jewish Establishment," in the *New York Review of Books* 57, no. 10 (June 10, 2010).
5. In his new book, *No End of Conflict: Rethinking Israel-Palestine* (Lanham, MD: Rowman & Littlefield, 2016), former Mossad officer Joseph Alpher tries to disentangle 1948 from 1967 not merely philosophically but also in a practical sense, in order to properly assess and tackle the problems that emerge from each stage of history.
6. Pew Research Center, *A Portrait of Jewish Americans*.
7. The concept of Palestinian nationalism is a hotly contested one, with Jewish and Arab scholars arguing (not always along predictable lines) over two key, interrelated elements: chronology and the degree to which Palestinian nationalism *reacts* to Zionism or exists *independently* of it. See, for example, H. Gerber, *Remembering and Imagining Palestine: Identity and Nationalism from the Crusades to the Present* (Basingstoke, UK: Palgrave Macmillan, 2008); R. Khalidi, *Palestinian Identity: The Construction of Modern National Consciousness* (New York: Columbia University Press, 2010).
8. Ze'ev Jabotinsky, "The Iron Wall," *Rassvyet*, November 4, 1923; Engish trans. in the *Jewish Herald*, November 26, 1937.

9. Shabbat *Musaf Amidah*, perhaps the most famous, though far from the only, prayerful expression of this sentiment.
10. W. E. Kaegi, *Heraclius: Emperor of Byzantium* (Cambridge: Cambridge University Press, 2003).
11. A. Cuffel, "Call and Response: European Jewish Emigration to Egypt and Palestine in the Middle Ages," *Jewish Quarterly Review* 90 (1999): 61–101.
12. Gershom Scholem, *Major Trends in Jewish Mysticism*, rev. 3rd ed. (New York: Schocken Books, 1995), especially the seventh lecture.
13. D. Carpi, "The Activity of the Jewish Community of Padua on Behalf of the Poor of Eretz Israel: 1584–1620" [in Hebrew], *Studies in Jewish History Presented to Professor Raphael Mahler on His Seventy-Fifth Birthday* (Merhavia: Sifriat Poalim, 1974), 24–46.
14. V. Jabotinsky, *The Jewish War Front* (London: Allen and Unwin, 1940), 218: "The Jewish and the Arab ethno-communities shall be recognized as autonomous public bodies of equal status before the law."
15. P. Mendes-Flohr and J. Reinharz, eds., *The Jew in the Modern World*, 3rd ed. (New York: Oxford University Press, 2011), 631–35.

To Be a Post-nationalist Zionist
A Theo-political Reflection

RABBI DR. HAIM O. RECHNITZER

> But you the Eternal took and brought out of Egypt, that iron
> blast furnace, to be God's very own people, as is now the case.
> —DEUTERONOMY 4:20

THE POPULAR ISRAELI SONG "*Ein Li Eretz Acheret*" (I have no
other country) starts with the words "I have no other country
/ even if my land is burning / only a word in Hebrew / seeps into
my veins, my soul / with anguished body, with famished heart /
my home is here." The song was written during the First Lebanon
War (1982) by the Israeli songwriter and Israel Prize laureate Ehud
Manor (1941–2005). "I have no other country" is a protest song
directed against the incompetence of the Israeli leadership that led
to the pointless deaths of Israeli soldiers in an unnecessary war.
However, within a few years after its first recording in 1986, the song
was adopted by Israeli Jews from the entire political spectrum and
has become an anthem, a psalm to be sung at various public events
such as political demonstrations and national memorial services.[1]
The song has become a virtual psalm of Israeli civil religion.[2] Its lyrics strike directly into the heart of our discussion by exposing that
which is often overlooked—the fundamental schism between Israelis and the rest of world Jewry. This song, unlike many other canonical Israeli popular songs, cannot be sung in good faith by Zionists
living in the Diaspora, whose mother tongue is other than Hebrew.
The song attests to the existential and ideological fusion between
land, language, and the individual as a private person who is a member of a national community. Similar to the effect of participating
in a religious ritual, singing this song alone or at public events may

evoke strong emotions. Here the song describes the very emotions it evoke, a national sentiment that runs through the innermost feelings of the individual, manifesting the self as woven into the tapestry of the group.

The song's correlation between love of one's country and of one's culture while still being a critique of the country's shortcomings makes it a particular, sublime expression of an Israeli national sentiment—not of a Jewish or a Zionist one. The distinction among these three modes of identity—Israeli, Jewish, and Zionist—is the base of our quest for "post-nationalist Zionism": what does post-nationalist Zionism mean, and what might a "post-nationalist" theo-political engagement with the State of Israel and with contemporary Israeli civilization look like?[3] My goal here is to outline a basic political-theological perspective on the question of Zionism.

By "political theology" I mean the use of a theological matrix within which political reality receives its meaning and interpretation. It also refers to the use of theological language and myth to provide the meta-narrative for the political entity—its past, present, and future—and thus to portray the concept of *good* for society while, inter alia, critiquing the present state of affairs in society.[4] For example, is the State of Israel and its establishment "the beginning of our redemption," that is to say, is it a step in the progression of eschatological history, or is it a practical solution to the Jewish problem? The different answers to this question yield different understandings of the historic events in June 1967: Is the outcome of the Six-Day War attributed to a brilliant military campaign or to a revealed miracle that marks another stage of a messianic redemption? Are the conquered lands of Judea and Samaria occupied territories or the freed land of our ancestors, a restoration of our "Days of Old"?

"Zionism" is an umbrella term for many ideologies within various cultural, political, spiritual, or religious traditions. First and foremost, however, Zionism is a modern national movement rooted in nationalist ideology. It has strived to promote a territorial existence for a collective of people that share, in varying degrees, language, ideology, memory, culture, and ethnicity. These components are nourished by, even while transcending, other collective identities that exist within the nation such as class, race, gender, and religious affiliation. As a political principle, nationalism, and Zionism as such, "holds that the political and the national unit should be congruent." It requires that "ethnic boundaries should not cut across political ones,"[5] meaning that the national aspect of the collective identity may feed back into, disturb, or change the collective identities that exist, so to speak, under the nation's dominant presence, such as religions, subcultures, or ethnic minority groups.[6] As a national movement, Zionism's raison d'être is to secure a body politic under one geographical territory for the Jews and to form a Jewish state. This very fact means that it moves across and against the collective Jewish identities that existed before Zionism's appearance on the historical scene or newer identities that are not anchored in nationalism. The nationalist aspect of Zionist ideology is also in inherent discord with Jewish collective identities that affirm the existence of Jews outside of its geographical, political, and cultural zone, that is, outside of the Jewish state. This can explain the inherent tension between Israel and the Jewish Diaspora and between the national Zionist identity and other Jewish identities, whether they are based on universalistic worldviews, as Reform Judaism, or Haredi worldviews.[7] From a nationalist point of view, the existence of such groups, which are perceived as part of the nation, is a disturbance and violation of the national principle and can be accepted only as a temporal and transitive state. The other option to mend and ease the sense of violation of the national principle is to differentiate between such groups and the national group.

These processes have taken place since the establishment of the State of Israel. As with any political entity, the principle of identification and demarcation of the other, the nonmember, is a defining component of the group. Therefore, in spite of the shared past with other Jews in the Diaspora, we witness a growth of political and cultural differentiation and separation between diasporic Jews and Israeli Jews. It is worth recalling Ernst Renan's characterization of a nation:

A nation is a soul, a spiritual principle. Two things . . . constitute this soul, this spiritual principle. One lies in the past, one
in the present. One is the possession in common of a rich legacy
of memories; the other is the present-day consent, the desire
to live together, the will to perpetuate the value of the heritage
one has received. . . . To have performed great deeds together, to
wish to perform still more—these are the essential conditions
for being a people. . . . One loves the house that one has built.[8]

Since the establishment of the State of Israel, the spiritual components (i.e., all cultural manifestation of the human spirit in conjunction with a national sentiment) that constitute a nation have
intensified and are not necessarily shared with non-Israeli Jews.
By now, Israelis have accumulated a significant shared legacy and
"have performed great deeds together." Israelis have accumulated a
significant mass of a "past" that is not shared with other Jews. That
is to say, the content of the Jewish collective memory has less and
less binding commonality between Israelis and Jews outside of the
"national home," i.e., the State of Israel. The idea that there is one
Jewish people is not sustainable in the long run. Israelism, including
the varieties of "Judaisms" within this civilization, will become more
and more particular and different from other Jewish cultures outside of Israel. Even the "Israeli Progressive Movement," the offshoot
of American Reform Judaism, is in the process of becoming more
"Israeli" than "Reform." It has more in common with other Israeli
denominations and subcultures than with its "mother" movement,
at least so long as the Reform Movement keeps its universalistic
humanistic theology. The recent political struggle to ensure equal
access to the Kotel for women and Reform prayer services is a case
in point, illustrating how Israeli Reform ideology is influenced by
national-religious Zionist sentiment. Since the Six-Day War of 1967,
the Kotel has increasingly become a site that fuses nationalist sentiment with religious fervor. It is a central symbol of the Israeli civil
religion, a "holy site" where induction ceremonies for IDF soldiers
and Israeli police cadets, as well as the Israeli Memorial Day ceremonies, are celebrated. The place of the Kotel within Israeli society

has become the epitome of the fusion between the national-political sphere and the Jewish religion, making the latter the theological rationale for the State of Israel.[9] Thus, by interlocking the fight for religious freedom and women's rights with the right to pray at the Kotel, the Reform Movement propels itself straight into the fusion of religion and state in Israeli society and culture. It is an unfortunate case of confusion between a national sentiment with feminism, which in turn influences, deviates, and distorts the American Reform agenda and its theology.

Zionism has accomplished its primary goal with the establishment of a sovereign state. From that moment on, the physical, political, cultural, and religious processes that have taken place within the borders of the State of Israel continuously contribute to the evolving Israeli civilization. It is important to note that in this context the term "Israel" denotes the national unit existing under the political entity that is the State of Israel. This is not to be confused with either the historical or the theological term "Israel," although some aspects of the latter are indeed fused into and nourish the modern political entity. A demarcation between "Israelis" and the "others"—other nations, other peoples, and other Jews who are not Israelis—was born with the establishment of the State of Israel. As Israeli civilization continues to develop according to its own inner forces and its particular political and cultural contexts, the demarcation line becomes progressively more pronounced.

The term "Zionism" is used today by Israelis and non-Israelis alike in three ways. The first is in reference to the historical phenomenon labeled "Zionism"—its past congresses, ideologies, projects, leadership, and so on. It is also used in a polemic context regarding Israel's legitimacy by reproducing or recalling the basic rationale of Zionism. However, it is also used in a third way, which is misleading and anachronistic in nature, to refer to ideology regarding society's concept of the good and to policies for realizing a good society. Thus, the question "What is a contemporary Zionist ideology?" and questions facing the State of Israel regarding its furtherance of a "good society" become equated. These kinds of questions are national questions and translate to decisions about war and peace, distribution of resources, education, integration of minority groups, and so forth. These questions—important, comprehensive, and ideological as they may be—are not particularly "Zionist" questions, but rather *national* questions. They are "Israeli" questions in the same manner that in France they are French questions or in the United States, American questions. They are "normal" questions that every nation must face. As the Israeli philosopher Natan Rotenstreich notes, "The existence of the State of Israel can explain the disappearance of the Zionist ideology insofar as any realization of a broad social-political goal may make the guiding ideology obsolete."[10] It behooves us to distinguish between the question "What should the Israeli society aspire to become?" and the question "What is Zionism after the establishment of the State of Israel?" in a way that does not overlap with the national-based questions. Zionism, as it was when it first appeared, is a group of ideologies that moves in two directions: a fundamental critique of the present cultural, spiritual, and political condition of the Jewish people and the presentation of a vision for a different future for Jewish people as a modern nation rooted in a state. In this sense it is utopian and messianic at its core. In the present state of things, Zionism that is not equated with nationalism should situate itself "outside" of the Israeli social-political arena, outside of the nationalist-centered point of reference. Such Zionism, a post-nationalist Zionism, can be the compass by which both Israel's *concept* of "the good society" and its *policies* are measured and critiqued. As does any compass, it should align itself to a field of influence that transcends the powers of the immediate perimeter. It should measure contemporary Israeli civilization according to ideals that are not rooted in nationalism and cannot be reduced to it. It should aim to put forth ideals and visions that transcend the State of Israel and that can continually pull Israeli civilization toward a dream greater than itself, a vision for humanity at large, to become a "light to the nations" (Isaiah 42:6, 49:6)—first and foremost by never reducing the messianic-utopic vision to a national one.

Where can we find resources for such a vision?

The most immediate answer is inscribed in Israel's Declaration of Independence: "[Israel] will be based on freedom, justice, and peace as envisaged by the prophets of Israel." However, Scripture—that is, our prophets—can be interpreted in various ways, some of which are even conflicting. Suffice it here to mention one such interpretation, that of Rabbi Abraham Isaac Kook and his son Rabbi Zvi Yehudah Kook and the religious right in Israel. Their messianic vision is a fusion of the national and the theological. They emphasize the national particularistic elements of the prophets' vision of redemption. We, post-nationalist Zionists, are seeking a vision that transcends the national realm and pulls it forward and up toward a universal ideal such as that described by Isaiah, "For My house shall be called a house of prayer for all peoples" (Isaiah 56:7), which connects between the redemption of Israel and the rest of humanity. We can turn to philosophers such as Hermann Cohen and Franz Rosenzweig for inspiration. Both put the Jewish people's center of gravity "outside" of the prevailing modern national worldview. However, here I would like to illustrate the basic parameters for "post-nationalist Zionism," with the aid of two Jewish philosophers more closely aligned with the Zionist vision: Martin Buber and Leo Strauss.

In a lecture series titled "Israel and Palestine: The History of an Idea,"[11] Martin Buber (1878–1965) distinguished between a "normal" national concept and that of the people of Israel. A normal national concept is "when a people makes its unity, spiritual coherence, historical character, traditions, origins and evolution, destiny and vocation the objects of its conscious life and the motive power behind its actions."[12] However, the essence of the Israeli national identity goes beyond this. Israel's national concept is captured by the name "Zion," the city of God. It is the belief in a divine leadership of a divine mission that can only be accomplished by a unique association between the people and the Land of Israel. The divine vision cannot exist in spirit only but must be situated to take part in history, mending and innovating through history. And though it puts vision into practice, it must constantly push against the reduction of vision to pragmatic considerations, in order to translate it into a secular modern concept of nationality. "It is not simply a special case among the national concepts and national movements: the exceptional quality that is here added to the universal makes it a unique category extending beyond the frontier of national problems and touching the domain of the universally human, the cosmic and even of Being itself."[13] It is a nation that moves beyond the nation and a land that cannot be reduced to the concept of a state. Thus whenever Israel's social-political ideologies and policies are solely an expression of realpolitik, of a nation-centered worldview or chauvinism, post-nationalist Zionist must present a universalistic perspective that is inspired by Jewish tradition's social justice concepts and relations to the ger, the stranger, the other. Post-nationalist Zionism echoes and offers modern implementation of the Torah's injunction "You shall not wrong nor oppress a stranger, for you were strangers in the land of Egypt. You [communal leaders] shall not ill-treat any widow or orphan. If you do mistreat them, I will heed their outcry as soon as they cry out to Me" (Exodus 22:20–22).[14]

Leo Strauss (1899–1973) presents us with a radical teaching regarding the political sphere, Jewish or otherwise, via his interpretation of the prayer Aleinu.[15] Strauss refers to the prayer as the "great Jewish prayer . . . surpassing everything that any present-day man could write."[16] The prayer, Strauss states, is a testimony to the unique fate of the Jewish people, which is to be a "living witness for the absence of redemption."[17] In modern times, the Jewish people stand against new idols, new "vain things and emptiness . . . gods which cannot save."[18] These modern idols, according to Strauss, are a confidence, or we may say, a dogmatic faith, in secular redemption via scientific progress and the modern political organization of the state. That is, Strauss warns us against the idea that scientific progress guarantees spiritual and moral advancement of humanity. In Aleinu we proclaim, "It is our duty to praise the Lord of all things . . . Since He has not made us like the other nations of other lands, and He has not placed us like other families of the earth . . ." Strauss reminds us that the Zionist attempt to solve the Jewish problem by way of national assimilation—that is, to become a normal nation—cannot be the last and ultimate phase of the Jewish civilization. The prayer includes a statement of coronation of God over the nations: "to You every knee must bend and every tongue must swear allegiance." The crowning of God as the ultimate sovereign is at the same time the recognition that no human sovereign and no human political structure can ever become the ultimate answer for the human condition. The prayer plants an anarchistic seed at the heart of every human association. It helps form a spiritual and intellectual disposition that is always suspicious of the state and demands that it look beyond itself. Inspired by Strauss's suspicion of the state, of any state, we might imagine the next phase of Zionism, a Zionism after the establishment of the sovereign State of Israel, as post-nationalist Zionism. Such Zionism introduces a contemporary Jewish critique of the modern state in general and the Israeli state in particular. Israel is by its own accord "a Jewish state." Its actions, therefore, are a manifestation of that which Israelis understand "a Jewish state" to be. And thus, all those who have a stake in the Jewish tradition and the Jewish future can and should engage in its critique.

This critique should strive to constantly encourage the Israeli state, its leaders and citizens, to not lose sight of the universal message of the Jewish tradition. It demands of them to make sure that realpolitik, and more so a nationalist-separatist worldview, never be the sole judge of the sociopolitical situation and the prescriber of political and social action. Israel is not merely a place of refuge; it was conceived to be, and must yet strive to become, "a light unto the nations." History will judge it by its ability to overcome and transcend "that iron blast furnace" (Deuteronomy 4:20) of the present, the geopolitical threats and the internal strife. When Israel can demonstrate that a nation and its state are not ends in and of themselves, but rather temporary vehicles to accomplish human spiritual and physical prosperity, it will become "a name and a praise among all the peoples of the earth" (Zephaniah 3:20).

NOTES

1. See, for example, the memorial gathering in Tel Aviv commemorating ten years since Prime Minister Yitzhak Rabin's assassination on YouTube at https://www.youtube.com/watch?v=o3LIcdy3Qn4.

2. On civil religion in Israel, see Charles S. Liebman and Eliezer Don-Yihya, *Civil Religion in Israel: Traditional Judaism and Political Culture in the Jewish State* (Berkeley: University of California Press, 1983). On popular songs and Memorial Day as part of Israeli civil religion, see Haim O. Rechnitzer, "Haim Guri and Rabbi David Buzaglo: A Theo-Political Meeting Place of Zionist Sabra Poetry and Jewish Liturgy," *The Journal for the Study of Sephardic and Mizrahi Jewry* 2, no. 1 (Summer 2008).

3. I use the term "civilization" in the same manner that was used by Mordecai Kaplan to describe Judaism as a civilization: "the accumulation of knowledge, skills, tools, arts, literatures, laws, religions and philosophies which stand between man and external nature and which serves as a bulwark against the hostility of forces that would otherwise destroy him"; Mordecai Menahem Kaplan, *Judaism as a Civilization: Toward a Reconstruction of American-Jewish Life* (New York: Schocken Books, 1967), 179.

4. See Menchem Lorberbaum, "Making Space for Leviathan: On Hobbes' Political Theology," *Hebraic Political Studies* 2 (2007): 78–100; and Haim O. Rechnitzer, "Tell Me What Your Questions Are and I Will Tell You Who You Are: Some Reflections on 'The Proposed Taxonomy for a Twenty-First-Century Theology of Reform Zionism' by S. M. Davids," *CCAR Journal* 54, no. 3 (Summer 2008): 29–37.

5. Ernest Gellner, *Nations and Nationalism* (Ithaca: Cornell University Press, 1983), 1–2.

6. See, for example, John Hutchinson, *The Dynamics of Cultural Nationalism: The Gaelic Revival and the Creation of the Irish Nation State* (London; Boston: Allen & Unwin, 1987).

7. The interpretation of Judaism according to Western-Christian values (which are perceived as "universalism") was and remained the basic interpretive lenses of Reform Judaism in spite of the fact that "official" Reform platforms such as the Pittsburgh 1999 platform mark an acceptance and appreciation for the "unique qualities of living in ארץ ישראל (*Eretz Yisrael*) and, the land of Israel, and encourage עליה (*Aliyah*) immigration to Israel." See Pittsburgh Convention Central Conference of American Rabbis, "A Statement of Principles for Reform Judaism," CCAR, https://ccarnet.org/rabbis-speak/platforms/statement-principles-reform-judaism/. For a critique of the Pittsburgh Principles, see David Aaron, "The First Loose Plank: On the Rejection of Reason in the Pittsburgh Principles of 1999," *CCAR*

Journal 48, no. 4 (Fall 2001): 87–116. For a perspective on the Reform relation to Israel and Zionism as reflected by the Reform prayer books, see Peter Knobel, "A New Light upon Zion? The Liturgy of Reform Judaism and Reform Zionism," CCAR Journal: The Reform Jewish Quarterly 54, no. 2 (Spring 2007): 69–83.

8. Renan Ernst, "What Is a Nation," in Nation and Narration, ed. Homi K. Bhabha (London: Routledge, 1882 [1990]), 19.

9. See Liebman and Don-Yihya, Civil Religion in Israel, 158–61. A religious critique of the nationalization of the Kotel is best presented by the Israeli thinker Yeshayahu Leibowitz in his essay "Discotel," a play on the words "discothèque" and "Kotel"; Yeshayahu Leibowitz, Yahadut, am Yehudi, u-medinat Yisrael (Yerushalayim: Shocken, 1975), 404. On Leibowitz and his critique of the fusion of religion to the state in the case of the State of Israel, see Haim O. Rechnitzer, "Judaism and the Idea of the Law: Leo Strauss and Yeshayahu Leibowitz' Philosophical and Ideological Interpretation of Maimonides," Hebrew Union College Annual 79 (2008): 165–191; "Redemptive Theology in the Thought of Yeshayahu Leibowitz," Israel Studies 13 (2008): 3.

10. Nathan Rotenstreich, Zionism: Past and Present (Albany: State University of New York Press, 2007). 115.

11. The lectures were published in Hebrew in 1944. The English edition was published in London and New York in 1952. Martin Buber, On Zion: The History of an Idea (New York: Schocken Books, 1973).

12. Ibid., xvii.

13. Ibid., xx.

14. The halachah expands the instruction not to mistreat them to a positive commandment to be responsible for their well-being. See, for example, Maimonides, Mishneh Torah, Hilchot Dei-ot 6:10. Moses Maimonides, The Code of Maimonides, translated by B. D. Klein (New Haven: Yale University Press, 1949).

15. "Why We Remain Jews: Can Jewish Faith and History Still Speak to Us?" (lecture at Bet Hillel, Chicago University, February 1962). The transcript of the lecture was published twice: in Kenneth L. Deutsch and Walter Nicgorski, Leo Strauss: Political Philosopher and Jewish Thinker (Lanham, MD: Rowman & Littlefield, 1993), 43–80; and Leo Strauss and Kenneth Hart Green, Jewish Philosophy and the Crisis of Modernity: Essays and Lectures in Modern Jewish Thought, SUNY series in the Jewish writings of Leo Strauss (Albany: State University of New York Press, 1997), 311–58.

16. Strauss and Green, Jewish Philosophy and the Crisis of Modernity, 414.

17. Ibid., 327.

18. From *Aleinu Leshabeach* prayer. Nosson Scherman and Meir Zlotowitz, *The Complete ArtScroll Siddur: Weekday, Sabbath, Festival* (Brooklyn: Mesorah Publications, 1985), 158. This sentence was perceived by Christians as a direct condemnation of Christianity. The sentence was omitted from most Ashkenazi prayer books by the eighteenth century due to fear of Christian Censorship. I deemed it appropriate, as did Kenneth Hart Green, who edited Strauss's lecture, to include this sentence in particular because in this lecture Strauss emphasizes the religious nobility of Jewish martyrdom during the Crusades and because he refers to this prayer as "a stumbling block to many." He also spoke about this prayer as an invocation of God against idolatry. Please see Green's elaborate explanation in Strauss and Green, *Jewish Philosophy and the Crisis of Modernity*, 352, n. 28.

An Evolving Covenant
Renewing the Liberal Commitment
to a Jewish Democratic State

R ABBI R ACHEL S ABATH B EIT -H ALACHMI , PhD

The Liberal Jewish Dialectic

L IBERAL J EWS live with inescapable complexity because of our
multiple and sometimes conflicting commitments. Whatever
the issue, a serious, thoughtful liberal Jew often lives in the unambiguous tension between modern liberal values and ancient Jewish
text and law. Simultaneously we are utterly dedicated to universal
values. These values include a commitment to liberal ethics, to religious, racial, and gender equality. At the same time liberal Jews are
committed to our inherited particularistic tradition, with its ideals
and ancient covenantal narratives. Regardless of the issue, however,
the challenges of modernity and postmodernity often lead Jewish
leaders to ask: how much should universal values or Jewish values
influence our response? Liberal Jews have just as often responded:
why must we choose? Because at times these values are in irrevocable
tension—a dialectical tension. Yet this is precisely the tension that
has pushed Jewish law and life to evolve and remain ethical, relevant,
and meaningful in ever-changing contexts.

In theory, Reform Judaism teaches that we can balance these tensions and even live in them. But in practice, our multifaceted commitments challenge us as individuals and as a community to make
difficult decisions. With limited resources, should a Jewish community prioritize aiding all the needy or primarily those Jews in need?
Should we favor in-marriage, or is intermarriage equally sacred and
thus can even our clergy be in interfaith relationships? For Jews, the
aspiration both to thrive in a culture of universal values and also to

thrive in a more particularistic community can be fraught with conflict and ambivalences. Yet as American Jews, our role in the public sphere and our commitment to the civic culture of the United States has made us great advocates for minorities and for religious freedom in the United States and throughout the world.

Our evolving understanding of the interconnectedness of universal values and Jewish values is what makes our Judaism far from static. In each phase of modern Jewish life, new questions challenge liberal Jews and often elicit new ways of thinking and living. In fact, Judaism itself is an ever-evolving tradition that is based on a broad and complex set of ancient ideologies and theologies interpreted by scholars over time. At the heart of Jewish theology is a multifaceted covenant—a covenant between us Jews and God and between each of us and other Jews. In the modern era, we have also expanded our sense of covenant with and responsibility for humanity and for the world. Today we remained covenanted with God and with our people's evolving relationship with the world.

From the early modern writing of philosophers like Moses Mendelssohn and Hermann Cohen, questions emerging from the encounter of Judaism and modernity started to become clear.

Famously, some early modern thinkers like Moses Mendelssohn (1729–1786) argued that one should strive to "be a Jew in your home and a man [sic] outside it." To what degree should Jews embrace the new opportunities available in the modern world, and to what degree should they remain distinct and separate as a religious community? To what extent should modern Judaism embrace the ideals of egalitarianism and change practices regarding the roles of men and women? Each of these new ideals creates a tension between ancient commitments and modern values. When do we dispense with old notions, and when must we reinterpret? When do our modern meta-ethics demand that we expand our understanding of the other? Each of these challenges forces uncomfortable choices between values. Yet not to choose the possibilities that modernity affords Jews would be to stifle the capacity to evolve and participate fully in the development of the broader society. Inevitably, while much is gained in these transformations, aspects of tradition are also lost. In addition, many Jews intellectually and spiritually fully embraced modern ideas such as egalitarianism and were awakened by the possibilities of Jewish nationalism. Modern democracy allowed us not only to survive as an otherwise often subjected minority, but also to flourish dramatically and to fully participate in society.

A New Zion? Democracy as a New Covenant

With the emergence of Reform Judaism in the early nineteenth century, traditional ideologies were challenged, and Jewish theology, texts, and rituals were reinterpreted. Among the most radical reinterpretations was the reevaluation of the biblical and Rabbinic ideal of the return to the Land of Israel and the rebuilding of the Temple. The opportunities that the emancipation afforded to Jews throughout most of Western Europe led Jewish thinkers to view modern states and societies as the context for Jewish "redemption," the opportunity to create a "new Zion" in the Diaspora, and to be full participants in creating a spiritually pure and ideal society. New thinking about the very nature of the human being, religion, and political life led some Jews to embrace the Diaspora as the new Zion, while others saw in modern nationalism the opportunity to redeem all Jews through the establishment of a Jewish state in the Land of Israel. We can only be fully human if we are fully free, and only in exercising our freedom to influence our own democratic culture can we find the possibility of redemption for our society and for ourselves.

Perhaps modernity would enable the Jewish people finally to respond fully to God's original call to the first Jew, Abraham (Genesis 12), not only to be a nation, but also to be a source of blessing for all. Simply put, without the protection and possibilities that democracy has given us, we could not fulfill our destiny as Jews. Our commitments to modern democracy and an evolving Judaism are not in conflict with each other, but rather they are deeply and mutually sustaining. These mutually reinforcing commitments inspire enormous hope in the goodness and maybe even the redemption we, as liberal Jews, can bring about precisely because of our commitment to and influence in two sovereign democratic states with enormous power.

While liberal Jews have long embraced the idea that law and ritual should evolve, the full engagement of liberal Jews with notions of Jewish nationalism was the cause of some debate. Again a tension arose in the late nineteenth and early twentieth century: should we focus on becoming "citizens of the world," where permitted, and/or should we focus on creating a Jewish state where every Jew could find refuge and become an equal citizen? These tensions are at the heart of how liberal Jews came to embrace Zionism: both/and. While we engaged fully in every society to improve it, we also sought to help build a state that not only would protect and defend every Jew, but would also have a positive impact on the world. And as Liberal Zionists, we have been committed to our political role in our people's ancient homeland and the right to Jewish sovereignty. Our prevailing sense of the evolving nature of Jewish law and life motivates us to ensure that all our values are upheld in a pluralistic society both in North America and in Israel. These commitments have been at the core of the liberal covenant with God and with Zion.

Liberal Jewish Zionism and the "Salvation" of Democracy in Israel

Perhaps, as the great modern Jewish thinker Mordecai M. Kaplan (1881–1983) taught, democracy might still be the source of our salvation. In his teachings, writings, and institutional leadership, Kaplan helped American Jews rethink Jewish life, prayer, and purpose in radical ways. According to Kaplanian theology, "God is the power that makes for salvation."[1] Not only is God the power that makes for freedom and the power that makes for righteousness, but God can also be found in the positive power of democracy, because it is a vehicle for our total individual and collective realization. Democracy, in fact, shares many of the same goals as those of Jewish life: a whole culture built upon the encouragement of certain values and certain kinds of behavior essential to an ethical life. If we engage fully in both, we will achieve not only a collective worthy of redemption but our own personal fulfillment and salvation as well. If we fail to participate, we fail to be engaged in our own salvation as a people both in Israel and in the worlds.

Just as Kaplan wrote in the 1930s and 1940s that America can offer full "salvation" by and for Jews, I often think that the salvation of Israeli democracy—and perhaps of even Israel itself—will be possible because liberal Jews both inside and outside Israel are so absolutely committed to democracy, equality, and religious pluralism for all of Israel's citizens. The establishment of a sovereign Jewish state offers the Jewish people a historic opportunity to test our values, to expand Jewish culture and thought, and to allow, as David Hartman (1930–2013) argued, for the healthy development of Jewish law.[2]

Do these commitments to ethics, pluralism, and democracy change when we think about Israel? No. For many American Jews, there can be a profound disconnect between the ideal moral standards we demand and the political and military consequences taking place in reality. For some, it means that Israel is related to wholly differently than any other country. For others, it means distancing themselves from an Israel that doesn't meet their high ideals.

After the Israeli army was accused of failing to prevent a massacre in Lebanon in 1982, David Hartman wrote a profound essay entitled "Auschwitz or Sinai?"[3] Core to his discussion of power and responsibility, Hartman stresses that indeed sometimes there are unintended consequences of Israel's use of its power. However, a mature society can take responsibility for its actions, hold itself to the highest of moral standards, take responsibility, repent, and work to prevent such consequences in the future. In this way Israel won't perpetuate its narrative of itself as a society of victims beyond rebuke, but rather create a narrative based on Sinai, of a society always striving to become more moral.

Israeli liberal Jews have been particularly forceful in working to ensure that Israel continues to hold itself to those high standards and remains as democratic as it is Jewish. In fact, as some of my Israeli colleagues have argued, Israel can *only* be as Jewish as democracy allows. Conversely, Israel cannot be only as democratic as Jewish law allows, for running a theocracy according to traditional Jewish law would profoundly compromise Israel's founding principles and raison d'être. So our liberal faith in the power and possibilities of democracy can put us liberal Jews in conflict with more conservative and ultra-Orthodox elements of the society and government, who argue often for Jewish values to overpower modern democratic standards and even human rights. Ironically, liberal Jews at times have a discourse of values more in common with non-Jewish minority populations than with some Jewish groups in Israel and beyond. We live in a dialectic of values and commitments.

While the sixty-nine-year reality of a Jewish democratic state dramatically expands our capacity to combine the best of Judaism and the best of democracy, consequently granting us the possibility of fulfilling our destiny as a sovereign people, the knowledge also lurks in every Jewish mind and heart that democracy's weaknesses have revealed themselves even in the "best" of cultures. Moreover, for liberals committed to the equality of every human being, the fifty-year occupation of another people is beyond intolerable and indefensible for a modern democratic state of any kind. Alongside all the valid security and political arguments, and together with all the conflicts and wars of the last decades, and precisely because of each of the failed attempts at an enduring peace, it remains impossible to argue that the Occupation is a Zionist necessity. While the exceptional wonder of Israel has achieved so much and survived such horrific threats—some of which I have personally witnessed—it is nevertheless marred by significant challenges to fulfilling its humanistic and democratic mission for all in its realm of protection and control. I do not believe, as some have said, that Israel has lost its way. Rather I believe that Israel has been necessarily trapped fighting for one essential aspect of the sacred Zionist project, the sacred mission of survival through the wise use of hard-won military power. As Israel developed its ethically founded right to self-defense, it developed extraordinary military power. And with power came complex responsibilities. While varying political ideologies and military concerns have often trapped Israel into continuing its control over territories and peoples for more than a generation, these endeavors have seriously compromised our deeper Zionist and Jewish values and prevented Israeli society from developing as it could have and still should. I am an unabashed Zionist, a lover of Israel and the Jewish people. But often, as a rabbi and as a person committed to justice, and more often than I wish, I have felt morally and Jewishly compelled to critique some Israeli policies. I have sought to be thoughtful and responsible when I have joined publicly with others in criticizing some aspect of Israeli society, but it has always come from a place of covenantal love and active personal commitment. As an Israeli citizen, the wife of a former IDF officer, and the mother of three Israeli children, I find many of these questions to be deeply personal and profoundly existential for my immediate and extended family. But I am also a student of ethics and Torah. Even my enemy was created *b'tzelem Elohim*—in the image of God. I know that Israel was created not so that we could abuse the human rights of others. I know that land itself is not more sacred than life, and I know that our Torah was given to us in order to fill the world with more blessing, not with more suffering.

While there have been days of despair and shame, at least as many days have been filled with pride and fulfillment. My children were born into a country where Jewish values of time and space embraced them. It is a place where health care is universal and where maternity leave and child support are largely guaranteed. The Muslim and Christian women giving birth in the rooms next to mine received the same first-rate medical care as I did, just as their newborns received the same care as my Jewish Israeli babies. Many members of my family serve in a Jewish defense force to ensure that no Jewish community will ever again face extermination. The siblings of my children's grandparents and their great-grandparents were *murdered* because they were Jews. On a daily basis my children and many members of my family and community have been particularly threatened as Jews and Israelis. And at the same time we have enormous power and influence. It is a miraculous historical privilege that we have created a country and a national military to protect ourselves. We have had the opportunity to create entirely a society according to our particular

Jewish values. The blessings of power are enormous and existentially redemptive. Because of Israel, our people has been redeemed, our language reborn, and our little country can bring much blessing to many others. Israel wasn't meant just for us, but for the world. It isn't just about the ethical necessity of creating a safe haven for the tormented Jew or about the right to self-defense and self-determination. It must be all of that but it must also be more. Israel must have universal impact; it must be transformative for all its citizens and for all of humankind. That is how I understand my Liberal Religious Zionism.

Against the reigning wholly political Zionist doctrine, the philosopher Martin Buber argued for a Zionism that was also inspired by Jewish humanist values rather than just simply by Jewish nationalism. As he wrote in a profound essay, "Hebrew Humanism," first published toward the beginning of the twentieth century, decades before the establishment of the State of Israel:

> By opposing Hebrew humanism to a nationalism which is nothing but empty self-assertion, I wish to indicate that, at this juncture, the Zionist movement must decide either for national egoism or national humanism. If it decides in favor of national egoism, it too will suffer the fate which will soon befall all shallow nationalism, that is, nationalism which does not set the nation a true supernational task. If it decides in favor of Hebrew humanism, it will be strong and effective long after shallow nationalism has lost all meaning and justification, for it will have something to say and to bring to mankind.[4]

For Buber, Zionism must be the teaching and realization of righteousness. This is what Liberal Zionists and Reform Zionists must continuously recommit to creating in the state and in the Land of Israel.

Much of what the cultural and humanist Zionists argued remains true for Liberal Zionists today inside and outside the State of Israel. Reflecting on nearly seventy years of the modern State of Israel, we see both disillusionment and hope. Have we succeeded in fulfilling their legacy of pluralism and tolerance? Is the Israeli Declaration of

Independence a source of inspiration and a living presence in Israeli society, or does it hang on our wall, silent, allowing us to conveniently forget its demands?

The latter, I fear, is closer to the truth. Israel of today has, to be sure, come a long way in cultivating its ethos of democracy and human rights—no small feat in a region in which such notions are so foreign. At the same time, however, Israeli society in general still gives very little room to alternative political, religious, and ethnic voices. There is still much to be done by way of bridging center and periphery, establishing gender equality, instituting minority rights, and, most importantly, accommodating different religious ideologies and lifestyles. Ironically, the Jewish state founded on the commitment to "freedom of religion, conscience, language, education and culture" has failed to recognize any form of Judaism save one.

While Israel today is witnessing a religious renaissance, with more and more Jews searching for diverse expressions of spirituality and religious meaning, Orthodoxy still holds exclusive control of the country's religious public sphere, institutions, and funding. We are still a far cry from the freedom of religion envisioned by the founders of Israel.

Standing as we do in an era of new kinds of challenge for the Jewish people and the world, it is our evolving Reform theology—of particular and universal redemption, of unmitigated standards of ethics and democracy together with the political vision of Israel's Declaration of Independence—that can inspire us to renew our commitment to Israel as a Jewish democratic state. Only such an evolving but ever-deepening commitment to these values and a deep pluralistic respect of all human beings will ensure that the Israel of the future can fulfill the vision of the past.

I believe, like Buber did, that Zionism must be the teaching and realization of righteousness. Ensuring that Jewish values and modern democratic principles continue to mutually reinforce the possibilities of that realization is filled with an ongoing dialectic. But perhaps this dialectic can serve also as a source of renewal. In the 1951 letter that Martin Buber wrote to Mordecai Kaplan in honor of his seventieth birthday, Buber considers how we will continue to be transformed and transformative:

> Liberalism and tradition are contrasts, liberty and tradition are none. Tradition is true and living only if it renews itself constantly in liberty and the will to preserve brings forth inner transformations. And as to liberty, from where shall it take the substance of its work, if not from the depths of tradition? This cooperation manifests itself most strongly in times of great crises.[5]

Liberal Judaism, with its multiple covenantal commitments thoroughly embodies this cooperation between liberty and tradition. Such a mutual upholding is how our covenant has evolved and will be how our commitment to a Jewish democratic State of Israel will continue to be renewed.

Notes

1. Mordecai M. Kaplan, *The Meaning of God in Modern Jewish Religion* (New York: Behrman's Jewish Book House, 1937), 57–58.
2. See David Hartman, *A Living Covenant: The Innovative Spirit in Traditional Judaism* (Woodstock, VT: Jewish Lights, 2012); *A Heart of Many Rooms: Celebrating the Many Voices within Judaism* (Woodstock, VT: Jewish Lights, 1999); or *The God Who Hates Lies: Confronting and Rethinking Jewish Tradition* (Woodstock, VT: Jewish Lights, 2014).
3. David Hartman, "Auschwitz or Sinai? In the Aftermath of the Israel Lebanese War," in *A Heart of Many Rooms*, 259–66.
4. Martin Buber, "Hebrew Humanism," in *Israel and the World: Israel in a Time of Crisis*, ed. Martin Buber (New York: Schocken Books, 1948).
5. Mordecai M. Kaplan letters, archived at the Library of the Jewish Theological Seminary of America.

Social Justice and Universalism *versus* Jewish Peoplehood and Particularism, and the Security of the Jewish State

Joshua S. Block

> If I am not for myself, who will be for me? But if I am only for myself, who am I? If not now, when?
> —Hillel, *Pirkei Avot* 1:14

THERE ARE OVER SEVEN BILLION people in the world, and roughly thirteen million Jews. There are six million Jews in America, and about the same in Israel, with the remainder scattered about the globe. So that leaves about just six million Jews in their natural habitat; if we were of the animal kingdom, the Jewish people would be an endangered species. It seems the world will do more to preserve the spotted owl in its natural habitat than the last remaining Jews in theirs. Perhaps Israel, the nation-state of the Jewish people, should be like a bird sanctuary, and the world should make it a special crime to kill a Jew.

The Jewish people are special. There aren't many of us left. The perils of assimilation are not new. However, the catastrophic results of our collective failure to give our children an adequate sense of Jewish identity and experience, of Jewish specialness—the depth of this weakness in the fabric of our collective identity, which saps the will of young Jews to stand apart when it's uncomfortable, to support the Jewish state when it's unpopular—this is new. And the impact is accelerating.

The problem is not Zionism itself; it is not in the imperfections of the nation-state of the Jewish people. The problem, rather, is that too many Jewish leaders fetishize a wonderful 1960s' version of social justice that no longer exists in today's world. Instead of preparing our kids to understand the postmodern attitude that devalues Jewish identity and the too often radical and occasionally violent reality of social justice as it exists today, we are giving them none of the grounding in the particularism of being a Jew and sending them out drunk with yesterday's universalism into a dangerous and very different world.

The Reform Movement and much of the unaffiliated American Jewish community has failed to adapt to this change, failed to understand its responsibility to our children and the urgent need to pivot away from the older romantic ideas of "social justice" and to recognize the beast that has now taken over the use of its name. This failure acutely threatens not only Jewish continuity and the community's future in America, but also our ability to imbue among this or the next generation of Reform and unaffiliated Jews the very notion of the necessity and rightness of a Jewish-defined state.

"A Jewish state, she says? Who defines themselves that way anymore?"

A son rolling his eyes at his mother's Zionism: Imagine the pain of the Jewish parent who shared such an exchange with a speaker at a recent event at a major Reform synagogue in the Northeast. The pain of knowing you failed to give your child a reason to see being Jewish as special or to sense responsibility to the Jewish future, linked to our people's past, despite years of temple attendance and *b'nei mitzvah* and confirmation classes.

If only that were an isolated experience. Today's Jewish kids are swamped with the peer pressure of universalism, the need to assimilate, the need to check their love of Israel at the door if they are to take part in the Women's Day rally. Ask yourself: Is your child proud enough of her Judaism, rooted enough in her belief in Jewish nationalism and self-determination after millennia of powerlessness and subjugation, to stand up and fight for her Zionism? For the importance of Jewish self-determination after millennia of subjugation and anti-Semitism?

Over the past decade or two, the Reform Movement has increased its emphasis on social justice as a central focus in the expression of Jewish practice. At the same time, however, the concept of "social justice" underwent a transformation: a postmodern, moral-relativist zeitgeist, one that is almost unrecognizable to the older form of liberalism, suddenly broke out of its theoretical, academic confines and began flooding the consciousness of social progressivism, especially on campuses, and almost always in the movements to which young Jewish activists are attracted.[1]

Something important has changed in the meaning of "social justice," and our community has failed to grasp the shift or adapt to it.

It is critical to understand that today's postmodern social justice does not have the same goals as that of the 1960s, which sought equal rights and opportunity and was rooted in the traditions of Western law and philosophy—and ultimately of Judaism. To the contrary, today's postmodern social justice seeks not equal treatment for all under the law, but the equality of outcomes[2] by delegitimizing the systems that developed law and history. It embraces a relativist basis to judge human conduct and seeks to delegitimize the foundations of history upon which Zionism and the rights of the Jewish people rest.

In today's climate, speaking the truth about those who do physical violence to Jews is itself called violence. Speakers on campus who speak uncomfortable truths are greeted with mob violence. At the University of California at Berkeley, where a controversial speaker encountered a riot including Molotov cocktails and attacks on police resulting in over $100,000 in damage to the university, the school newspaper ran an op-ed explaining that "violence helped ensure the safety of students."[3] Read that again.

When Oberlin professor Joy Karega was poisoning her campus community[4] with accusations that Israel was behind ISIS and the Paris terrorist attacks, that Jews controlled world media and invented AIDS, it was the postmodern reaction that cast her as the victim of a racist establishment unfairly judging a professor of color.

It may be hard to hear, but postmodernism is a threat to Western civilization, to the legitimacy of Jewish history and the expression of history itself, and to the system of nation-states that gives legitimacy to the modern and only expression of Jewish nationalism, the State of Israel.

In an essay entitled "How French 'Intellectuals' Ruined the West: Post-Modernism and Its Impact, Explained," Helen Pluckrose describes the factors behind the social justice river into which we are today pouring all our energies of Jewish action and self-definition:

> Morality is culturally relative, as is reality itself. Empirical evidence is suspect and so are any culturally dominant ideas including science, reason, and universal liberalism. These are Enlightenment values which are naïve, totalizing and oppressive, and there is a moral necessity to smash them. Far more important is the lived experience, narratives and beliefs of "marginalized" groups all of which are equally "true" but must now be privileged over Enlightenment values to reverse an oppressive, unjust and entirely arbitrary social construction of reality, morality and knowledge. . . .

Despite all the evidence that racism, sexism, homophobia, transphobia, and xenophobia are at an all-time low in Western societies, Leftist academics and SocJus activists display a fatalistic pessimism, enabled by postmodern interpretative "reading" practices which valorize confirmation bias. The authoritarian power of the postmodern academics and activists seems to be invisible to them whilst being apparent to everyone else.[5]

This postmodern view, which holds a liberal democracy, Israel—besieged by ahistorical lies and an intransigent, terror-addicted region—to be the evil, illegitimate party, is what animates distorted, anti-Semitic views of the Jewish state and Jews in general today.

In fact, we Jews have an empirical history, values that are universal and that have given rise to the modern view of human dignity, but these count for nothing in a world where postmodern social justice puts daily demands on our children to dismiss Jewish identity, uniqueness, and rights as just one more illegitimate view produced by white men of privilege.

Adrift after Soviet Jewry

Since the movement to free Soviet Jews ended in victory in 1990, with the dissolution of the USSR and the emigration of over a million Jews to Israel, Jews in America have failed to coalesce around a single, particularistic issue—one that uniquely affects fellow Jews and can unite people across the faith spectrum of Reform, Conservative, and Orthodox.

During the 1980s and 1990s, an impressive machinery of social justice activism was built around the cause of assisting and freeing the Jews of the Soviet Union, whether that involved smuggling in matzot for the celebration of Passover or vocally publicizing the cases of refuseniks (those denied permission to leave the USSR for Israel). That communal architecture included organized religious and secular social service branches across the Jewish community. However, when the cause of Soviet Jewry disappeared, the organizations, employees, and foundations behind these noble efforts did not. But they had no central, organizing cause.

Simultaneously, in the late 1980s and mid-1990s, Jewish synagogue participation underwent a generational shift. Those who are today's grandparents were at the time transitioning into the age bracket of temple-going prospects. But unlike their parents, who in prior decades were drawn to temple for traditional religious reasons or to seek out a warm, embracing Jewish community amid a world of non-Jewish strangers and occasionally career-stifling anti-Semitism, these increasingly assimilated Jews were looking for more than just old-fashioned concepts about religion to make it worth their time. The meaning they sought in synagogue had changed, modernized.

Synagogues, and in particular those within the Reform Movement, embraced this desire among their congregants to be part of larger causes, but after the success of the Soviet Jewry movement, they were faced with a challenge: Where could all this pent-up social justice energy be channeled?

The answers that were chosen by many clergy, congregations, and Jewish organizations put an increased emphasis on universal causes in pursuit of a better world, and in parallel on the betterment of Israel itself in its own pursuit of social justice. Both of these were laudable in and of themselves and when seen in isolation.

Yet when combined, the universal vision and the desire to criticize or "improve" the particularist Jewish state created a framework in which young Jews will inevitably be judged—and judge themselves—unfavorably for their commitment to Israel and to Jewish people-hood more generally. This has undermined the crucial role of Jewish communal synagogue life in developing our children's individual and collective Jewish identity and sense of communal belonging.

The synagogue's central and irreplaceable role of creating a rich and sustainable commitment to the Jewish collective has been grad-ually eroded, and a new generation of Jews has emerged as adults who simply don't relate, emotionally or intellectually, to the bond of peoplehood that for generations steeled us against the forces of assimilation, anti-Semitism, and apathy.

The sense of mutual responsibility, which had always been bal-anced against universal responsibility, now became an irrational, archaic source of tension, which could be most easily resolved by defaulting to the universal. The idea that Jews have a special respon-sibility to protect and nurture not just themselves but the broader Jewish family has atrophied over time.

This notion of Jews bearing special responsibility to protect other Jews is not an invention, however. It is a God-given commandment.

At the same time, a new spirit has entered North American cam-puses, in which universalism has taken on a much harsher form. The new radicalism to an astonishing degree replaces rational conver-sation with relentless pressure to choose sides. Jewish students are now on the defensive on account of their very identity. If, in the past, Jewish students drew upon centuries of historical persecution, as well as the biblical call to "remember you were strangers in Egypt," as the basis of a Jewish imperative to protect the oppressed, today's identity politics labels the Jew as beneficiaries of unwarranted "priv-ilege," who have no right to "safe spaces" and no just claims against "microaggression." In this new universalism, Jews are structurally left out, and a kind of subtle anti-Semitism has increasingly gained legitimacy.

At exactly the moment when Jewish students most desperately need a well of historical self-awareness and mutual commitment, they find that well dry.

By teaching our children to value postmodern universal values above their own identity in the specific continuum of Jewish history and peoplehood, we are betraying ourselves, our children, and our communities—and sawing off the limb of collective Jewish commitment on which Jewish universalism has always rested, leaving them terribly ill-equipped for the unique challenges of the campus environment and cut off from any public discourse that values Jewish particularist identity and institutions—and especially the Jewish state—at a time when such identities are the antithesis of current postmodern culture.

The Universalist Bar Mitzvah

These days, when our children are introduced to their bar or bat mitzvah year, in most liberal congregations they are told that they must undertake a "mitzvah project"—a wonderful endeavor that helps those on the cusp of adulthood understand that they have responsibilities far beyond themselves. This is a laudable goal, but one whose practice has produced deeply problematic and lasting consequences.

When I became bar mitzvah, I was twinned with a young Jewish boy in the Soviet Union—a boy who could not have a bar mitzvah ceremony in a land where he wasn't free to be Jew. Many Jews of my generation participated in similar programs.

That simple twinning, born of the movement to free Soviet Jewry, gave a young bar or bat mitzvah a true gift—one that is desperately absent from today's emphasis on social justice and universalism. As I know from my own experience, it taught every American-Jewish child three powerful things:

Something about being a Jew: You are not alone, but part of a people.

Something about being an American: You are free while others are not. Your unique Jewish identity is a privilege that must be cherished and protected.

Something about totalitarianism: The people of the Soviet Union were not free, and neither are many of the nations of the world today. So don't take your freedom for granted. Work to protect your people, your Jewish values, and by extension the freedom and rights of others.

I realized something else too: that I was lucky to have been born during a time of unprecedented freedom for Jews in the Western world, following the ravages of the Shoah. The creation of the State of Israel provided us not just with a potential sanctuary, but a society that we in America could help build, as well as a platform to bring the global Jewish community together. Even more fundamentally, I could live free of the fear and violence that consumed our ancestors in their day-to-day lives.

But the flip side of this freedom is that it gives us the opportunity to abandon our particularism.

Today, rather than using the bar or bat mitzvah as an opportunity to impart critical lessons that will help ground our children in a common identity and an authentic commitment to protecting Jewish lives, far too often we are encouraging them to skip all that and go directly to causes that are essentially universal. These causes are praiseworthy in their own right, but the shift in emphasis has meant that the role of an individual Jew is simply to do something good, for anyone, for any cause, because we are Jewish and we seek to repair the world. Yes, it is still labeled as "Jewish," but without the core elements of history, peoplehood, and textual heritage, that label has become increasingly hollow. What sets apart a Jew who helps others from a non-Jew who does the same?

I recently attended a joint bar and bat mitzvah ceremony for two children coming of age. For them, the choices for the mitzvah project were telling. One raised money for a camp for children who had lost a parent (she was fortunate to have both her parents looking on with pride). The second raised money to fight genocide in the Darfur region of Sudan. Both represented a kind of universal selflessness, a beautiful act to help "the other." But there was nothing to emphasize the responsibility to ourselves or to show in a significant way how those mitzvot are part—though not all—of an authentic liberal Judaism.

Is that why we go to temple? While I am deeply committed to social service and social justice, my primary interest in temple is the one thing that it can provide that we can't get anywhere else: the health, well-being, and strong continuity of the Jewish people; to be surrounded by other Jews. There are many opportunities in my life to pursue causes of universal concern, from the Rotary Club and Toys for Tots, to signing petitions and joining political actions in support of my beliefs. But none of those provide the framework for the continuity of Jewish peoplehood or for my kids to become vested in a love of Israel.

There needs to be a crucial shift to Jewish pride for its own sake to replace the overemphasis on social justice.

There are nearly endless opportunities for me to take my kids to learn about and participate in the pursuit of social justice. What is far more precious and is what I want from my Reform synagogue and community is Jewish togetherness. I belong to temple to be around other Jews, and I want my kids to be at temple, not to prize social justice, but to prize being part of the Jewish people—for it to be cool to hang out and have fun with other Jews—to understand their history, treasure their Jewish identity, and find a reason to stand up for the right of the Jewish people to have a homeland and the modern expression of Zionism.

In many parts of America today, country clubs are losing money and closing or merging with others. It is well past time that Reform congregations start merging with such country clubs to create sustainable centers of Jewish communal flourishing where the focus is not simply on worship, but also on play and nature. Imagine the outdoor programming, fun of Jewish practice, and organic pride that could result from year-round Jewish experience in a camp-like setting.

Studies show that participation in Jewish activities increases when the things people are doing together are fun and active—biking, hiking, cooking, and yes, even social service projects. Many congregations are having tremendous success with Rock 'n' Roll Shabbat services and other creative, nontraditional activities. Much research has shown that children who know the details of their family's history—where their grandparents went to school, what their assimilation journey was like, or what their careers entailed, both the ups and downs—are far more likely to succeed in life in general. So it is in their willingness to be part of Jewish life, to see themselves as a link in the chain of Jewish continuity, and feel a sense of responsibility to stand up for Zionism, the right of the Jewish people to exercise self-determination, and to openly confront anti-Zionists, those who deny Jews that basic right, as anti-Semites.

A primary role of Jewish institutions, including Reform synagogues, should be to inculcate a strong bond among the Jewish people and a sense of particularistic values and communal commitment, as the core basis for universal action—and as a basis for pride in Zionism and the willingness to speak out for the rights of Jewish people, here in America, as well as in Israel.

Take the example of opposing public school prayer. I am against prayer in public schools. I support the separation of church and state. But I hold these beliefs not because I am a universalist, but primarily because I am against religious coercion—and especially the coercion of my own children—a belief born of my appreciation of Jewish history and experience. A doctor must herself be healthy before she can treat others. Similarly we need to teach our children some useful self-awareness, if not selfishness, in order to give them the path to useful *selflessness*.

If those we seek to engage in Jewish life believe that the universal good always outweighs the needs of the Jewish collective, we will not have a Jewish collective a generation from now. Why, therefore, am I against prayer in school? Not simply because I am for everyone, but because I am also for myself.

Yet this ideological framework, this careful symbiosis between particular and universal so common in liberal Jewish institutions just a generation ago, is no longer driving our teaching or our ways of creating Jewish togetherness, practice, and pride—and we are paying an intolerably heavy price.

Israel Is a Particular Country

This combination, of exclusively universalistic teaching as the core of Judaism, with a social justice environment that assaults all expressions of Jewish particularism, makes it extremely hard for any Jewish student who has emerged from the Reform Movement to find the spiritual resources necessary to stand up publicly for the idea of a Jewish state in the world—or, for that matter, to act on behalf of any particular Jewish cause, such as opposing anti-Semitism in Europe or helping needy Jews in the former Soviet Union. After all, why speak out for Jews so far away when there are pressing universal causes, like racial justice, that all their friends are involved in here at home? Especially if those same friends keep whispering to them, with no understanding of what they are saying, "Don't you know that Israel is a racist apartheid state?"

The prioritization of universalism also acts as a powerful disincentive against support for Israel any time the Jewish state takes actions that any nation-state must take to protect itself—whether in its military defense or its actively deepening Jewish content in its schools or connection to the ancestral homeland. To the universalistic Jewish student, even the farthest-left Zionist party in Israel triggers a sense of disquiet, because Zionism is itself a glaring form of Jewish particularism.

Most of these Jewish students won't become anti-Israel activists, but they will find an apathetic stance toward Israel to be a path of least resistance on their road to self-discovery at college. Nor is the problem limited to their social environment; in the classroom they will discover that many courses on the Middle East take it as axiomatic that Jews are not indigenous to Israel, that the Palestinian refugee issue is a consequence of deliberate ethnic cleansing, and that Israel's military operations are aimed at causing as much harm to civilians as possible. Few people, especially when they come from a liberal, educated, and cosmopolitan community, would want to be associated with this presentation of Jewish history

For those who remain engaged on issues facing Israel, their stunted sense of Jewish particularism will also leave them unqualified to adopt positions or join movements that contribute positively to Israel's future. American Jews may convince themselves we are immune to the forces of history, but protecting and preserving Israel means not only holding it to a high moral standard, but also being acutely sensitive to real-world particularistic problems: staying safe amid shifting geostrategic threats, preserving Jewish identity in its institutions, crafting a national ethos out of a cornucopia of immigrant communities, protecting Israelis from terror attacks—while simultaneously preserving a commitment to liberal democracy and the full and equal rights of Jewish and non-Jewish citizens.

But that is not where we are headed. Ironically, Jewish particularism has become acceptable only when it involves vehement critiques of Israel, whether over its policies toward the Palestinians or its very existence as a sovereign state. When young Jews come together in such a framework, the net result is to make Judaism and Jewish history a source of shame instead of pride—to the point where students interpret the anti-Semitic demand for dismantling the Jewish state as a positive demonstration of opposition to racism and "colonialism."

When universalism trumps particularism, it's only natural that Jewish groups, lacking any sense of history or collective bond, will come together and attract young people, dedicated mainly to criticizing other Jews for their perceived particularistic failings, all in the name of "improving" Israel, or "holding it to a higher standard." While such groups, operating outside of Israel and the Hebrew discourse, have virtually no effect on Israel's actual behavior, they do have the potential for enormous harm to the Jewish collective by adding fuel to global efforts to demonize not just Israel but Jews as a whole. Most Jewish students think they are doing good for their people when they start down this path, not ever really gaining the values, tools, and historical perspective and instincts necessary for the preservation of our people.

And so, when a professor at Oberlin publicly declares that Israel was responsible for 9/11 and that the world's central banks are controlled by a Jew named Rothschild,[6] we discover members of the campus chapter of J Street U siding with the professor (on the grounds of "academic freedom") against the alumni who raised a protest.[7] The line between universalism and overt anti-Semitism has suddenly become very blurry.

Nor are they aware that all too often they are actually being played by forces with much darker intentions. Money flows, alliances are built, and groups with innocent-sounding names like "Jewish Voice for Peace"[8] attract students unaware that when you sit in America and publicly call Israel an "apartheid state," you are doing nothing to "improve" Israel, but are in fact marching in lockstep with the global machinery of hate and delegitimization that fuels violence against Israel and, automatically, against Jewish communities around the world. This problem is even more acute when organizations like J Street, who claim the pro-Israel mantle, legitimize anti-Zionist groups like JVP by inviting them to speak and share the stage at their national convention;[9] or when once-respected voices like Peter Beinart[10] seek to champion, and urge others to embrace, those who share their relentless, and occasionally valid, criticisms of Israel, while ignoring these same organizations' and individuals' anti-Zionist beliefs[11] and their desire for elimination Israel.

In other words, the de-prioritization of particularism can some-times mean robbing the next generation of the ability to tell when they are being recruited into efforts whose ultimate goals are to stigmatize the Jewish state and create a false choice—between, for example, a distorted version of feminism led by the likes of Linda Sarsour and the convicted terrorist Rasmea Odeh, on the one hand, and a belief in the justice of Jewish self-determination, on the other. Sarsour insists that Zionism and feminism are incompatible. Such false choices are a cudgel commonly wielded by heavily funded anti-Israel groups, and when our kids join these efforts they become unwitting weapons in a global war against both Israel and the Jews.

That Jewish students don't know this intuitively is the inevitable result of years of being taught in their synagogues that to celebrate and cherish and protect the particularism of Judaism is somehow inferior to the embrace of universalism, when in fact they should be seen as two inseparable parts of the unique Jewish whole. Speaking out against Linda Sarsour and her demented demand for the anti-Zionist credentials of progressive activists as a price of admission in support of feminism or other values, and educating others that there is a better, more effective way to accomplish shared progressive goals without the anti-Semitic context, is more rooted in Jewish values than embracing her ideas and urging others to ignore the hate she is peddling in pursuit of justice. If we are not for ourselves, who will be?

How Do We Fix This?

It used to be the case that Jewish commitment to universal social action flowed directly from the Jewish collective commitment—whether it was through identification with the oppressed because of a sense of Jewish history or through a reverence for the prophetic moral tradition and the teachings of Jewish thinkers like Rabbi Abraham Joshua Heschel, for whom marching to Selma with Dr. King was an ultimate expression of his deeply informed, elevated, and energized Jewish spirit. Jews were universalist not despite their Judaism but because of it. Jewish commitment was the fount of universal wisdom and the key to its sustainability over time and transmission from one generation to the next.

While Jewish values certainly do demand from us and from the Jewish state that we seek to alleviate the suffering of others, including the stranger, the Torah commands us to disobey God if it means saving our life or the lives of others.

This core teaching, famously captured in Hillel the Elder's dictum "If I am not for myself, who will be for me? But if I am only for myself, what am I?" (*Pirkei Avot* 1:14), seems to have been erased in liberal Judaism today—not because Jewish institutions fail to teach universalism, but because they fail to teach a love of Jewish particularism and the commitment to Jewish peoplehood without which Jewish universalism cannot be sustained. Much good can be done for the world over a lifetime of activism, but the role of the temple is above all to ensure that Jews build their universal activism on a foundation of Jewish belonging and learning, through an immersion in Jewish history, texts, and communal initiatives to spend time with, and develop a sense of mutual responsibility toward, other Jews.

This is also part of the explanation as to why many temples are, frankly, not doing well. Jews used to feel a bond into which they were born and from which they could leave only with great difficulty. Today, however, the market of potential affiliations and identities is more free and fluid than ever. With every swipe of their smartphones, younger Jews are choosing new identities and rejecting others. If being Jewish is primarily or only about universalism, and not also about being part of a long arc of Jewish history or a living community that takes care of its own, if being Jewish is just another "brand" of universal activism, then it's much easier to just cut yourself off from Jewish identity altogether—for what value does it add, and at what cost? For many students, the jump from "just Jewish" to "just human" is an easy decision: all the benefits without any of the burdens.

The failure among younger Jews to stand up for Israel is, in other words, just a symptom of what is really a much deeper problem: the failure to truly care about fellow Jews, as members of a great family to which you are privileged to belong and who must be helped above others in times of need—that there are times when one must prioritize the particular. There are no longer a million Jews locked behind an Iron Curtain. But there is no shortage of Jewish causes that could be made into a core element of the activism of younger Jews: there are Jews who live in poverty; there are Jews who feel a tightening noose of anti-Semitism; there are Jews who live under the threat of terror. That we rarely see such mitzvah projects—supporting Jews as Jews—suggests we have lost our way.

Jewish life in America is a miracle in its freedom and rebirth, given the millennia of powerlessness and vulnerability that defined our entire existence until just a few decades ago. The life of Jews in America has become so richly modern. Indeed, our success and desire to assimilate, to transcend and leave behind that grounding specialness, and to be accepted by the non-Jewish world as just another American are so great, it seems we have begun to prioritize others over the strength and preservation of ourselves—only seventy years removed from the most horrific destruction visited upon our people.

In the past, liberal movements in Judaism emphasized their universal teaching as a way to set themselves apart from the particularism of Orthodoxy and show their embrace of modernity. Today, however, the greatest threats to our community come not from tradition but from the same forces that threaten modernity itself—from the postmodern mutation of "social justice" that lures Jews into a false sense of universal good while attacking the core of their Jewish identity and the very idea that Jews have collective rights, including the right to a sovereign homeland, and which forces them to choose between the universalism they've always been taught to prioritize and the underlying value of being Jewish in the first place.

Yet who will make the argument that Jews are special and must be celebrated and secure, if not us? Who in the future will defend the justice of a Jewish state when our community does not prioritize inculcating a Jewish identity and the responsibility to strengthen ourselves and fight for our own survival?

We have failed to internalize these changing conditions and now find ourselves in a trap of our own making: the need to show our greatness to others has wrecked our ability to be great to and for ourselves.

Instead, we need to go back to telling ourselves and our children how special we have been, and can be in the future, if we survive and celebrate the Jewish tradition that has given the world the foundations of Western civilization and human dignity, of law and rights and humanity. This comes through intense education of history, text, and culture—but also through fun and recreation, through sports and cooking and dance, with fellow Jews, building the bonds of uniquely Jewish relationships and love of community. At a time when real friendships are everywhere being displaced by massive on-line social interaction, the need for real human contact and communal consciousness has never been greater. And the central institution where this should happen is the synagogue, the citadel of essential Jewish thinking and teaching.

Jewish communities must adapt if they are to survive. Instead of using social justice as a draw, especially as its new postmodern manifestation is threatening to obliterate our perspective on history, we should shift our communal practice to drawing in families and participants in ways that speak to their lives as they live them and that fosters ways for Jews to spend time together, remembering the particular specialness of being with other Jews.

Hillel's famous saying poses a question at the very heart of our role as Jews, in service to God and in pursuit of the everyday spectacular citizenship that our great country allows. Yet it also provides an equally important, and perhaps overlooked, template for prioritizing where we rest our energies at times of peril for the Jewish people. When the "me," the I, is alone and at risk, it comes first. Even as we pursue a self and society where we look beyond ourselves, if there is no me, nothing is possible. While always in tension, the need for self-preservation is always prioritized above other mitzvot.

Until confronted by the uncomfortable reality of anti-Semitism surging around them since the 2016 election, many on the Jewish left and their champions in organizations, from J Street to If Not Now to the anti-Zionist Jewish Voice for Peace, turned up their noses at the notion that anti-Semitism remained pervasive in the rarified air of the early twenty-first century. Such ideas, they claimed, were only promulgated by wild-eyed fanatics seeking to justify the need for a Jewish state in the world. The nation-state to them was at best vestigial, at worst an expression of fascism, rather than an expression of the Jewish right to self-determination and self-defense.

In July 2017, the director of the American Civil Liberties Union's human rights program said on Twitter, "Israeli leaders exploit horrible acts of anti-Semitism to encourage Jews to move to Israel. Judaism ≠ Zionism. Anti-Zionism ≠ Anti-Semitism,"[12] an anti-Semitic remark that drew a direct rebuke from the Anti-Defamation League's national president, but silence from those in the community who claim to speak for progressive Jews.

One *New York Times* opinion page editor, Matt Seaton, publicly dismissed the idea that anti-Semitism among Palestinians, inculcated in their classrooms and pervasive in their culture, deserves special attention, saying it would only be meaningful when the Palestinians "have a sovereign state to discriminate with."[13] Yet as awful as that attitude may seem, it is widespread among today's New Left and Liberal Zionist proponents of the BDS (Boycott, Divestment, Sanctions) movement, both in the Jewish community and beyond. But the reality and threat of violence against Jews, and the easy manner in which hatred of Jews is conveyed under the more acceptable cover of anti-Zionism or critique of Israel, betray the cold reality. It should serve as an opportunity to educate. How many young Jews today know that while Jews total about 2.2 percent of the U.S. population, we are the victims—according to an FBI report released in late 2016—of over half of the religiously motivated hate crimes in America?[14] No other minority comes even close, with Muslims the second most-victimized group, at two out of ten incidents.

And while many Jews are intensely and justifiably alarmed by violence threatening African Americans, women, Muslims, Hispanics, the LGBTQ community, and others, the only group that always seems glaringly left out from the list of victims of bigotry that define the debates on campus and beyond is Jews. As *Tablet* editor Alana Newhouse, that generational talent of Jewish pride and twenty-first-century Jewish hipness, put it in a recent essay, "The absence of Jews from the lists of those whose vulnerability merits attention is a measure of how far the disease of anti-Semitism has spread in sectors of society that otherwise pride themselves on their compassion for minority groups."[15]

That silence too often today includes Jews—Jews who, while not being driven by anti-Semitic hatred, are nonetheless enabling those who are. For by turning a blind eye to the relentless and often violent assault on their own people, they are failing to teach their children about the reality that Jews face, failing to imbue the pride required to recognize, let alone confront, the diminishment of Jewish value. And they are failing to create the conditions for the next generation of Jews to enjoy and celebrate, rather than mask, the particular specialness of being a Jew.

For the tide to turn, however, we need to rediscover our Jewish institutions, foremost among them the temple, as a unique source of Jewish wisdom, peoplehood, heritage, and collective self-love—and we must act quickly, before we find ourselves with little left to save.

Notes

1. Nathan Heller, "The Big Uneasy: What's Roiling the Liberal-Arts Campus?," *New Yorker*, May 30, 2016, http://www.newyorker.com/magazine/2016/05/30/the-new-activism-of-liberal-arts-colleges.

2. Bari Weiss, "Jonathan Haidt on the Cultural Roots of Campus Rage," *Wall Street Journal*, April 1, 2017, https://www.wsj.com/articles/jonathan-haidt-on-the-cultural-roots-of-campus-rage-1491000676.

3. Juan Prieto, "Violence Helped Ensure Safety of Students," *Daily Californian*, February 7, 2017, http://www.dailycal.org/2017/02/07/violence-helped-ensure-safety-students/.

4. TheTower.org Staff, "Daily Beast: Oberlin Students Who Protest Other Injustices Are Silent about Anti-Semitism," *Tower*, April 5, 2016, http://www.thetower.org/3187-daily-beast-oberlin-students-who-protest-other-injustices-are-silent-about-anti-semitism/.

5. Helen Pluckrose, "How French 'Intellectuals' Ruined the West: Postmodernism and Its Impact Explained," *Areo Magazine*, March 27, 2017, https://areomagazine.com/2017/03/27/how-french-intellectuals-ruined-the-west-postmodernism-and-its-impact-explained/.

6. David Gerstman, "Oberlin Professor Claims Israel Was Behind 9/11, ISIS, Charlie Hedbo Attack," *Tower*, February 25, 2016, http://www.thetower.org/3012-oberlin-professor-claims-israel-was-behind-911-isis-charlie-hebdo-attack/.

7. William A. Jacobson, "Oberlin Student Senate Condemns Witch Hunt against Professor Joy Karega," *Legal Insurrection*, September 20, 2016, http://legalinsurrection.com/2016/09/oberlin-student-senate-condemns-witch-hunt-against-prof-joy-karega/.

8. Daniel Mael, "On Many Campuses, Hate Is Spelled SJP," *Tower Magazine*, October 2014, http://www.thetower.org/article/on-many-campuses-hate-is-spelled-sjp/.

9. Jewish Voice for Peace YouTube channel: Rebecca Vilkomerson at J Street, supporting BDS movement, https://www.youtube.com/watch?v=wbH-dZOjH8dI&feature=youtu.be.

10. Josh Block, "We Were 100% Right to Highlight Anti-Israel Hate—Whatever Peter Beinart Says," *Forward*, June 27, 2017, http://forward.com/opinion/375632/we-were-100-right-to-highlight-anti-israel-hate-whatever-peter-beinart-says.

11. Josh Block, "What Do TIP and the Dyke March Have in Common? Absolutely Nothing," *Forward*, June 30, 2017, http://forward.com/opinion/national/376048/israel-project-dyke-march-common-nothing-josh-block-peter-beinart/.

12. Jamil Dakwar, https://twitter.com/jdakwar/status/881497780560302080.

13. Shiryn Ghermezian, "New York Times Opinion Editor Explains Why Paper Won't Address Palestinian Racism," *Algemeiner*, October 30, 2014, https://www.algemeiner.com/2014/10/30/new-york-times-opinion-editor-explains-why-paper-wont-address-palestinian-racism/.

14. JTA, "FBI: Anti-Muslim Hate Crimes Up 67 Percent; Anti-Semitic Hate Crimes Up 9 Percent," *Haaretz*, November 15, 2016, http://www.haaretz.com/world-news/u-s-election-2016/1.753231.

15. Alana Newhouse, "Hitler's Babies: Anti-Semitism, America, and the Jews," *Tablet Magazine*, November 23, 2016, http://www.tabletmag.com/scroll/218520/hitlers-babies.

Between Judaism and Democracy
Arab-Palestinian Citizens of a Jewish State

YOAV SCHAEFER

> When strangers reside with you in your land, you shall not
> wrong them. The strangers who reside with you shall be to you
> as your citizens; you shall love each one as yourself, for you were
> strangers in the land of Egypt.
> —LEVITICUS 19:33–34

S HORTLY AFTER the United Nations' vote to partition Palestine
in November 1947—which paved the way for the establishment
of a Jewish state—David Ben-Gurion, Israel's most revered and
visionary statesman, gave a speech at a meeting of the Labor Party.
"It is incumbent upon us," Ben-Gurion told the Labor Party leadership, "to think in terms of a state, in terms of independence, in terms
of full responsibility for ourselves—and for others too."[1] For the
state, he said, would include not only Jews but non-Jews as well. All
members of the state "will be equal citizens . . . in all respects without
any exception—that is, the state will be their state as well."[2] Only in
the realm of immigration, Ben-Gurion made clear, would the state
actively discriminate against its non-Jewish citizens. This, he felt,
was justified by the historical experience of the Jewish people, since
he considered Israel's raison d'être—in the aftermath of the Holocaust—its existence as a place of refuge for Jews in times of need.
With the exception of immigration, however, he declared that the
Jewish state would ensure "full and real equality, de jure and de facto,
of all of the state's citizens."[3] To accomplish this goal, he continued,
the state would work toward the "gradual equalization of the economic, social, and cultural standard of living of the Arab community
with that of the Jewish community."[4]

Ben-Gurion's speech is deeply revealing. He understood that
societies were measured, above all else, by how they treated their
weakest members, especially their minorities. Yet he feared that the
Jews, given their lack of experience with political sovereignty, were
ill-prepared for the demands of democratic governance and that
they would fail to extend to their minorities the same rights and
equalities that they had sought and so often been denied throughout
their long dispersion.

Ben-Gurion's egalitarian vision would ultimately be enshrined in
the State of Israel's Declaration of Independence, which promises
to "ensure complete equality of social and political rights to all its
inhabitants irrespective of religion, race or sex."[5] And yet, Israel has
failed to live up to the ideals of both its founding document and its
founding father. Ben-Gurion's hope that the Jews would establish in
Israel a society in which all of its citizens, regardless of their religious
or national identity, could be full and equal members has yet to be
fully realized.

Jewish Israelis—and Israel's supporters around the world—
must confront an important but painful truth. The establishment
of a Jewish national homeland has come at a heavy cost for Arab-
Palestinians.[6] Not only were Arab-Palestinians dispossessed as a
result of the destruction of a civilization in Europe for which they
bore no responsibility, but Israel's Arab-Palestinian citizens are
subject to manifold forms of racism and discrimination, which, in
effect if not in intent, render them second-class citizens in their own
state. The disenfranchisement of Israel's Arab-Palestinian minority
raises difficult moral and political questions about Israel's ability to
be a home to all of its inhabitants. The rightward shift of Israeli politics, the normalization of racist forms of political nationalism, and
recent attempts to undermine the legitimacy and ethos of Israel's
democratic institutions have only further exacerbated the precari-
ous situation of Israel's Arab-Palestinian minority.

A Jewish Democracy: A Contradiction in Terms?
It is sometimes alleged that Israel's designation as a Jewish state is to

blame for much of the racism in Israeli society. Israel's Jewish character, so it is argued, violates the democratic principle of equal treatment and is therefore inherently discriminatory. According to this
view, ethnicity and culture, like religion, have no place in the public
sphere of a democratic state and ought to be limited to the private
life of the individual citizen. Only when Israel becomes a neutral
state—a state that neither endorses nor privileges any particular cultural or national group—can it be a genuine democracy.

On its face, this argument seems flawed. For one thing, Israel's
designation as the nation-state of the Jewish people is by no means
unique. Many countries in the world—including a good deal of
democratic ones—are nation-states in which the public-sphere,
national institutions and symbols are organized such that they
reflect the unique linguistic, cultural, or historical heritage of the
dominant ethnocultural group. Germany, Finland, Greece, Ireland,
Iceland, Armenia, Serbia, Romania, and Turkey are all examples of
nation-states, to name just a few. Like Israel, these countries implement special policies to institutionalize and protect the unique
identity and culture of a particular national group (e.g., immigration policies and citizenship rights, special links with and privileges
accorded to members of diaspora communities, a unique status
granted to a particular religion).

Indeed, most countries in the world today are closely tied to the
language and culture of the majority national group. And this is
hardly undemocratic. In fact, quite the opposite is true: questions
concerning the public sphere in democratic countries will often,
given the majoritarian nature of democracy, reflect the preferences
of the majority. Minorities, due to their marginal numbers, will have
a limited capacity to shape the public sphere and culture of the state.
To be sure, being governed by an alien public sphere may at times
be uncomfortable for minorities, but it is not necessarily discriminatory. Nor can it be said, prima facie, to infringe upon their basic
civic rights.

Inherent in every state, then, is a tension between minority and
majority groups. This has led many Jewish Israelis to assert that

there is no more need to demonstrate the legitimacy of Israel's status as a Jewish state than there is to justify the legitimacy of any other state. The issue, they therefore argue, is not whether Judaism and democracy are reconcilable in Israel. The issue is whether liberalism, with its commitment to individual rights, is reconcilable with the collectivist spirit of nationalism.

Israel's Second-Class Citizens: Separate and Unequal

This argument would be correct, it seems to me, were "Judaism" in Israel defined in terms of culture alone. The problem, I want to suggest, is not that Judaism and democracy are inherently irreconcilable, but that the vast majority of Jewish Israelis interpret the Jewish character of the state in hegemonic—rather than cultural—terms.

Many Jewish Israelis regard it as axiomatic that the right to self-determination implies the right to complete hegemony over the entire state. Said differently, the hegemonic conception of sovereignty to which many Jewish Israelis subscribe suggests that the dominant national group has the right to control most, if not all, aspects of the public and political life of the state. It implies, in short, ownership over the state and its institutions. The result is that Jewish Israelis enjoy almost exclusive control over education, resource allocation, state symbols and national institutions, culture and language, religion, security, immigration and repatriation policies, and official holidays. Simply put: Israel's ethnocultural bias, while by no means unique, is often unprecedented.[7]

As such, the hegemonic interpretation of the right to self-determination implies, in both theory and practice, an unequal status for non-Jewish citizens, effectively barring them from full integration into Israeli society. It is not only that Israel's public sphere and national culture—including its national symbols—are inimical to the full inclusion of Israel's Arab-Palestinian minority, which makes up a significant subset—over 20 percent—of the population. Jewish Israelis have yet to understand what it took the United States nearly a century of Jim Crow laws and the historic ruling in *Brown v. Board of Education* to acknowledge: that "separate but equal" is decidedly unequal.

Israel has, as a result, systematically rendered its Arab-Palestinian minority second-class citizens in ways that go far beyond that of most other nation-states. This is true in the realms of resource allocation, welfare, education, and political representation, where significant disparities exist between Jewish and Arab-Palestinian Israelis. More fundamentally, most Jewish Israelis simply do not see Arab-Palestinians as deserving of full membership in Israel's public or political life. For example, a recent poll by the Pew Research Center found that 79 percent of Jewish Israelis believe that Jews deserve preferential treatment in Israel. Astonishingly, 48 percent of Jewish Israelis believe that Arab-Palestinian citizens of Israel should be either expelled or transferred from Israel altogether.[8] Another poll by the Israeli Democracy Institute found that a majority of Israeli Jews (56.6 percent) oppose the presence of Arab parties in the government or the appointment of Arab-Palestinian ministers; 42.5 percent of Jewish Israelis believe that Arab-Palestinian citizens have not reconciled themselves to the existence of a Jewish state and support its destruction, while 39 percent of Jewish Israelis believe that they constitute an imminent security threat.[9]

What such figures reveal is that many Jewish Israelis consider it self-evident that Arab-Palestinians cannot become full and equal citizens of the state. Even more, they demonstrate a fundamental misunderstanding of the basic underpinnings of democracy on the part of, if not the majority, then a significant number of Jewish Israelis. The democratic rights of Arab-Palestinians are taken to be contingent upon either the benevolence of Israeli Jews or the loyalty of Arab-Palestinians to the state, not something that they inherently possess by virtue of their membership in the body politic. Arab-Palestinian citizens of Israel are regarded, at best, as leaseholders but not rightful owners of the state; at worst, as unwanted inhabitants, even enemies of the state bent on its destruction. In short, Arab-Palestinians are not called upon to be full and equal partners in the Israeli national project.

A Moral Vision for the Jewish State: A Shared Civic Identity

It is hard to imagine Jewish Israelis renouncing their more hegemonic interpretation of the right to self-determination. It is even more difficult to imagine them relinquishing their exclusive control over many realms of the political and public life of the state, especially over the state's symbols, the military, and immigration policies. Of course, there may be historical and moral justifications for the hegemonic status conferred upon Jewishness in Israel and the preferential treatment granted to Jews. Furthermore, exclusive Jewish control over certain realms of the state—especially those of security and of immigration—may be justifiable given the historical experience of the Jewish people and the seriousness of Israel's security concerns. The question is whether those justifications, however valid, are enough to justify the cost imposed upon Israel's non-Jewish citizens. The crucial question, in other words, is not whether Israel has the *right* to define Jewishness in hegemonic terms. Rather, it is whether defining Jewishness in such a way is conducive to building a society that reflects the highest values, ideals, and aspirations of the Jewish people and the Jewish state. Such questions are, to be sure, profoundly difficult and complicated. They allow no easy answers. As Isaiah Berlin pointed out, there are no simple or perfect answers to political questions.

Admittedly, the idea of an American-style civil rights movement emerging in Israel, with Jews and Arab-Palestinians marching side by side and demanding equal rights for all Israelis, is difficult to envision. A few notable exceptions aside, Jewish and Arab-Palestinian Israelis live parallel but entirely separate existences. There are, it is important to note, glimmers of hope breaking through the darkness. In recent years, a handful of civil society initiatives dedicated to building and bolstering crosscutting cleavages among Israelis of all backgrounds have emerged. But these initiatives are the exceptions that prove the rule. The vast majority of Jewish Israelis have yet to embrace the integration of Israel's non-Jewish citizens as an imperative. Nevertheless, that is hardly a reason that such an integrationist ideal should not be pursued. Ideals set an infinite task: they are like an ever-receding signpost toward which we continuously strive but never fully reach.

To realize such an integrationist ideal, it is not enough to merely pay lip service to the values of inclusivity and equality when it comes to Israel's Arab-Palestinians citizens. Nor is it a matter of simply improving their welfare and their participation in the political and public life of the state, although these are good initial steps. Israelis must create a thin layer of civic identity with which all of Israel's citizens can identify, regardless of their religious or ethnic background. Only then can the inclusion and integration of Israel's Arab-Palestinian minority be possible.

Creating a shared civic identity in Israel and integrating non-Jewish citizens into the Israeli mainstream are moral and political imperatives. Discrimination, whether de jure or de facto, has a corrosive effect on democratic societies. It undermines the basic social fabric that binds citizens to one another. Moreover, it renders impossible the idea of an overlapping consensus upon which the very possibility of democratic politics is contingent.

Of course, Ben-Gurion knew all of this to be true. He understood that integrating Israel's non-Jewish minorities was both morally and politically necessary. Israel's future, Ben-Gurion recognized, would ultimately depend on its ability to defend itself not only militarily but also morally. In his mind, morality and politics, far from being mutually exclusive realms, were reciprocally linked. "No regime and no rule," he said, "will endure by brute force alone. And no political claim will succeed for long if it does not rest upon a strong moral foundation."[10] The success and future of Zionism depend on us heeding Ben-Gurion's words. Building a more egalitarian and democratic Israel—in which all of Israel's citizens can be equal and full participants—is at once Zionism's most difficult and vital task. No matter how inconceivable or daunting this realization may seem, we are not free, as our tradition teaches us, to desist from it.

NOTES

1. Quoted in *The Jewish Political Tradition*, vol. 2, ed. Michael Walzer, Menachem Lorberbaum, and Noam J. Zohar (New Haven, CT: Yale University Press, 2000), 524.

2. Ibid.

3. Ibid., 525.

4. Ibid.

5. The Declaration of the Establishment of the State of Israel. https://www.knesset.gov.il/docs/eng/megilat_eng.htm.

6. Following several prominent scholars, I use the term "Arab-Palestinians" to emphasize and distinguish between the ethnic and linguistic identity (Arab) and national identity (Palestinian) of Israel's Arab-Palestinian citizens. Arab-Palestinians consider themselves not only a religious or ethnic minority but a national minority as well.

7. For a more comprehensive and detailed exploration of Israel's ethnocultural bias relative to other nation-states, see Chaim Gan's illuminating study: *A Just Zionism: On the Morality of the Jewish State* (Oxford: Oxford University Press, 2008).

8. See the Pew Research Center's recent report: "Israel's Religiously Divided Society" (March 2016). http://www.pewforum.org/2016/03/08/israels-religiously-divided-society/.

9. See the Israel Democracy Institute's report: "The Israeli Democracy Index" (2015). https://en.idi.org.il/centers/1159/1519.

10. Quoted in *The Jewish Political Tradition*, vol. 2, 524.

In the Classroom and on Campus

Educating for Ambiguity

RABBI LISA D. GRANT, PhD

Three Scenes

SCENE 1: A conversation before Shabbat services. I am speaking with a second-year law student, who is telling me about a friend of hers who is spending the year in Israel. She says, "That would be hard for me to do. I'm not so Zionist anymore. I have a lot of questions." She then says, "I'm a little suspicious of anyone who doesn't have questions about Zionism today." I concur. She then proceeds to tell me about her semester on the Eisendrath International Exchange program as a high school student and her semester at Ben-Gurion University as an undergraduate. Lastly, she mentions that she and her fiancée are planning to visit Israel during their winter break from school. She says, "She's only been on Birthright, so she hasn't really seen Israel. I'll get to show her a lot of what I think is important about Israel."

SCENE 2: A facilitated small-group discussion about Israel on a Thursday night at the synagogue. About forty people divide themselves into circles of eight or so people each. In my group, one woman in her forties emphatically says, "Israel has absolutely no place in my understanding of Judaism." A man in his fifties says, "I grew up in a very Zionist home, but now I am so disheartened. I hate what Israel is becoming." A high school senior says, "I didn't know what to think about Israel until I went on a program last summer that was a mix of Americans and Israelis of very different backgrounds. Being in conversation with them all summer in Israel made me realize the situation is so different from what we mostly hear and see and talk about here."

SCENE 3: A member of the Knesset from the Labor Party in Israel speaks to the congregation during Friday night services. Almost twice as many people as typically show up are there. She speaks briefly, mostly in tribute to Shimon Peres, z"l, whose funeral was that day. During a question period after her remarks, someone asks, "What can we do as American Jews?" Her response: "Don't give up hope. Don't write us off. We need your support and your partnership."

These three snapshots capture a lot about American Reform Jews' conversations about Israel today. There are those who remain curious and committed, wanting to remain connected in some meaningful way. There are those who have effected a divorce, asserting Israel has no place in their lives. And there are those who are ambivalent, filled with questions, not sure what they think and feel. Many would consider the last two categories a failure in cultivating a passionate connection to Israel. I disagree. It seems to me that any conversation about Israel that engages people in open, honest exploration of issues and expression of questions and concerns is an educational success. After all, even the woman in the second scenario who said Israel isn't part of her Jewish identity came to an event to talk about Israel! We often say that we don't know how to talk about Israel. My question in response to this is: what is the Israel that we don't know how to talk about?

The prevailing assumption, and indeed there is much evidence to support this, is that conversations about Israel in American Jewish life today are filled with vitriol, divisiveness, and dismay. Indeed, there is an abundance of opinion pieces in the Jewish press that reflect this reality, with titles like "We Need Dialogue, Not Demagoguery"[1] and "Why We've Left Zionism Behind."[2] On the other side of the spectrum, and perhaps even more common, there is silence. Many communities either tacitly or implicitly avoid doing much at all to engage in any serious learning or conversations about Israel either for fear that it will result in polarization and alienation within the community or simply because it is not a high priority among the many other more pressing and immediately felt local and national issues and concerns. Exacerbating matters is what many see as a progressive deterioration of core democratic and Jewish values in Israel with a nonexistent peace process, increased settlement development in the West Bank, a vilification of the left by the right and the right by the left, continued efforts of the religious establishment to block any forms of religious pluralism, and what seems like an endless cycle of violence perpetrated on and by Palestinians. This galvanizes some into action, but it likely confuses and paralyzes many others.

Though the situation seems particularly disheartening at this point in time, ambivalence about Israel is far from new in American Jewish life in general and American Reform Jewish life in particular. As we know, the early American Reform Jews dismissed Zionism as irrelevant, writing in the Pittsburgh Platform of 1885 (see p. 287) that "we consider ourselves no longer a nation, but a religious community, and therefore expect neither a return to Palestine, nor a sacrificial worship under the sons of Aaron, nor the restoration of any of the laws concerning the Jewish state."[3] This outright rejection softened considerably by the Columbus Platform in 1937 (see p. 261), but the language made clear that the upbuilding of the Jewish homeland was for "many of our brethren," but not really for us. American Jews were to help from a distance, supporting the creation of "not only a haven of refuge for the oppressed but also a center of Jewish culture and spiritual life."[4] In 1997, the CCAR issued a platform devoted exclusively to Zionism,[5] in recognition of the centenary of the First World Zionist Congress in Basel, Switzerland (see p. 271). The language of this platform is quite clear about Reform Jewish support of Israel, but it also takes pains to affirm "the authenticity and necessity of a creative and vibrant Diaspora Jewry." For the first time, the Reform Movement states a position about *aliyah*, encouraging it "in pursuance of the precept of *yishuv Eretz Yisrael* [settling the Land of Israel]."

The 1997 platform was followed soon after by the broader 1999 Statement of Principles (see p. 277), which seems to overshadow the earlier document.[6] This document includes a statement of support of Israel tinged with ambivalence, suggesting a sense of distance in rejoicing in the accomplishments of our distant cousins, affirming that living in Israel has certain "unique qualities," and again encouraging *aliyah*.[7] Though each new platform was intended to replace the earlier, themes and attitudes of each are still resonant in Reform Jewish life today.

This can be seen by considering just a few questions and conundrums one hears posed by thoughtful Reform Jews:

- As Reform Jews who believe in a universal God, universal ethics, and universal entry into the world-to-come, how can we support an increasingly particularistic, nationalistic, exclusionary country?
- If Israel is the homeland of the Jewish people, how come they don't recognize so many of us as Jews?
- If we do not read the Torah literally, why should we understand the "Promised Land" as a literal piece of geography?
- Israel as a safe haven makes no sense today. It is an incredibly unstable and dangerous region, and we can't really think a new Holocaust is likely.
- Why should Israel be the spiritual center of our faith? Why do we need a piece of land as our spiritual center? Aren't God and Torah the spiritual centers of our faith?

These are challenging and rich questions that deserve thoughtful consideration, and yet much of our educational initiatives assiduously avoid questions such as these, for fear that addressing them seriously may result in further distancing from Israel. The goals for Israel education in many Reform Jewish settings most likely still fit with what Barry Chazan identified more than forty years ago. They are "low-level and ambiguous . . . reflect[ing] no ideological principles beyond the assumption that Israel is important, nor do they delineate any clear sense of meaning of Israel for Jewish life."[8]

Our inability to articulate a compelling vision for Israel education may lie in our unwillingness to accept the inherent ambiguity in our stance toward Israel. Rather than embrace this ambiguity, we seek to harmonize and instrumentalize Israel so that it fits with the not-so-hidden curriculum of American Jewish education, which is, in essence, how to function as an American Jew. Inasmuch as Israel education can be used as a way to reinforce *American* Jewish identity, it is viewed as a positive. This has resulted in a "mythic" representation of Israel that, as Jonathan Sarna pointed out, has, "for well over a century... revealed more about American Jewish ideals than about Israeli realities."⁹ Jewish education has reinforced this idealization of Israel to a great extent so that Israel can remain consistent with American conceptions of "Zion as it ought to be."¹⁰ This means that we keep Israel at a distance through episodic and rather superficial encounters. We teach old conceptions and old narratives about Israel, because they are "safe" and because we don't know what else to do. Indeed, it seems that a tacit assumption is made that only by first cultivating an uncritical "love of Israel" can we hope to engage American Jews at all.

To be sure, approaches that cultivate love can be effective for some. For increasing numbers, however, such approaches lead to dissonance, alienation, anger, and outright rejection, especially when they come to realize the mythic vision of Israel they were taught is vastly different from the much more complicated and often distressing reality. And, teaching only the "lovable" parts leaves our learners with, at best, a superficial understanding of *why* Israel is or could be significant in American Jewish life. We don't teach only the "lovable" parts of American history and society. Why should we do so with Israel?

I want to propose that we accept the fact that that being ambivalent about Israel is a productive educational goal. This may be unsettling for some, but it is far from a novel idea. Almost a century ago, the great Hebrew poet and writer Chaim Nachman Bialik wrote that "the phenomenon of dualism in our psyche [is] a fundamental characteristic of the Jewish people."¹¹ This dualism is not a black-and-white choice between opposing forces, but rather a formative tension that allows for productive negotiation and growth. This kind of dualism is woven throughout Jewish life, belief, and practice, with manifold tensions between Zion and Sinai, sacred and profane, Israel and Diaspora, exile and redemption, religion and peoplehood, blessing and curse. Bialik claimed that the desire both to expand from the center and to contract toward it is what has kept

Judaism and the Jewish people a dynamic and thriving civilization. "Because the people did not tie its fate to one of these and because they remained in equal power, the rule of this dualism in our group character has survived to this day."[12]

Much more recently, Michael Marmur offered the idea of "confident inadequacy" as another kind of dualism in formulating an inherently ambiguous stance as a Reform Zionist.[13] Drawing on the image of a half-full cup, such a stance both acknowledges all that is good and at the same time recognizes that there is much to be done. Marmur wrote that a totally unambiguous identity is impossible. We must learn to live with the tensions and contradictions inherent in Israel. But this is not just a problem of Israel. Rather, this is a problem of Jewish life broadly speaking and simply in being human today. It is the reality of the search to construct meaning in a time when our grand narratives have been exposed as inadequate to address the manifold complexities of our world today.

What would it look like to intentionally embrace such an ambiguous stance toward Israel and Jewish life? For this, I draw on the ideas of Parker Palmer, a Quaker thinker, writer, and educator who has had a profound impact on American education. His book *Healing the Heart of Democracy* examines how to deal realistically and hopefully with the political tensions in American society "without the shouting, blaming, or defaming so common in our civic organizations and faith communities today."[14] These lessons are wholly applicable to conversations about Israel today as well. He offers five principles, but in a recent appearance on the radio program "On Being with Krista Tippett," Palmer said if five was too many, we really need only two: chutzpah and humility.[15] Palmer explained that "chutzpah" gives us the confidence to speak out, to acknowledge that we have something worth saying. "Humility" tempers this confidence, however, reminding us that we don't know everything and may have only a partial understanding of the truth of any given situation. We need to stay in balance both with ourselves and with each other. Leaning too far in either direction results in either silence or arrogance, neither of which affords for learning or growth.

Palmer's ideas about chutzpah and humility align beautifully with Bialik and Marmur and offer us a conceptual framework for rethinking what Israel education might be. There are, in fact, models of what intentional teaching for ambiguity around Israel might look like in progressive Jewish life. A prerequisite to this approach is for clergy and educators to reflect their own sense of confident inadequacy in how they talk about Israel—acknowledging their points of view are incomplete, their knowledge only partial, and their willingness to learn from others welcome. This demands the creation of a safe space for open, honest conversations that expose our vulnerabilities. It means sharing fears, anger, and pain with others who may have totally different perspectives or no perspective at all. It requires strong and active facilitators who can create and preserve this safe space, who guide us in learning how to listen more deeply to each other and to ask each other questions that are grounded in genuine curiosity rather than a desire to prove the other wrong. The organization Resetting the Table[16] exemplifies this kind of facilitation and has done work across the country in training facilitators to convene programs in synagogues, Hillels, Jewish Federations, and other organizations to learn to speak across difference and live within the ambiguity.

Another prerequisite for this stance is the willingness to take the time to engage a wide variety of synagogue community members in thoughtful and substantive planning to identify goals for Israel education that align with the community's broader goals for Jewish life. Temple Shaaray Tefila (TST) in New York City is one example of what the fruits of this kind of work might yield. This congregation has made an explicit commitment to integrate Israel into all aspects of congregational life. In a multiyear process, a task force identified core principles to guide them in this work:[17]

- Increased Israel engagement will not be the result of programming alone.
- Increased Israel engagement requires a culture where Israel is integral in all that we do and how we think.
- Increased Israel engagement requires a nuanced

understanding of Israel and its issues. Israel is complicated, its issues are complex, and we need to understand
that complexity.

- We agree that we unconditionally support Israel and its
right to exist. Unconditional support does not mean
that we cannot be a place where controversial issues are
discussed or criticism of Israel is raised.

While they don't use the words "confident inadequacy," the above principles suggest that this congregation is grappling with how this idea can and should undergird their thinking about Israel engagement. Embedded in these principles is the idea that Israel is both integral to the life of the community and also imperfect, that there is a need for serious learning about Israel and also space for serious disagreement.

Translating a "nuanced understanding of Israel" into educational practice is a multilayered process that could start even with how the geography of Israel is taught. What maps are displayed on the walls? Do they mark the Green Line? Do we teach only about Tel Aviv, Haifa, and Jerusalem, or do we also include units on Kfar Kana, Um el Fahm, and Sakhnin? Do we focus only on the kibbutzim of the north or also teach that 50 percent of the population of the Galilee is Muslim, Christian, or Druze? When we plan a *mifgash* (encounter) with Israelis, whether virtual or real, do we include meetings with Palestinian citizens of Israel or only Jews? Does our investigation of social justice initiatives in Israel extend only to issues of religious pluralism that pertain directly to Reform Jews, or do we also study about educational and/or social justice organizations that are striving to attain a shared citizenship across religious, ethnic, and political differences?

These are just a few of the questions worth considering when thinking about developing an intentionally ambivalent educational approach to teaching Israel. Embracing this ambivalence does not preclude me, however, from starting with the *chutzpadik* claim that Israel is integral to Jewish life wherever it is lived. That sets a boundary that is clear but also flexible. For me, Israel is a key dimension of what it means to be a Jew. Like the Psalmist, I believe that forgetting Israel can be likened to losing the use of a limb.[18] One can still live without one's right hand, but the loss is an attenuation, a diminishment, far from desirable. But, this chutzpah is tempered with a lot of humility. Understanding Israel as integral but not central allows for and even endorses a range of different personal commitments and connections. Israel as integral means that there is no one right way or one right level of intensity to be connected. Just as with every other aspect of Jewish life, Israel education can provide individuals with the resources and experiences to become informed and then make their own choices as to the nature and extent of their involvement. Just as all would agree that God, Torah, and Shabbat are integral to Jewish experience but that different Jews have different beliefs and practices, the same can be said about Israel. There is no one right way to engage with Israel, but engaging is an essential aspect of Jewish experience. Just as educators strive to help Jews find meaning in God, Torah, and Shabbat and cultivate the motivation, knowledge, or skills that enable them to be develop their own set of practices, so should they work to help Jews engage with Israel, each on their own terms, yet as part of the collective Jewish project.

What this means is that we must accept that our communities can and need to welcome a wide range of views, understandings, feelings, and actions about Israel. This seems all the more pressing and essential today in order to build thriving Jewish life and to sustain a relationship with and connection to Israel. It means having faith and hope in the Jewish people, that expressing our differences will help us to listen more carefully to each other with open hearts, knowing that the choices we make build us up, enrich us, and allow Jewish life to continue to thrive in a multiplicity of ways.

NOTES

1. Jon A. Levisohn and Miriam Heller Stern, "We Need Dialogue, Not Demagoguery, When It Comes to Israel," JTA, September 23, 2016, http://www.jta.org/2016/09/23/news-opinion/opinion/we-need-dialogue-not-demagoguery-when-it-comes-to-israel.

2. Hasia Diner and Marjorie N. Feld, "We're American Jewish Historians: This Is Why We've Left Zionism Behind," Haaretz.com, August 1, 2016, http://www.haaretz.com/opinion/1.734602.

3. The Pittsburgh Platform, 1885, https://www.ccarnet.org/rabbis-speak/platforms/declaration-principles/.

4. The Columbus Platform, 1937, https://www.ccarnet.org/rabbis-speak/platforms/guiding-principles-reform-judaism/.

5. Reform Judaism & Zionism: A Centenary Platform, "The Miami Platform," 1997, http://ccarnet.org/rabbis-speak/platforms/reform-judaism-zionism-centenary-platform/.

6. In my many years of teaching at Hebrew Union College–Jewish Institute of Religion, students have often created a model lesson on the CCAR platforms. Rarely is the 1997 Miami Platform included, even when the lesson is focused on Reform Zionism.

7. Central Conference of American Rabbis, "A Statement of Principles for Reform Judaism," 1999, https://www.ccarnet.org/rabbis-speak/platforms/statement-principles-reform-judaism/.

8. Barry Chazan, "Israel in American Jewish Schools Revisited," *Jewish Education* 42, no. 2 (1979), 10.

9. Jonathan Sarna, "A Projection of America as It Ought to Be: Zion in the Mind's Eye of American Jews," in *Envisioning Israel: The Changing Ideals and Images of North American Jews*, ed. Allon Gal (Detroit: Wayne State University Press, 1996), 41–59.

10. Ibid.

11. Chaim Nachman Bialik, translated by Zali Gurevitch, "Jewish Dualism," in *Revealment and Concealment: Five Essays* (Jerusalem: Ibis Editions, 2000), 27.

12. Ibid., 38.

13. Michael Marmur, "Happiness inside the Jewish State: Toward a Liberal Theology of Israel," *CCAR Journal: A Reform Jewish Quarterly* 54, no. 2 (Spring 2007): 84–97.

14. Parker Palmer, *Healing the Heart of Democracy*, http://www.couragerenewal.org/resources/books/.

15. Parker Palmer, "On Being with Krista Tippett," http://www.onbeing.org/program/parker-palmer-and-courtney-martin-the-inner-life-of-rebellion/transcript/8946#main_content, aired on September 22, 2016.

16. Resetting the Table, http://civility.jewishpublicaffairs.org/resetting-the-table/.
17. "TST Project: Gateways and Tents," internal document shared by Hope Chernak, Temple Shaaray Tefila's director of youth and informal education, September 25, 2016.
18. Psalm 137:5, "Should I forget you, Jerusalem, may my right hand wither" Robert Alter, *The Book of Psalms: A Translation with Commentary* (New York: W.W. Norton and Company, 2007), 474.

Metaphor and Meaning 101
The College Campus as Battleground

Rabbi Leah Cohen, DMin

THE JEWISH TRADITION is rich with metaphors to express ideas that are complex and nuanced. One of the best-known examples of metaphor in the Jewish lexicon comes from the High Holy Day liturgy. The prayer *Ki Anu Amecha* ("For we are Your people") offers a list of metaphoric possibilities as the basis for a relationship with God, including the following:

> We are Your flock, and You are our Shepherd.
> We are Your vineyard, and You are our Guardian.
> We are Your creatures, and You are our Creator.
> We are Your Faithful, and You are our Beloved.

The language of *Ki Anu Amecha* is effective because it helps us with a difficult, yet important aspiration, namely connecting with God on the most sacred day of the year. In this prayer, though we feel the power of the metaphor, we do not confuse the language of metaphor with the language of experience. On Yom Kippur we do not actually mistake ourselves to be sheep or vineyards. This prayer constructively uses metaphor to create a unifying framework for collective worship, yet allows for nuance in personally reflecting on our relationship with God. This metaphor serves to expand our thinking in imaginative ways as we envision a bond we care greatly about, but which remains complicated nonetheless.

Just as our relationship with God is understood and expressed in a variety of ways, so too is our connection with the State of Israel. The role of Israel in the lives of American Jews has become an increasingly divisive topic and nowhere more so than on college campuses.

This essay examines the subject of Israel on American campuses, starting with a critique of one of the most common metaphors to describe this relationship. The next section discusses a number of variables that impact the role of Israel on campus. Finally, the last section proposes criteria for describing Israel on campus and offers some new possibilities for framing this critical issue. My goal in writing this piece is twofold: first, to help those who are not steeped in campus life better understand the complexities and shades of the Israel/campus relationship; and second, to challenge us to be self-reflective and to think critically in choosing language to describe this relationship.

Critique of the Battleground Metaphor

I start with the example of *Ki Anu Amecha* to demonstrate metaphor in the Jewish world that is effective in contrast to metaphor that is less so. As early as 2002, and increasingly so in the last decade, the declaration that "college campuses are the new Israel battleground" has appeared in countless articles in the secular and Jewish press.[1] This phrase began gaining traction within Jewish circles with the rise of the BDS (Boycott, Divestment, Sanctions) movement. The origins of the BDS movement can be traced back to the UN World Conference against Racism in Durban, South Africa, in 2001 and the parallel conference, the NGO Forum. At the NGO Forum, a document known as the NGO declaration was produced, in which Israel was declared a "racist, apartheid state that was guilty of racist crimes including war crimes, acts of genocide and ethnic cleansing."[2] This declaration established an action plan promoting "a policy of complete and total isolation of Israel as an apartheid state . . . the imposition of mandatory and comprehensive sanctions and embargoes, the full cessation of all links (diplomatic, economic, social aid, military cooperation and training) between all states and Israel."[3] Although this language was not used in the final Durban Strategy document, it was widely circulated and had a tremendous impact.

Shortly thereafter in 2001, Students for Justice in Palestine (SJP), a student group at the University of California, Berkley, initiated a campus divestment campaign in conjunction with the San Francisco chapter of the American-Arab Anti-Discrimination Committee. SJP chapters spread to other campuses around the country. In 2002, the first campus divestment vote in the United States took place at Wayne State University. In 2005, the "Palestinian Civil Society Call for BDS against Israel" sought to link its divestment strategy to a movement focused on human rights and international law, instead of the anti-Semitic NGO Forum of the 2001 Durban conference.

Today, the BDS movement has spread to over one hundred college campuses in the United States. Over the last decade, BDS on campus has taken the form of academic boycotts (a movement to boycott Israeli academics from serving as faculty or visiting lecturers) and economic boycotts (a movement to compel the university to divest from or boycott Israeli companies or those doing business with Israeli companies). Student involvement has been primarily focused on economic aspects, whereas faculty involvement, in general, has been connected to academic boycotts.

The BDS strategy employed by student organizations such as SJP or Jewish Voices for Peace (JVP) has failed on campus from an economic perspective. To date, regardless of how the vote in the student government or even in cases of campus-wide referendums has turned out, no American university has divested from doing business with Israel. Nonetheless, the toll is quite draining on Jewish students who are involved in testifying against BDS in student senates and working in general to prevent a BDS resolution from passing. The burnout factor among Jewish campus leaders after such a vote, regardless of the outcome of the vote, can be significant.

Under these circumstances, and in light of the increase in anti-Semitic and anti-Israel rhetoric and incidents occurring on some college campuses across the nation, it is easy to see how the battleground metaphor has gained currency. In a battle, there is a sense of urgency that allows no room for apathy. There is a clear distinction between friend and foe. There is a unifying call that sets petty differences aside in order to address the more pressing issue of war. Campus as the new Israel battleground is indeed a compelling image.

However, I believe we have now crossed a critical line. These days, I hear this expression used too often not as metaphor, but as an ontological truth. This expression is inaccurate and potentially harmful in describing and dealing with the subject of Israel on campus. I wonder how many people who use this phrase have ever been on a battleground. I haven't, but I have spent the last four years on a college campus; we do not have soldiers or generals here. Deadly weapons are not distributed, nor does academia function with anything that remotely resembles military discipline. Students do not dodge bullets darting along bloody streets on their way to class, nor do they study in libraries strewn with dismembered body parts. On campus, the contest for life and death is greatly surpassed by the struggle to find interesting friends, juggle extracurricular activities, and turn papers in on time.

If the battleground metaphor were only inaccurate, it would not be so bad. But describing college campuses as battlegrounds perpetuates an obsession with crisis as the primary paradigm for engaging with Israel. Crisis mentality fosters attitudes and behaviors that are contrary to the overall purpose of higher education. To a person with a hammer, everything looks like a nail. To those who call campuses battlegrounds, everything looks like a war.

Colleges do not exist to perpetuate war. Rather, they exist to instill in the next generation the capacity for critical thinking; to expose young adults to new ideas; to educate students on content and structure across a range of subjects; to foster skills of self-expression, independence, and resiliency; and to imbue a sense of service and purpose in those who will be responsible for society in the future.

To these primary aims, Jewish college students face an additional set of expectations. College is recognized as a time of profound identity formation and psychosocial development. The Jewish community recognizes this fact and is sensitive to the opportunities and challenges therein. Although several Jewish organizations have a presence on college campuses, Hillel International is the world's largest Jewish campus organization, with affiliates on over 550 campuses in the United States alone. Hillel makes clear its priority in regard to campus and Israel in their vision statement: "We envision a world where every student is inspired to make an enduring commitment to Jewish life, learning and Israel."[4]

Given the reason colleges exist and the additional expectations for Jewish college students, I would argue that the battleground metaphor is inherently incompatible with the primary purpose of higher education and is ineffective for engaging college-aged students with Israel. The biggest problem campuses face with Israel engagement does not come from those who are for or against anything having to do with Israel. Rather, the reality is that a vast majority of Jewish students are completely indifferent to anything related to Israel. Telling someone there is a war going on about a subject they have shown little interest in is not usually a compelling reason for them to get involved. Furthermore, for those students who are involved with Israel, the battleground image presumes that allies and foes are easy to identify and that clearly foes must be destroyed. That paradigm is simply not how campus alliances work. The battleground mentality is a framework that is alienating and polarizing to many college students.

As the American Jewish community has become more divisive on the topic of Israel, it is not so clear who is fighting whom in this "battleground." For example, what began as a simple BDS versus the Jewish community battle has become much more about various elements of the Jewish community fighting among themselves and projecting these unresolved issues onto American college campuses. It is time to reassess the situation and consider language that is more fitting to the reality of Israel on campus today.

Analysis of the Variables Impacting the Role of Israel on Campus

The battleground framework, which has been espoused by both the left and the right, is an oversimplified model. By its binary nature, it is not adequate to capture the many variables that shape the role of Israel on campus. The reality of Israel relations and American campuses is ever changing. The following summary attempts to portray a snapshot of the current state of affairs across three interactive dimensions—student variables, campus variables, and external variables—with the goal of deepening our understanding of what is happening on campuses today.

Student Variables

Let us start from the perspective of the student. Jewish students come from a variety of backgrounds, and once on campus, they have a range of experiences in regard to all aspects of Jewish life, including Israel. Students who went to day schools, had parents who were strongly affiliated with congregations, received supplemental Jewish education, visited Israel with their family or congregations, or went to Jewish summer camps have often been exposed to the subject of Israel before they arrived on campus. Many Jewish students, however, grew up in homes where none of the above occurred and their first engagement with Israel is on campus.

Interestingly, there are pros and cons with both types of students when it comes to the issue of Israel engagement. Those with little background are easily swayed by the argument of the day, because they have no educational basis of comparison nor any emotional loyalty to Israel based on their upbringing. On the other hand, those who do come from strong Jewish backgrounds in which Israel was a part of the curriculum often suffer from a credibility gap when encountering Israel on campus. They are shocked to learn about Palestinians and a more multifaceted version of Israel's history that includes aspects they have never heard about growing up. This subset of the Jewish student population is often very angry and feels deceived by their parents, teachers, and rabbis. Once exposed to another narrative, they are often eager to learn more as a way of "finally finding out the truth." They can be gullible at times to the lies of Israel haters, simply because they now discount anything they learned before once they found out it was not the whole truth.

An important distinction considering Israel education on campus is the issue of advocacy versus critical thinking as the underlying rationale for offering this education. There are adherents and programs for both. However, my observation is that at this time pure advocacy training is looked down upon by most students as being too one-sided and unsophisticated. They often find it insulting or entertaining, and it tends to have the opposite effect from the one desired by those who attempt to use it. Students tend to be more interested in developing their critical thinking skills and can recognize when that is what is being offered to them.

In attempting to offer "talking points" that portray Israel in a good light, educators sometimes make a mistake that comes across as "changing the channel." For example, when difficult issues related to Israel come up, such as checkpoints or embargoes, what happens at times is that instead of staying with a contentious issue, the educational strategy has been to "change the channel" and start talking about Israel's exemplary record on LGBTQ rights (known as "pink washing") or divert attention to Israel's excellence as the "start-up nation." Students are suspicious and resentful of this technique, and it unfortunately winds up detracting from many of Israel's excellent achievements. The technique known as *hasbarah*—translated as either "public diplomacy," "public relations," or even more strongly, "propaganda"—in the guise of education, is usually rejected even among the most ardent Israel supporters on campus.

Most college undergraduate students are between eighteen and twenty-one years old. This age was defined by the great psychologist Erik Erikson as "late adolescence," the time when young people are tasked with integrating the sum of their past learning and experiences into a new coherent identity as an emerging adult. For Jewish college students, this integration can involve the topic of Israel in challenging ways when elements of Israeli reality are at odds with each other or with the individual's values. For example, how Israel is both Jewish and democratic and how that is played out in real life is something that Jewish students grapple with on campus these days. At other times, the reconciliation of values and priorities is thrust upon Jewish students by other students. Thus, when a student group that focuses on social justice activities challenges a Jewish student who wants to join because they question her ability to be both pro-Israel and pro–social justice, this can initiate profound moral confusion.

Issues of ego integration appear frequently with students who do not identify with the actions and statements of the current Israeli administration in regard to women's rights, religious pluralism in Israel, economic disparity, Palestinians, and a host of other topics. Resolving the integration of their values creates a fluidity in student relationships that may be difficult for those who are not familiar with this age group to fully appreciate. Students may get involved with one group that espouses a particular Israel rhetoric, then change several times throughout their time at college. For those observing college life, it is important to remember this aspect of student development in regard to Israel engagement. Exploration is part of what this age does, and the more forbidden something is, often the more enticing it can become. As Jewish college students attempt to assemble the pieces of themselves into a coherent, mature identity, deepening and expanding the conversation about Israel is more authentic to who they are at this age than is restricting certain topics.

Campus Variables

The climate of Israel engagement varies greatly from campus to campus. For the vast majority of campuses, Israel engagement is simply not a priority, either pro or con. In cases where Israel is a topic of interest, the nature of the campus will greatly determine the tenor of the relationship. For example, if the campus has a culture of activism, then it is more likely to have an activist attitude in regard to Israel. If the campus has a STEM focus (science, technology, engineering, and math), there will usually be little interest in Israel from a political perspective. Other factors such as campus size, location, and private versus public will impact the Israel environment as well.

Another campus factor that strongly influences the climate around Israel engagement depends on the Jewish community on campus. If the Jewish community is strong, with a diverse range of religious and political expressions, as well as a wealth of resources in terms of staff, faculty, finances, physical space, and student leadership, then the opportunities for Israel engagement are numerous and enticing. However, if the opposite is true and the campus is characterized by strong antagonism within the Jewish community, that campus becomes more vulnerable to anti-Israel efforts, with a special emphasis on recruitment among alienated members of the Jewish community.

Jewish centers on campus must negotiate the ideal of inclusivity with the need for Jewish safe space at times. Jewish students need to be able to express their concerns and criticisms without feeling that their vulnerabilities will be taken advantage of, that their Jewish authenticity will be challenged, or that open discussion and questioning will be perceived of as airing dirty laundry.

Similarly, the nature of the Muslim community on campus can strongly impact the Israel engagement climate. In schools where there are good relations between the Muslim and Jewish community, starting at the top (clergy/director level) and permeating to all levels of the campus, where there are intentional Muslim/Jewish student groups, and where both communities take advantage of opportunities to support one another, Israel on campus will be just one of many topics for discussion in respectful terms, even when there are deep disagreements. On these campuses, the Muslim students are usually second- or third-generation Americans and often their parents or grandparents came from places all over the world. By and large, these students' aspirations are to achieve the American dream of succeeding professionally, socially, and personally. They plan on living and working in the United States and consider America their home. On campuses where there are first-generation Palestinian students who have come to America to study (often on university scholarships) and who plan on returning to their homes in the Palestinian territories, there is often a very different attitude toward Israel on campus. In these situations, Palestinian students may see studying at American campuses as an opportunity to delegitimize the State of Israel through campus activism.

Furthermore, the relationship between the Jewish student organizations and other ethnic student groups can have a direct impact on the tone of Israel engagement for that campus. For example, during the fall semester of 2015, issues of racial injustice became central to several campuses across the country. In some situations, anti-Israel sentiment became linked to issues of racial injustice. On other campuses, the alliance between the Jewish student groups and the African American, Asian, Native American, and Latino student groups was strong enough to withstand this linkage.

It has been a long-standing strategy of anti-Israel groups to connect Israel and apartheid in ways that are meant to draw on the sympathies of ethnic minorities. For example, the summer of 2014 saw riots in Ferguson, Missouri, sparked by claims of racial injustice, which coincided with the Gaza War that same summer. Shortly thereafter, a campaign called "From Ferguson to Gaza" was launched on campuses around the country in an attempt to draw parallels between these two events and to elicit anti-Israel sentiment among students of color. The recent anti-Israel statement within the manifesto of the group Black Lives Matters is an example of where these efforts of linkage have been successful.

In addition, 10 to 20 percent of Jews in America today identify as people of color. Intersectionality, "the interconnected nature of social categorizations such as race, class and gender as they apply to a given individual or group, regarded as creating overlapping and interdependent systems of discrimination or disadvantage,"[5] has become a sensitive and hot topic on campus, with implications for Israel engagement as well. For example, imagine an LGBTQ, African American, female Jewish student. She might have experienced discrimination as a result of any one of these characteristics or from people within one of these groups against her. In relationship to Israel, she might identify with Jews of color from Israel or relate to Israel negatively because of how Jews from North Africa fared in society during Israel's history. She might recognize Israel's positive track record on LGBTQ rights but feel marginalized by some of Israel's policies that discriminate against women. She may have negative experiences from her Birthright trip when Israelis she met questioned her Jewishness, or she may have felt her Jewish *n'shamah* resonate with being in the Jewish spiritual homeland.

Relations between the Jewish community, the college administration, and faculty also impact the role of Israel on campus. Some
college presidents and key college representatives have been openly
supportive of Israel and have warm relations with the Jewish community on campus. Others have been more distant or reluctant to
take a stand. Faculty can be a source of introducing anti-Israel teaching and activism on campus. When matters reach a certain level of
anti-Israel activity, students, alumni, parents, faculty, and Jewish
professionals on and off campus will intervene with the administration in an effort to adjust the campus environment. Due to faculty
tenure and hiring procedures, the process is usually quite time-
consuming and circuitous.

External Variables
In addition to the student and campus variables, Israel engagement
on campus is greatly influenced by factors outside of the campus.
One such factor is political events in Israel and the United States. For
example, the Second Intifada (2000–2005), Operation Protective
Edge (2014), and the recent American presidential election (2016)
increased anti-Israel and anti-Semitic activities on campuses around
the country. Jewish students are at times expected to respond to
these situations when even politicians, diplomats, and scholars are
stumped. Sometimes students opt out of the whole Israel conversation because they are burned out or confused.

The role of the media in regard to Israel and campus life is often
not helpful. The media has chosen to focus on campus life only when
they perceive a problem. In self-serving ways, they often agitate the
situation when it comes to Israel and campus life. On campuses
where there has been an active BDS campaign, managing the media
becomes a time-consuming and frustrating part of the Jewish professionals' work, often detracting from the real work of addressing
the situation on campus. Social media can also be a source of divisiveness when it comes to Israel on campus. Posting on social media
is easy to do, often anonymous, and requires no verification of facts.
Therefore, comments about Israel can be false, can quickly escalate,

and can appear to be more widespread or important than they might actually be.

Beyond the media, there are a host of other players outside of campus who, while trying to be helpful, are often less so when it comes to Israel/campus relations. Whether on the left or the right, an increasing number of philanthropists, nonprofit agencies, Jewish organizations, lobbying groups, and so forth, have chosen to make American college campuses their playing field to advance their own agendas vis-à-vis Israel. The result can be helpful at times, when the outside organization respects the needs of the students and works with the existing Jewish campus community taking their lead from them. There are a number of generous individuals and organizations that truly understand how to work with Jewish campus life and serve as wonderful resources in helping connect Jewish students and Israel. Sometimes, however, outsiders perceive themselves to be "experts" and cause greater harm than good. They have the luxury of moving on, while those who work on campus are left to deal with the repercussions of their "help."

When trying to understand the role of Israel on campus, perhaps one of the biggest challenges comes from the generation gap between college students and older adults, usually over the age of forty. Much has been written on the differences between these groups as regards the Israel connection, Jewish identity, institutional affiliation, and a host of other characteristics. When older adults look at Jewish college students and their relationship with Israel, they don't always take the time to understand the students. Rather, they are often quick to judge this generation as lacking and feel they need to "fix" the problem in the younger generation. Sadly, most older adults fail to realize that American Jewish college students are the product of the times they grew up in and the education they received from our synagogues, schools, camps, and communities. Now is a time for generous intergenerational listening and shifting from a policy based conversation to a values-based one when it comes to the topic of Israel. We can strive to understand what values motivate each of us in regard to our relationship with Israel. This understanding is the basis for helping to bring back together a community that has become way too divisive.

Israel and American College Campuses: Choosing New Language

I contend that once we begin to grasp the complexities of Israel on campus, we can see why the battleground metaphor and all it entails is less than ideal. In choosing language to describe the relationship between college campuses and Israel, we must take into account the broader role of higher education and the range of issues that exist in regard to Israel on campus. At the same time, we should reflect critically on the underlying assumptions in our choice of language. The words we select say as much about ourselves as they do about anything happening in Israel or on American college campuses. In choosing language to describe this relationship, we would do well to consider how a particular metaphor might

1. help students develop their relationship to Israel and succeed at their primary tasks as students,
2. help those who are not on campus better relate to what is happening on campus, and
3. help heal the divisiveness in the larger Jewish world on the subject of Israel.

In thinking about Jewish metaphor, I cannot help but reflect on such powerful images as Franz Rosenzweig's *t'shuvah* as he plunged his hands into "the ancient treasure chest of Judaism" to reclaim what he already owned;[6] or Natan Alterman's poem "The Silver Platter," written right before 1948 in response to Chaim Weizmann's statement "The Jewish State will not be given to the Jewish people on a silver platter";[7] or even the entire Song of Songs, which so eloquently portrays the endless pursuit and eternal yearning between the Jewish people and God. These are images that inspire and draw people together even while making room for interpretation and subtlety. These metaphors are serviceable because they help people reach that which they aspire to and do not confuse metaphor and reality.

In exploring alternative metaphors to describe the relationship between college campuses today and Israel, let us begin to analyze some of the complexities and subtleties that are part of this relationship but are not fully expressed in the overly simplified metaphor of battleground. What might replace the "battleground" image?

Might colleges be the new Israel *shuk*—noisy, jostling, a place of rubbing shoulders, of buying and selling in an unregulated, even tumultuous way? You can pick up and examine produce at will, but buyer beware. Know that everything has a cost, so choose wisely! Let the best product succeed! The trade metaphor encourages students to master the skills of relationship building, discernment, promotion, and negotiation. For the broader community, commerce is not negative; rather it is a normal give-and-take framework, and not a crisis-oriented one.

Perhaps the college campus is the new Israel text. Jewish text comes with layers of commentaries that interpret and speak to each other. We have precedent to disagree without being disagreeable. In fact, we engage through disagreement. The beauty of text is that we all start with the same verses, but we keep turning it and turning it to find new truths. Those who do not agree with us are not bad or wrong; they are expressing other perspectives with which we are free to agree or disagree. Israel as text teaches the skills of interpretation, articulation, and critical thinking that are the hallmarks of a quintessentially Jewish approach.

Maybe campus is the new Israel bimah, a place of elevated performance, ritual, drama, and dance. Who is the audience? Who is performing? What are the props? What happens on campus is really symbolic, at best a proxy for what is happening in Israel. As I was recently reminded by a politician in Israel, "It's not like I'm waiting in Jerusalem to hear how the BDS vote went in order to decide what we should do next." Perhaps it would help students and those who are overly worried about campus to put things in this perspective. Life is a stage, and our students can learn how to act as an important life skill.

The possibilities are endless, yet finding the right language is not easy to do, especially during these complicated times. However, I challenge all of us to strive for a richer, more nuanced, imaginative, and useful way of describing Israel, especially on campuses. Hyperbole does not serve us at this time. Language matters immensely in shaping thought, dialogue, and relations. We can do better and we should do so—for our students, for our people, and for our future.

NOTES

1. Annette Koren, Leonard Saxe, and Eric Fleisch, "Jewish Life on Campus: From Backwater to Battleground," in *American Jewish Year Book 2015: The Annual Record of the North American Jewish Communities*, ed. Arnold Dashefsky and Ira M. Sheskin (New York, Springer: 2016), 45–88; Anthony Del Signore, "College Campuses: The American Battleground for the Israeli-Palestinian Conflict," *IVN*, September 8, 2014, https://ivn.us/2014/09/08/college-campuses-american-battleground-israeli-palestinian-conflict/.

2. Mitchell Bard, "American Jews and the International Arena (April 1, 2015–April 15, 2016): US-Israel Relations in a Crisis, a Hiccup, or a Healthy Alliance?" in *American Jewish Yearbook 2016*, ed. Arnold Dashefsky and Ira M. Sheskin (New York, Springer: 2017), 127–152.

3. Article 425, NGO Forum, World Conference Against Racism, Racial Discrimination, Xenophobia, and Related Intolerance, Durban, South Africa, August 27–September 1, 2001, http://www.i-p-o.org/racism-ngo-decl.htm

4. "About Hillel," Hillel International, http://www.hillel.org/about.

5. *Oxford Dictionary*, s.v. "intersectionality."

6. *Franz Rosenzweig: His Life and Thought*, ed. Nahum N. Glatzer (New York: Schocken Books, 1961), 95.

7. As cited in "Think About It: Revisiting the 'Silver Platter'" by Susan Hattis Rolef, *Jerusalem Post*, November 1, 2015.

Coming Clean on Israel

An Honest Assessment by Two Rabbinic Students of Priorities for Our Future Rabbinates

MAX CHAIKEN AND ERIC ROSENSTEIN

OUR LOVE FOR ISRAEL is unconditional, but to be honest, right now we've got other priorities. Both of us grew up in a sort of "golden age" of Liberal Zionism. Our religious schools adorned their walls with maps of Israel and posters of famous Israelis. Our summer camps hosted dozens of Israeli *sh'lichim*—ambassadors of the Jewish state—whom we adored and who made the State of Israel a concrete reality in our young lives. We learned to love Israel because it was a Jewish state and a refuge for historically persecuted Jews, even though we ourselves never really experienced any such persecution. Our love for the State of Israel grew naturally from our love for the Jewish people. Our desire to spend time in the state and get to know it firsthand grew from the soil of optimism and love.

We knew, of course, that there was conflict and occasional violence in Israel. When Rabin was assassinated, for instance, our communities mourned. Yet the pain and grief of that incident, and other reminders of political instability, quickly faded back to the optimism of the late 1990s. We remember the heartache expressed in our communities when the promise of peace at Camp David failed and the Second Intifada began, but it remained a distant pain, not quite our own.

In the twenty or so years since, our relationship to Israel has evolved. We still recall fondly the ease with which we could wear our Zionism in our formative years; and yet like an old jacket, it gets harder and harder to squeeze into it each fall.

We find ourselves deeply disturbed by the ongoing realities of fifty years of occupation. We find ourselves dismayed at the fact that so many in the Jewish world are willing to ignore or push aside the drive of another people for self-determination—the very same drive that the founders of the Jewish state fought and died to achieve for themselves and for our people. As proud Americans and Reform Jews, the myriad roadblocks to true religious freedom and pluralism still astound, frustrate, and alienate us. Of course there are parts of our Zionist identities that still fit quite easily: we continue to believe in the right of the State of Israel to exist, and we remain proud of its role as a beacon of democracy in a turbulent region.

Yet as we look toward our careers as rabbis, we need to come clean about something: we imagine a rabbinate that needs to demote Israel and Zionism at large to a lower priority.

Several related factors lead us to this conclusion. To begin with, Diaspora communities provide a fully Jewish identity without ever needing to set foot in Israel. Jews have known this and have made the choice to remain in Diaspora ever since the Edict of Cyrus in the sixth century BCE allowed Jews in Babylonia to end their exile and return to Israel. Jews who stayed in Babylonia enjoyed unprecedented prosperity, built up the only home they knew, and developed a flourishing culture. Today, the United States provides an unprecedented level of freedom and opportunity to Jewish citizens, who continue to negotiate a hybrid identity. We benefit from the freedom and openness of our society, which in turn informs the values we strive to live by as Reform Jews. We love visiting Israel and experiencing mundane moments in our holy language. As the streets quiet for Shabbat, we appreciate what it might mean to live within a Jewish culture, but we have no intention to leave the United States or to cede the freedoms and privileges that come with citizenship of this great nation.

When we think back to the narrative that informed our love for Israel, we remember the promise of a "Jewish and democratic state," the miraculous victories against those who would destroy us fought by a brash but moral army, the flowering of science and technology that caused the desert to bloom and created a "start-up nation," and the freedom to live in a Jewish culture, in Jewish space and Jewish time. But we won't ignore the fact that far too often, Israel falls short of its Liberal Zionist promise. We watch as it relinquishes its democratic character in the attempt to remain Jewish. A half-century of occupation taints the miraculous victories of 1967. The Israeli high-tech economy, so often lauded, contributes to an unsustainable income inequality. And the ones who define Jewish space, time, and identity do not recognize—or else relegate to a low priority—our commitment to religious pluralism, egalitarianism, or the progressive value of choice. The realities of the State of Israel leave us disappointed.

Historically, one of the chief arguments for a sovereign Jewish state was the creation of a refuge for Jews as a historically persecuted people to be free of anti-Semitism and anti-Jewish violence. Although Jewish immigrants to America certainly faced trials similar to other immigrant populations, as well as anti-Semitism, we believe the America we know today still serves as a haven to Jews at least as well as Israel does. Perhaps this is a reflection of growing up in a generation that never really experienced anti-Semitism. But despite renewed instances of anti-Semitism, we maintain that Jews in the United States enjoy unprecedented safety, security, and religious freedom.

Finally, the freedom and equality we experience as committed Jews and Americans call us as individuals and as community leaders to address immediate and tangible concerns in our local contexts: promoting equality of rights, advocating economic opportunity for all, and pursuing a more just society.

These are the realities that stand before us and before our congregants. We successfully maintain full Jewish identities outside Israel. We find the realities of the current situation in the State of Israel antithetical to our Jewish values. To the extent that Jews still face existential threats, we aren't convinced that Israel defends against them better than the United States does. And we care deeply about using whatever power we have to improve our local communities and our home country.

Don't misunderstand: the current realities of political and

religious life in the United States trouble us as well. We see a broken culture all around us. We talk past each other, yell into echo chambers, and seek connection in our pixelated screens. We communicate across incredible distances at the blink of an eye but feel more isolated by the day. People increasingly disregard facts and turn instead to craft narratives that bolster the arguments they're already convinced are true and preach them to siloed communities. We hurl arguments past each other and villainize the other side, disregarding human complexity and seeing the worst in another's motivations.

This brokenness also applies to Israel and to the toxicity that pervades conversations about Israel among American Jewry. Ignorance or latent anti-Semitism fuels that toxicity from the outside, while passionate disagreement and raw emotion poison discourse from within our communities. Whatever cognitive distance we create between ourselves and the actions of the state, there are those who will associate us with Israel simply by fact of our being Jews. But if we allow this toxicity to set our agenda, we will find ourselves caught in a perpetual cycle of reaction; we will allow fear and worry to set our priorities and hijack our Judaism.

Although Zionism and Israel advocacy may be the entry for some into a more active Jewish life, for many of our peers, particularly those who are not fellow Jewish professionals, issues relating to the State of Israel and expressions of Zionism create stumbling blocks to Jewish engagement. In turn, some unquestionably tune out of Jewish life rather than be drawn further into the futile abyss of shouting past each other, further into the cognitive dissonance of squaring their ethical values with the current political realities in Israel. We refuse to allow Zionism to become the stumbling block to Jewish life.

We will become rabbis in this dynamic and broken culture in which affiliation and engagement are hard to come by. Yet we know that the texts, rituals, and holidays of our faith continue to create meaning and order chaos in our contemporary world. We affirm that Judaism contains infinite layers of wisdom to contribute to society if only we would turn it and turn it again. We want to engage and welcome people into the doors of Judaism, in whatever way we can, allowing them to reclaim their role in Jewish life. This societal context, along with these tensions and constraints, fuel our need to promote the various other aspects of our Jewish identity over our Zionist convictions in our teaching, our preaching, and our civic engagement.

This recognition comes with deep sorrow. We wish we didn't have to make tough choices about how to fulfill our calling to serve the Jewish people, but we are limited by time. Effective rabbis, like effective leaders in every field, make difficult decisions every day about how to manage divergent or conflicting priorities. Stephen Covey offers one way to think about this leadership dilemma. He distinguishes between our circle of concern and our circle of influence and urges leaders to focus their energies on the latter.[1] As rabbis and Liberal Zionists, we keep Israel and Israelis very much in our circle of concern. We follow the news regarding Israel with great interest. We worry that a Jewish democracy continues to lose viability the longer a Palestinian people go without statehood. In equal measure we worry about the State of Israel maintaining the safety and security of the Israeli people as rockets fall, terrorists build tunnels, and violence threatens the routines of daily life. Our hearts ache and our *kishkes* turn to knots during these difficult moments, testifying to our unconditional love for the place and the people. Yet such grand and overarching worries typically lie only in our circle of concern— far beyond our ability to influence events.

And so we ask ourselves: What can we influence? How do we use the precious time we have serving our future communities to strengthen Jewish identity and engagement? What choices can best transmit and translate the wisdom of our faith tradition to a new generation?

The relationships we build within communities through prayer, song, learning, and counsel serve that cause. The creativity we can bring by acting through hope, and not fear, serves that cause. Drawing upon the particular texts of our tradition that express the universal yearnings of humanity serves that cause. For some, learning and programming about Israel *can* still open a doorway to Judaism, and we will be the first to walk through that doorway when they open it. But for the young adult with a burgeoning sense of Jewish identity or the baby boomer returning to our house of worship with qualms about Israel, trying to engage them on Zionism will not be a worthwhile use of time unless *they* approach *us* with specific questions or interest. In other words, when we inevitably choose between keeping the door open to Jewish engagement and blocking that door with the daunting questions shrouding Israel, we will always choose the larger project of Jewish engagement.

We acknowledge that rabbis hold symbolic power to curate and embody living Judaism for their communities. What we omit from our priorities carries as much weight as what we choose to include. Were we to cut out Zionist engagement completely, symbolically signaling no importance whatsoever, one might argue that our choice to prioritize other aspects of Jewish life amounts to cowardice at best or a betrayal of Jewish peoplehood at worst. However, we maintain our symbolic role when we shape priorities for our communities in a way that reflects a diversity of understandings of Israel and Zionism. Our communities need to remain spiritual homes for the congregants for whom Zionism continues to be part of a balanced Jewish identity. And our communities also need to remain spiritual homes for those for whom Zionism may never be part of their Jewish identity. For the latter group, we must represent other avenues to a vibrant Jewish identity by allowing ourselves and our communities to prioritize other aspects of our tradition, communal life, and commitment to justice.

So will we preach about Israel from time to time? Yes. Will we still take the limited actions within our circle of influence to stay current with the news and activities of the Israel-focused organizations we trust or even lobby elected officials from time to time? Absolutely. Placing our Zionist identities *lower* within our priorities does not mean neglecting those identities completely. We do not abdicate responsibility to muster our influence when issues concern us and our communities.

But we will also meet our congregants where they are, with the limited time and influence that we have. We will not allow Zionism to become a stumbling block to Judaism. As leaders of our communities, we cannot operate out of the toxicity that so often infects discourse on Israel. We cannot lead from sadness, frustration, anger, and fear. So we will unapologetically focus our energy on other facets of Jewish life, and we expect to prioritize those elements over Israel. Facing the stark reality of our limited time on this earth, we will embrace the richness of a Jewish life for ourselves, our families, our communities, and our people, and we will do whatever we can to pass that richness on to the next generation.

NOTE

1. Stephen R. Covey, *The 7 Habits of Highly Effective People: Powerful Lessons in Personal Change* (New York: Simon & Schuster, 2013), 88–99.

*Conversations across Generations
and Continents*

Old Words, New Vision
The Talmud and Liberal Religious Zionism

JESSE PAIKIN

O NCE, AS I ALIGHTED from a train in Paris, I walked up to a food vendor and asked, *"Pouvez-vous me dire où est la rue La Fayette?"* (Could you please tell me where La Fayette Street is?). The vendor—detecting my stilted French Canadian accent, without missing a beat—impudently replied in English, "Oh, you're Canadian. Let us speak in English; it will be better for everyone." At once, my own French Canadian heritage was neutered, my pride shot, and I wondered what was the point of over a decade of French-language education.

Language is important. It plays a critical role in forging our sense of community. On the train platform in Paris, I thought I had a strong enough command of French to feel like an insider. But from the perspective of the native French speaker, I was a stranger.

Surrounded by those who sound like us, we tend to forget the role that language plays in how we understand our relationship to the world, how that relationship is structured across time and space, and how we consider the future.[1] Indeed, language underscores every relationship, letting us know who is like us, and—as the French baguette seller reminded me—who is different.

In their book *Jews and Words*, Israeli authors Amos Oz and Oz-Salzberger offer an innovative definition of Jewishness, suggesting that what unites Jews across history and geography is not religious or ethnic affiliation, but our common linguistic and textual heritage. It is not, as they put it, that we share a "bloodline," but rather a "textline."[2] It is the languages we speak, the stories we share, the texts we study, and how we integrate them into our lives that have always shaped how we understand ourselves:

> Jewish history and peoplehood form a unique continuum,
> which is neither ethnic nor political. To be sure, our history
> includes ethnic and political lineages, but they are not its prime
> arteries. Instead, the national and cultural genealogy of the
> Jews has always depended on the intergenerational transmittal
> of verbal content. It is about faith, of course, but even more ef-
> fectively it is about texts.[3]

As this is true for our understanding of our religiosity, our culture,
and our sense of peoplehood, it must be equally true for our Zionism.
In twenty-first-century North America, we often express our Zionism and affiliation with Israel in political terms. But this betrays the
deep cultural roots of Zionism, which is fundamentally about being
in relationship. It involves throwing your lot in with a wider group of
people and necessitates ongoing and active participation in a communal project. As a Progressive Religious Zionist, it is a tumultuous
time to be a partner in this relationship. I feel as though I share little either with fellow Progressive Zionists to my left or with fellow
religious Zionists to my right. From combating attempts by the
BDS (Boycott, Divestment, Sanctions) movement to discredit Israel,
to responding to increasingly disastrous policies toward the Palestinians by the Israeli government, I often feel as though I am speaking a language nobody else understands—or that everyone else is
speaking a language that confounds me.

Today, when Jews speak different languages and live in different
places, it is precisely our texts that have the power to drive our communal project. And this is not a new idea! As author Shulem Deen
argues:

> For 2,000 years, it was our texts, more than anything, that
> bound us as a people. Our biological bonds were often tenuous.
> Our religious practices varied. We did not speak the same lan-
> guage, wear the same clothes or eat the same foods. And yet...
> we shared the same texts: the Mishna, the Talmud and later,
> their commentaries, handwritten manuscripts traversing thou-
> sands of miles and reaching the farthest crevices of the Jewish
> Diaspora.[4]

What we Liberal Religious Zionists need is a way to reengage in the language of this two-thousand-year-old conversation. A command of Hebrew is a good start, but that alone does not guarantee that we are speaking the same language of ideas. Our textline—shared by all Jews, everywhere—is the foundation upon which we speak the ideas and values that are important to us. This is particularly pressing because if we do not own our texts, they may be used in ways that are troublesome to us. The use of the *Tanach* to justify expanded settlement growth, for example, should be a matter of concern for all Liberal Religious Zionists. But without a weighty claim on the texts ourselves, we are left out of the conversation. Furthermore, with the explosion of interest within Israel among liberal and secular Jews in deeply studying our canon, this matter is even more urgent. We cannot be left behind. We need to speak the same language.

To that end, what follows are four Talmudic texts. The ideas they contain and the questions they provoke form the backbone of my Liberal Religious Zionism: there is a divine relationship present whether we live in Israel or outside of Israel; fundamental equality is not a political issue, but a moral and religious one; we must strive at all costs to avoid humiliation and affirm the humanity in others; and our leadership must be based on a hopeful, not fearful, vision of the future.

Why the Talmud? Our canon is vast, with no shortage of sacred texts to inform this conversation. But so much of Jewish thought and practice emerges from and responds to the Rabbinic wisdom of the Talmud, particularly in the area of interpersonal relations. Moreover, when it comes to overcoming vast geographical and philosophical borders, it is the Talmud, as Shulem Deen argues, that models how Jews can do this sustainably.

Within our common language, there are many voices, even in our texts. A quick glance at a *daf* (page) of Talmud, with its multivalent commentaries and glosses, is enough to evince this. Thus, the interpretations on these pages should by no means be considered the exclusive understandings. Additionally, while liberal Jews should be steeped in the textline of the Talmud, it is by no means a liberal text itself. Writer Joseph Winkler reminds us that while it offers wisdom and guidance, the Talmud "is also a frequently prohibitive document of cruelty, of misogyny, of racism, superstition, and exclusion."[5] As such, it requires our attentive curiosity and a community of fellow learners to probe its nuanced wisdom. But *this* is precisely why it is such a ripe catalogue in which to ground Liberal Religious Zionism: it demands our active participation in a communal endeavor and a willingness to represent divergent viewpoints.

With this in mind, here are the four texts:

BT *Chulin* 92a: "Exile" Doesn't Have to Be Exile

> "For you have wrestled with beings divine and human" (Genesis 32:29). Rabbah said: The angel hinted to Jacob that two leaders were destined to come from him: the *rosh galut* (exilarch) in Babylonia and the prince in the Land of Israel.

Rashi explains how the "beings divine and human" correspond to the two major Jewish communities of the Talmud—Babylonia and the Land of Israel: Israel is seen as being closer to the Divine, while Babylonia is associated with the human. This fascinating gemara suggests that while distinct, the heads of the two great Jewish communities of old—Israel and Babylonia—descended equally from our patriarch Jacob. Today, a refrain often heard is that if one truly wants to have a stake in matters of importance to Israel, one needs to make *aliyah*. Anywhere outside of Israel is seen as *galut*—as exile—and *aliyah* is upheld as the true fulfillment of the Zionist dream. This argument sadly negates the reality of the majority of Jews worldwide, who, despite living physically elsewhere, can embrace a life in relationship with Israel.

This gemara comes to teach us that beyond there being a familial relationship between Jewish communities in Israel and the Diaspora, they both share the same divine origin. Liberal Religious Zionism must be grounded in an embracing of this relationship, which, like all families, carries with it both obligations and benefits. What might it mean for liberal Jews to look at all Israelis as our godly brothers and sisters, even if it means wrestling with them? This gemara prompts us to look both inward and outward: it enables us to respond to the invalid claim that Jews outside of Israel do not have an equal stake in the affairs of Israel, but it also demands that we treat leaders in the Land of Israel as our spiritual siblings.

BT *Gittin* 61a: Minority Rights and the Ways of Peace

> Our rabbis taught: We provide for the non-Jewish poor with Israel's poor, we visit the non-Jewish sick with Israel's sick, and we bury the non-Jewish dead with Israel's dead, for the sake of the ways of peace.

The Talmud is far from universalistic when it comes to the contours of relationships between Jews and non-Jews. Indeed, this text likely originates out of a desire to appease non-Jewish rulers out of fear of persecution.[6] And yet, it is precisely when confronting a fearful "other" that the Talmud is unequivocal about the absolute equality of non-Jews to Jews in certain matters for the sake of *darchei shalom* —the ways of peace.

Approximately 25 percent of Israeli citizens are not Jewish.[7] These "other" citizens, often marginalized, do not enjoy fully equal access to basic social services. The case for absolute equality under the law is clear from a humanist perspective. But these three principles— *tzedakah* (providing for the poor), *bikur cholim* (visiting the sick), and *l'vayat hameit* (burying the dead)—are not just social concerns, but fundamental religious obligations of every Jew. For the rabbis in this gemara, equality is not a question of left-wing or right-wing policies, but a vision of the responsibilities demanded by Jewish leadership. As such, Liberal Religious Zionism must be based on a vision of what it means to have sovereignty over both Jews and non-Jews. Today we might also ask how far this value reaches: to refugees who are not citizens of Israel? to Palestinians living under Israeli military control in the West Bank? How do we weigh protecting the rights of the most vulnerable against the legitimate concerns and needs of Israeli citizenry? This gemara advocates no monopoly over who has access to fundamental social services and that equality for the sake of *darchei shalom* forms the backbone of the just society for which we are striving.

BT *Bava M'tzia* 58b–59a: The Imperative to Not Humiliate

> *Mishnah:* You shall neither wrong a stranger, nor oppress them.
> . . . *Gemara:* One who publicly shames their neighbor is as though they shed blood. . . . Abayei asked Rav Dimi: "What do people most carefully avoid in [the Land of Israel]?" He replied: "Humiliating others . . . better that one throw oneself into a fiery furnace than publicly humiliate one's neighbor."

The extent to which this gemara decries humiliating another human being is exceptional. Our Rabbis were profoundly fearful of publicly degrading anyone, likening the sin to murder. Surely, they must have been intimately aware of what it feels like to be treated without equal dignity and rights.

Rav Dimi notes how this practice was a foundational code in the Land of Israel. He compels us to consider today what it means to fight for the rights of all within Israel. This should strengthen our conviction in the rightness of advocating for non-Orthodox Jews to practice Judaism with full equality; for Palestinians to have equal electoral, judicial, and labor rights; for asylum seekers and refugees to have equal access to basic human needs.

Each of these critically unresolved issues demands extensive systematic reforms to ensure full equality of law in Israel. We may not be able to effect this change overnight. But we can certainly begin by amplifying the absolute principle to not humiliate another human being as the driving motivator for social change and the core of our work.

One of the ways we risk humiliating others is by denying or denigrating their narratives. We see this when Israelis feel as though North American liberals negate their genuine narrative of isolation and existential threats. We see it when Palestinians feel as though Yom HaAtzma-ut negates the traumas of the Nakba. And we

Progressive Jews ourselves feel this when the Israeli Orthodox hegemony denies us religious equality.

Just as the Rabbis equated humiliating a human being with the other "big three" sins (murder, idolatry, and sexual immorality), we too must understand that the humiliation of others contributes to the breakdown of society. Our Zionism must address these matters from solid religious footing. To be a Liberal Religious Zionist is to understand that it is an essential obligation of Jews to not humiliate others.

BT *Rosh HaShanah* 17a: Leading from Hope, not Fear

> Rav Judah said in the name of Rav: Any communal leader who makes himself unduly feared by the community for purposes other than the religious will never have a scholar for a son.

Our gemara here speaks of those who lead from a position of fear. While we may rightly take umbrage with the Talmud's permission to use fear for religious purposes, the Rabbis expressly prohibit using undue fear for any other civil matter. The consequence of doing so is poetically just: if you lead others through fear, you will have no wise (male) children. While this idea may seem superstitious and sexist, there is sublime wisdom beneath the text's surface: if you lead your community from a stance of fear, you will have no wise followers and no hopeful future.

So much of the current discourse surrounding Israel and Zionism is rooted in fear—of an unknown future, of a menacing enemy, and of the stability of the State of Israel itself. Liberal Zionism, too, is not innocent of using frightening tactics to engender support. What would it mean for Liberal Religious Zionism to articulate a vision of Israel and Zionism that not only was responsive to the injustices we desire to right, but provided a proactive vision of a truly liberal and progressive Israel? What would it mean to vociferously counter the use of fear as a political tool within Israel and the Zionist world, by advocating for the kind of political leadership envisaged in the Talmud?

There is no room for thoughtful, measured, or inspiring leadership when fear is used to compel followers. And yet as we know far too well, when it comes to security concerns, Israelis have legitimate cause for fear. How do we embrace a desire for hopeful, forward-looking leadership, without succumbing to a naïve or facile understanding of reality on the ground? Our gemara seems to acknowledge the nuances of this debate in its careful wording. It does not preclude the possibility of real fears, but prohibits leading with *undue* fear. It is the systematic use of fear as a political tactic that is diametrically opposed to wise leadership.

No matter the gravity of the challenges it confronts, our Zionism must ultimately be one of hope. This has been the hallmark of our two-thousand-year-old dream, the clarion call so eloquently captured in *HaTikvah*. That hope has not yet been fully realized; the Zionist project is ongoing. And so, even when confronting real anxieties, we must advocate for leadership that is anchored in a hopeful vision of the future.

◎ ◎ ◎

OUR TEXTLINE and its stories shape how we understand our relationship with others and how we think about the future. As Amos Oz and Fania Oz-Salzberger assert, "Jews display a deeply rooted belief in the power of words to create and re-create reality, at times through prayer but at least as often by argumentative truth-seeking."[8] The key, for Liberal Religious Zionists, is to bring these words to the table, to speak the profound language of our people.

Some may suggest that turning to these texts is inappropriate given the state of Jewish literacy among wide swaths of contemporary Jewry. Others may argue that they represent too narrow a view of the Jewish canon and that there are just as many opposing texts that espouse a particularistic worldview.[9] Still others may argue that these texts represent too soft a vision in the world of realpolitik.

If these assertions are true, I wonder what need there is at all for a particularly religious expression of Liberal Zionism. Do we ultimately abdicate Jewish wisdom in deference to political expediencies? Are we content simply with modern, Western, liberal egalitarianism as the basis of our Zionist motivations? Or, might we instead firmly root our beliefs in an ancient textline that connects us to other Jews across history and geography? I believe in the latter. No matter how Jewishly literate one may be, these texts and the questions they provoke are accessible and inspiring. It is my hope that the study of our textline ignites substantive conversation about the wellspring of our values and how we bring them to the table.

Notes

1. Bonny Norton, *Identity and Language Learning: Extending the Conversation* (Bristol: Multilingual Matters, 2013), 45.
2. Amos Oz and Fania Oz-Salzberger, *Jews and Words* (New Haven, CT: Yale University, 2012), 1.
3. Ibid., ix–x.
4. Shulem Deen, "Why Talmud Is the Way to Be Jewish without Judaism," *Forward*, June 9, 2016, http://forward.com/my-heretical-year/342171/why-talmud-is-the-way-to-be-jewish-without-judaism.
5. Joseph Winkler, "Reading David Foster Wallace Led Me Back to Studying the Talmud," *Tablet*, February 10, 2014, http://www.tabletmag.com/jewish-life-and-religion/159711/david-foster-wallace-talmud.
6. While offering a vision of peaceful coexistence, it is indeed rooted in a fear of the "other." As Adam Kirsch notes, "Universalism was not a reality for Jews living in the Roman and Persian Empires in the first centuries CE. . . . Non-Jews were assumed to be hostile; Rome, in particular, was seen as Edom, an ancient enemy of the Jews, the destroyer of the Temple and persecutor of Judaism. The safest course for Jews was to have as little as possible to do with gentiles" (Adam Kirsch, "Jew vs. Non-Jew vs. Jew," *Tablet*, September 27, 2016, http://www.tabletmag.com/jewish-life-and-religion/214465/daf-yomi-179). See BT *Bava Kama* 114a or BT *Eiruvin* 62a for further examples of antipathy to and prohibitions against Jews living among non-Jews. See also BT *Bava M'tzia* 71a for examples of the particularistic imperative to care for the Jewish community first.
7. Israel Central Bureau of Statistics, *Selected Data on the Occasion of Jerusalem Day* (May 31, 2016).
8. Oz and Oz-Salberger, *Jews and Words*, 47.
9. A textual approach to Zionism must not succumb to picking and choosing quotes that merely substantiate already held beliefs. We must balance both

Jewish particularism and human universalism. As Daniel Gordis argues, our study and use of text "must be rooted in a broad read of the Jewish canon, not in sound-bites thereof. . . . Jewish discourse must not devolve into 'pin the tail on the rabbinic aphorism.' . . . Ideas, not 'greatest hits,' are what matter. We need a community-wide conversation, learned, frank and ongoing. . . . Are those books our guides, or just volumes in the library?" (Daniel Gordis, "A Responsibility to Speak," *Times of Israel*, November 26, 2012, http://blogs.timesofisrael.com/on-the-absence-of-outrage/).

A Letter to My Rabbi, from Your Favorite Twentysomething Congregant

LIYA RECHTMAN

D<small>EAR</small> R<small>ABBI</small>,

I am the member of your congregation trying to decide if I will stay in the community this year. I am not your colleague. I am not a fellow member of the rabbinate. However, I have been a lifelong member of Jewish communities. I have studied Jewish text, and Hebrew, and Israel. I am an alumna of URJ youth programming. I am one of yours.

This summer, I walked out of synagogue in the middle of services for the first time. Listening to a rabbi give her Friday night sermon, I watched as she pivoted from the Torah portion to her support of legislation against the BDS (Boycott, Divestment, Sanctions) movement. In a jump of logic, she rambled on about Israel as a scapegoat and the importance of anti-BDS legislation.

You see, generations are defined by formative experiences and collective political memory. My cohort knows a different Israel than our parents. We have, if not different politics, at least a new language for expressing ourselves. We don't talk much about "peace," mostly because we haven't seen signs of it in our lifetime. Instead, we discuss fighting for a two-state solution or stemming the ever-expanding settlement movement or the demolition of Palestinian homes across the West Bank. We talk about the Occupation.

For many of us, our love for Israel is tempered by our frustration with the all-too-often antidemocratic, racist reality of Israel today. My generation didn't grow up in the victorious wake of the '67 war. Instead, we took our first trips to Israel during the First and Second

Intifadas, when Israeli police responded with disproportionate violence to Palestinian opposition across the country. We didn't experience the hope of Rabin's '90s peace movement. Instead, we watched
Prime Minister Netanyahu rally support by calling on Jews to show
up to the polls to overwhelm Arab voter turnout. We were in college
for Operation Protective Edge.

None of this means that we aren't Zionists. I am a Zionist, but I do
not share my mother's or my grandmother's Zionism. I am a Zionist
in that I believe in the right of all peoples to self-determination. I am
a Zionist in that I, as a Jew and as an Israeli-American, care about the
future of my people, both politically and ethically. I am a Zionist in
that I am obligated to work in opposition to the Israeli occupation of
the Palestinian people and to Israeli human rights violations, toward
a vision of Jewish leadership informed by Jewish ethical values.

And yet, as I and other young Jews struggle to find our voices and
establish a new kind of loving relationship with Israel that includes
a harsh critique of the state, it sometimes feels like our Jewish communities are staging a witch hunt against those of us who dare to use
the word "Occupation." Our NFTY regions silence us; our Hillels
kicked us out; our professional Jewish community leaders fear that
we will be publicly "outed" as anti-Occupation. This year Simone
Zimmerman, a Jewish anti-Occupation community organizer with
If Not Now, was hired as the Jewish community outreach director
for the Bernie Sanders campaign. When it became clear that her politics were not in lockstep with an older Jewish establishment, leaders
across our community called for her to be fired. Her eventual dis-
missal exposed the intergenerational divide within our community
and demonstrated the constant threat that many of us often face as
young Jews working with the Jewish institutional world today.

Our reaction as a community to the BDS movement is even
worse. The institutional Jewish community refuses to engage with
pro-BDSers in our community and instead silences and alienates
progressives and young people.

This year, former Union for Reform Judaism president Rabbi Eric
Yoffie wrote in support of the Hillel International decision to ban

"anti-Zionist" organizations from operating under the Hillel banner. In an article in *Haaretz*, he calls supporters of BDS "enemies."[1] To whom are they enemies? And why do Zionism and rigorous criticism of Israel have to be mutually exclusive? To me, the proponents of both are friends and members of my Jewish community. More recently, Rabbi Yoffie wrote again,[2] this time about If Not Now, the Jewish organizing body that has taken a stand against Jewish institutions that refuse to acknowledge and work against the Occupation. He argued that because If Not Now had not formally distanced itself from BDS, this meant that they were not to be included within the Big Tent of the Jewish community. Rabbi Yoffie fails here to envision a new Big Tent.

I am not a supporter of BDS. I am currently sitting in a Jerusalem café sipping Israeli coffee next to my Israeli backpack and my cell phone with my Israeli SIM card. Twenty-seven members of my family are in the Israeli workforce and rely on this country's economy. I write this as an insider.

The official "BDS movement," devoted to divesting from all products of the State of Israel, is to be distinguished here from the boycott of goods produced in illegal Israeli Jewish settlements in the Palestinian Occupied Territories (i.e., the West Bank). I am not categorically opposed to the concept of boycott. Throughout history we have seen its enormous and productive impact, both moral and financial, on oppressive regimes and industries through boycotts, strategic divestments, and diplomatic sanctions. I take issue, therefore, with BDS not as a mechanism for change, but, more narrowly, as the appropriate response to Israeli occupation and or human rights violations.

And yet, as someone who does not support BDS, I am supportive of those who do. I have close friends, cherished colleagues, and respected classmates who are supporters of the movement. These people are not outliers or outsiders. They are full members of our Jewish community. Their beliefs come from a place of Jewish learning and practice. I don't agree with my friends who support BDS. However, my political, strategic, and financial disagreement with them about the benefits and consequences of this approach to ending the Occupation merits conversation, not disengagement. I am broadened and strengthened by encountering and loving those who hold views in opposition to my own.

The model of exclusion, witch hunts, and arbitrary red lines is both an outdated and ahistorical understanding of Zionism, Judaism, and the needs of our community. The treatment of BDS, If Not Now, and members of our community affiliated with other left-leaning organizations in our congregations is unproductive. Further, the Jewish support for legislation that cuts off funding to groups that support BDS is similarly ethically, Jewishly, and intellectually objectionable.

Our Jewish tradition of text-based study relies on moving toward truths through engaging with diverse ideologies. Rabbi Ethan Tucker, *rosh yeshiva* of the egalitarian Mechon Hadar in New York, teaches that Jews as a people are constantly in tension between the three ideals of pluralism, integrity, and community.[3] On pluralism and ideological diversity, he cites the American Orthodox rabbi Yitzhak Hutner:

> The extent of the power of Oral Torah is emphasized and revealed much more through disagreements than through consensus. Included in the idea that 'these and those are the words of the living God' is the fundamental principle that even a rejected *halakhic* opinion is a Torah view.[4]

In debating how to live our lives according to the highest possible standard of Jewish ethics, even the rejected is included and considered a Jewish (Torah) perspective. In Judaism, not only does the majority opinion hold weight, but the minority opinion is recorded and also considered valid. So, too, must we Jewishly understand the arguments from across a broad political spectrum regarding Israel, Zionism, and how we as a Jewish people can best move forward into the twenty-first century.

The Reform Movement has our own contemporary iteration of this ideology embodied in the current Audacious Hospitality initiative of the Union for Reform Judaism, led by URJ president Rabbi Rick Jacobs. Rabbi Jacobs has written of this initiative: "Audacious hospitality isn't just a temporary act of kindness so people don't feel excluded. It's an ongoing invitation to be part of community—and a way to spiritually transform ourselves in the process. Audacious hospitality is a two-way street where synagogue and stranger need each other, where we not only teach newcomers, but they teach us."[5]

Inclusion of diametrically opposing opinions is embedded in our text and at the center of the Reform Movement. Why, then, when we talk about Israel, do we draw bright lines and initiate witch hunts against heretical ideologies? We need supporters on the right, center, and left in our congregations. But having members with diverse ideologies is not enough. We need Jewish Voice for Peace and If Not Now members on the boards of our synagogues, Federations, and national institutions. We need radical, audacious hospitality, incorporation, and engagement.

And yet the question remains: What are the limits to inclusion? Where does political pluralism come at the expense of integrity and community, Rabbi Tucker's other two pillars of Jewish peoplehood?[6] Our intolerance for discrimination and hate lies at the outer limit of our capacity for inclusion and defines our Jewish communities as communities with integrity. Our desire to maintain peace within our communities leaves many a rabbi too afraid to speak out against injustice in Israel or to speak of Israel at all for fear of the response of her community. These values, at times, contradict one another.

So, how do we establish a continued relationship with Israel that allows for real, productive critique?

The solution to the problem of intergenerational and cross-political dissonance isn't to win over young leaders with institutional power. The solution is certainly not to ignore us or exclude us, either. We are at a critical juncture in history that requires us together to create new brands of Progressive Zionism and principled Jewish community formation. We must form a rigorous, critical Zionist ethic that actively engages with the wrongs done by the State of Israel in the name of the Jewish people while enabling dialogue within our communities.

Remember: We are you. We are a generation raised by you and your institutions. You taught us the value of inclusion, along with those of democracy and equality. You taught us to be critical thinkers, to question dominant voices, and to challenge authority. You taught us to be lovers of Torah, of Israel, and of the Jewish people. We are taking those values that you inculcated within us and responding, with you, to the world in which we have grown up, to the political climate that we face.

With love,
Your congregant

NOTES
1. Eric H. Yoffie, "No Home for BDS in Hillel," *Haaretz*, December 30, 2013.
2. Eric H. Yoffie, "IfNotNow Doesn't Deserve the Support of Left-Leaning American Jews," *Haaretz*, May 5, 2016.
3. Ethan Tucker, "Pluralism, Integrity, and Community: You Can't Have Them All, Part 1," https://mechonhadar.s3.amazonaws.com/mh_torah_source_sheets/CJLVPluralismIntegrityCommunity1.pdf, last accessed August 7, 2017.
4. Pachad Yitzhak, Hanukkah #3, R. Yitzhak Hutner, Israel/United States, twentieth century.
5. Rick Jacobs, "What Is Audacious Hospitality?," Union for Reform Judaism, March 17, 2014, https://www.urj.org/blog/2014/03/17/what-audacious-hospitality.
6. Tucker, "Pluralism, Integrity, and Community."

The Seventy Faces of Israel

Rabbi Danny Burkeman

We are the children of winter 1973,	אנחנו הילדים של חורף שנת שבעים
You dreamt us first at dawn at the	ושלוש
end of the battles,	חלמתם אותנו לראשונה עם שחר,
You were tired men that thanked	בתום הקרבות
their good luck,	הייתם גברים עייפים שהודו למזלם
You were worried young women	הטוב
and you wanted so much to	הייתן נשים צעירות מודאגות ורציתן
love . . .	כל כך לאהוב . . .
When we were born the country	כשנולדנו היתה הארץ פצועה ועצובה
was wounded and sad.	הבטתם בנו, חיבקתם אותנו, ניסיתם
You looked at us you hugged us you	למצוא נחמה
were trying to find comfort.	כשנולדנו ברכו הזקנים בעיניים
When we were born the elders	דומעות
blessed with tears in their eyes;	אמרו הילדים האלה הלוואי לא ילכו
They said: "We wish those kids will	אל הצבא
not have to go to the army."	

I DON'T REMEMBER when I first heard this song, but I do remember standing in Kikar Rabin (Rabin Square) and hearing it ring out. At the time, even though I didn't understand all of the words, I understood the power of what was being sung. I felt the depth of emotion, the sadness of the parents who had been unable to fulfill their promise of peace, and the strong resolve of the children who were prepared to serve and defend the country. It is part of my personal Israel soundtrack composed of the songs that I have heard at memorial services, *t'kesim* (ceremonies), and celebratory gatherings; it is one of the songs of my Israel.

Shmuel Hasafari, who wrote these words, is not a child of the winter of 1973; at that time he was a soldier fighting in the Yom Kippur

War. He wrote this song in 1995 for the IDF's Special Education Band, a group composed of people who were born in the aftermath of that war. He understood that the context into which we are born does, in a significant way, help to define the experiences that we have, and by extension the people that we become.[1]

In writing this song he intended it as a conversation between his generation, who had fought in the war, and the generation born in its aftermath. As he imagines it, the children of the winter of 1973 were born with the promise of peace from their elders; but despite the changes in the following years, they had to grow up and face the reality of war. As adults, despite all of the changes in Israeli society, they remained defined by a formative Israel experience that occurred just before they were born.

It is my belief that in many ways our relationship with Israel is determined by the context into which we are born and by our own formative Israel experiences. For the Jewish community that came of age before the Six-Day War, they encountered Israel as an almost impossible reality. It was hard to believe that this tiny state would survive surrounded by enemies on three sides and the sea on the other. Israel needed our help and support both for the establishment of the state and for its ongoing protection and defense. For this generation, the blue boxes and the collections for Israel were about the very survival of the fledgling state.

With the success of Israel in the Six-Day War this perception shifted, and it has continued to change in the years and decades that have followed. There have been times of war and times of (relative) peace, there have been periods of spectacular economic growth and technological innovation, and there have been intifadas and disengagements. There has been constant change, and therefore different generations of Diaspora Jewry have come to experience Israel through a wide variety of contexts and lenses. The question is how we, as a community, have been able to keep pace with this constantly changing landscape and whether we have actually been able to.

Many studies support the idea that in personal interactions, first impressions count. As Professor Frank Bernieri of Oregon State

University says, "First impressions are the fundamental drivers of our relationships. . . . In a sense, it's a little like the principle of chaos theory, where the initial conditions can have a profound impact on the eventual outcome."[2] And what is true in our relationships with people is also true in our relationships with countries and places. There is a first, formative impression, and it sticks with us, defining our relationship with that place moving forward.

On a personal level, with an Israeli mother and family living in Israel, I visited there on an annual basis from before I can even remember. My first impressions of the country were of Tel Aviv, the beach, and my family. But my formative Israel experiences came in the 1990s, as I began to see Israel as more than just the place where my family lived, but as my Jewish homeland. I experienced the Israel of Rabin and Peres, Israel celebrating peace on the White House lawn, and the Israel where thousands gathered to call for peace. I will always remember standing in Kikar Rabin in November of 1997, together with over two hundred thousand others as we mourned the assassination of Yitzhak Rabin. We cried, sang, and called for peace. Today, no matter how much has changed, this remains my Israel.

As an organized Jewish community we have tried to influence people's formative Israel experience. The focus on sixteen-year-old summer-in-Israel programs was a way of establishing a first impression of Israel that was filled with friends, positive experiences, and a person's coming of age. It established a positive foundation upon which one's Israel connection could grow and be strengthened. In a similar way, Birthright currently seeks to do the same thing over ten days for a slightly older population.

However, it is clear that a decreasing percentage of the Jewish community now participates in a summer-in-Israel experience, while Birthright, which is only open to those eighteen years old and above, may well be coming too late, with participants already having formed an impression of Israel from a distance. Furthermore, with the spread of social media and twenty-four-hour news cycles, our young people now encounter and experience Israel in arenas and contexts beyond the Jewish community and their families. Their first and formative impressions often come from the wider world, which can present a very challenging and difficult picture of the Jewish state.

It is hard to neatly divide and categorize the different generational connections with Israel. In broad dimensions one could suggest there was the Israel prior to 1967, an Israel that was threatened by her neighbors and needed support and aid from the Diaspora Jewish community. From 1967 until the early 1990s, there were times of Israeli strength and Israeli weakness, and it was a period in which the state continued to grow and develop, still requiring the support of the Diaspora. The 1990s was the decade of peace as Israel reached out to her neighbors and negotiated with the Palestinians; at the same time she definitively established herself as a thriving First World country. And since then, in this new century, Israel has been the "start-up nation," a hub of innovative technological growth, but also the place of intifadas and settlement expansion. Of course this is an oversimplification of what has happened, but it serves as a reminder of how much change has taken place in less than seventy short years.

What is clear is that despite this ever-changing landscape, a connection to Israel remains an important part of Jewish identity. According to the Pew Research Center's 2013 study of the American Jewish community, "about seven-in-ten American Jews (69%) say they are emotionally very attached (30%) or somewhat attached (39%) to Israel."[3] This is almost the same result as was found in the last National Jewish Population Survey, conducted in 2000–2001.

However, it is important to recognize that while broadly our connection to Israel has been maintained, the trends seen in the Pew study suggest a decline across generations. People over sixty-five are most connected, with 79 percent of respondents very attached or somewhat attached to Israel. There is then a sharp drop in those under fifty, where the study found that only 60 percent felt a similar connection to Israel.[4]

For those people with the strongest Israel connection, I would argue that Israel remains for them the small country that needs our help and support. Of course they have celebrated her triumphs and successes over the years, but first impressions and formative experiences are important, and this original connection still fuels their relationship. For this group, there is often a disconnect with the skyscrapers of Tel Aviv and Israel's now thriving economy; it does not fit with their picture of Israel. When I led a congregational trip to Israel recently, it was striking to see the shock on the faces of the older participants as they saw the extent of the building and growth that has taken place in Israel over the last few decades.

The disconnect between the Israel they first got to know and the Israel of today presents a major challenge when this generation tries to explain their Israel connection to, and motivate, a generation of people under the age of thirty. For the younger generation, this Israel, in need of support and always on the brink of destruction, is completely foreign and sounds almost unbelievable. They have grown up in a time when Israel is not just a fact, but a strong, vibrant, and powerful country; for them, she is a country with one of the world's leading militaries and is (allegedly) a nuclear power. For this generation, it is hard to imagine Israel as a small and weak country in need of support and defense.

When these two generations talk about Israel, it is often as if they are talking about different countries. Their first impressions and formative experiences are almost in opposition with each other. The gap between their perspectives causes a degree of distrust when the other is talking about Israel. It is most striking between these two generations, but it is present across the board, because over a very short history Israel has gone through dramatic periods of change. It has been hard for our pictures of Israel to keep pace with the way that the country has been transformed again and again.

It is said that the Torah has seventy faces.[5] Perhaps we need to now acknowledge that Israel also has a multiplicity of faces. As a community, we accept different interpretations and understandings of Torah, and we need to be able to do the same with Israel.

There is no one Israel, and our divergent and different formative experiences influence what Israel is for each of us. Every generation meets Israel and sees a different face staring back at them; these faces are all Israel, but they are all focused and nuanced differently. As an organized Jewish community, we have struggled to acknowledge the various ways in which people encounter Israel and as a result the different perspectives that people can have. All too often our communal vision and language remain rooted in that picture of Israel pre-1967; this is not just at odds with the way that younger generations view Israel, but it is in direct tension with the Israel they now experience. Our personal and communal experiences define the Israel that we see looking back at us, and we need to acknowledge the possibility for there to be a multiplicity of faces.

The challenge of how we, in the Jewish community, teach and talk about Israel is exacerbated by the modern world. Today, with the easy spread of information, the Jewish community is no longer the only or even the first place where a young person will encounter Israel. Information is disseminated in so many ways, and unfortunately many of them, unchecked and unfiltered, are breeding grounds for virulent expressions of anti-Israel feelings. In this arena old anti-Semitic tropes have been modernized to focus on Israel, and a consumer of this information could be forgiven for believing that Israel really is the global public enemy number one. And if, by some chance, their first Israel encounter has not come before college, then we know all too well that campuses today are unfortunately characterized by rabid anti-Zionism, with a monopoly for those who portray Israel as an aggressor, a colonial power, and an apartheid state. We need to remember that first impressions matter, and these are not the initial encounters we want people to have.

For those of us who love Israel and want to share that love with others, it is important that we recognize the different perspectives. No matter what generation we are a part of and what our Israel perspective is, we have to be open to a conversation with those who view Israel differently. Like Shmuel Hasafari, we have to be prepared to enter into a dialogue with a generation that is not our own. And through listening to the opinions of those younger or older than ourselves we will have the opportunity to deepen our own connection to Israel.

Most immediately we need to rethink the language we use to speak about Israel; we have to talk in terms, and of an Israel, that is relatable for all generations. We have to appreciate the complexities of contemporary Israel and recognize the different perspectives of multiple generations. When various groups and generations speak about Israel, it can often feel like they are speaking in different languages. The words they use are misunderstood, the descriptions appear incomprehensible, and the desired meaning is lost. We need to broaden the language that we use, to avoid speaking in exclusive terms and to accept the complexity of Israel.

This will be challenging at first, as it will require us to rethink some of the traditional language and programs we have used, and it will be difficult to recognize that "our Israel" is not the only Israel. Some of the words may sound foreign or be difficult to hear, but they will allow a greater number of people to be a part of the conversation. And it will allow us to present an Israel that is relatable to all, and once we do that we can share our love and connection in a way that others will be able to understand and hopefully share.

Alongside the development of a new language and a broader vocabulary to talk about Israel, we have to increase our investment in Israel education and engagement for our children. If we wait until our young people are at college to encounter Israel for the first time, we know what that experience is likely to be. We have to ensure that prior to setting foot on campus this generation have encountered and experienced an Israel that they can love and be proud of—an Israel that will be able to resist the slings and arrows of those who seek to attack her, an Israel built on firm foundations, and an Israel that is not black-and-white, but that reflects the real complexity of the modern state. We can offer them the seventy faces of Israel so that they can find the one or two that resonate for them and provide a base from which to grow. For this reason I would advocate for greater investment in the sixteen-year-old Israel experience, and I would want to find a way that Birthright could be offered to children before beginning college.

In today's information-driven world, people no longer view, or accept, information presented in black-and-white terms. There is a suspicion of representations that do not recognize the gray and the complexity of the real world. For a previous generation, Israel could be viewed very clearly and positively in definitive terms, but this representation no longer appears accurate or believable to generational groups that expect complexity. An experience of Israel that honors her complexity will prove far more resilient against attack from those who seek to demonize her. It is about acknowledging and recognizing those issues that trouble us, while at the same time being loud and proud in our support and celebration of Israel's successes and achievements.

As part of this complex Israel we have an obligation to move away from primarily responding to her in terms of war and peace. While it may be easier for many to relate positively to Israel when she is actively pursuing peace, we have to recognize that it is not entirely in her control whether or not she makes peace with her neighbors. And if our Israel experiences focus on only this one aspect of her identity, then it will always be far too delicate and too easily dismantled due to the actions of others. My division of Israel's timeline is hugely defined by war and peace; this is the way that it has largely been up to now, but moving forward it is a dynamic we need to change. This is just one element of Israeli society, and there is so much more that needs to be considered in painting a picture of the Jewish homeland.

My Israel will always be the Israel of Rabin and Peres, and as such no matter what happens I believe that she is a dynamic nation willing to take risks to make peace. With that first impression still nourishing me today, it is easy to be an *ohev Tzion*—a lover of Zion. This is not the case for everyone, and we need to nourish that love of Zion in her complexity, in her successes and failures, and in terms of the place that she really is. We need to recognize the seventy faces of Israel. And most of all we need to find a way to talk about Israel across generations and ideologies, so that all of our first impressions can be strong foundations upon which our relationship with Israel can be established, develop, and grow.

NOTES

1. Tarbut, http://tarbut.cet.ac.il/ShowItem.aspx?ItemID=49deec27-b9c0-4c7b-a445-f030462934ad&lang=HEB.
2. Rosie Ifuld, "Acting on Impulse," *Guardian*, March 6, 2009, https://www.theguardian.com/lifeandstyle/2009/mar/07/first-impressions-snap-decisions-impulse.
3. The Pew Research Center's Religion and Public Life Project, *A Portrait of Jewish Americans* (Washington, DC: Pew Research Center, 2013), 82, http://www.pewforum.org/2013/10/01/jewish-american-beliefs-attitudes-culture-survey/.
4. The study found 60 percent of the 18–29 category and 61 percent of the 30–49 category were very attached or somewhat attached to Israel.
5. The suggestion is found in *B'midbar Rabbah* 13:15.

An Intercontinental Dialogue
What North American and British Zionists Can Learn from Each Other

RABBI CHARLEY BAGINSKY and RABBI NEAL GOLD

SINCE ITS INCEPTION, a wide variety of ideological streams have nurtured the Zionist movement. The movement developed distinctive flavors and contours reflecting conditions in the different countries where it has flourished. The diversity of attitudes toward Israel within the North American Jewish community is significant; the same is true, of course, within the United Kingdom. By discussing the different histories and nuances of international Progressive Zionism, we can learn a lot from one another.

In an attempt to foster such a dialogue, Rabbis Neal Gold (United States) and Charley Baginsky (United Kingdom) conducted a cross-continent conversation.

What do you see as the historical roots of the Zionist movements in the UK?

CB: Despite holding an Israeli passport, I am British-born and work for a movement, Liberal Judaism, which is arguably defined by its birth within British society in 1902 (although it now includes under its auspices congregations in Dublin and Copenhagen) and retains idiosyncrasies, ideologies, and practices that are unique to this country and the time. British Jewry is not representative of all European Jewry and certainly not of its Zionism—Britain most definitely has unique differences from mainland Europe and that includes its Zionism as well.

Indeed it is very difficult to think about European Zionism as having some singular form, cohesion, or continuity, due to its complex history and the constant movement of Jewish communities. In a recent article written by Toby Greene and Yossi Shain,[1] they note the differences in the relationship with Israel within British and French Jewry. Britain, with 284,000 Jews, has the fourth largest Diaspora community, after the United States, France, and Canada. Unlike much of mainland Europe, Britain has managed to remain free of large-scale violence and expulsion since the Jewish community's resettlement under Oliver Cromwell in 1656. Additionally, it was the only major European community to escape Nazi occupation. They also note the impact of the British Mandate in Palestine and the following 1917 Balfour Declaration as defining moments in the formation of a peculiarly British Zionism.

In the early days of Progressive Judaism in the UK, Liberal Judaism[2] was opposed to the notion of modern Zionism, believing that Judaism was not a national identity but a religion and that one should not threaten the equal rights they had worked so hard to achieve within their country of residence. However, once the State of Israel was in existence, attitudes began to change. Notably, in 1951 one congregation requested permission to add a prayer for Israel into their services. Within five years, by the time of the Suez Crisis, Liberal Jewish practice often included an expression of strong support for Israel. By 1967, *Service of the Heart*, the new British prayer book for daily and Sabbath worship, included several prayers for the State of Israel and prayers for Israel Independence Day.

Does this have resonance at all for you when thinking about the roots of North American Reform Zionism?

NG: Unlike Europe, when you travel around America you're struck by the frequency of biblical names of cities and towns: Hebron, Bethel, Jericho, Salem, etc.—and many of them with the qualifier "New" in their name. For generations of Americans of a multitude of nationalities, the country was indeed a new Promised Land, and this was just as true for Jews who emigrated to the *goldene medina*. Therefore, enthusiasm for the Zionist cause in America was always going to be tempered by a real conundrum: in what ways do our historical Promised Land and our de facto one exist in tension with each other? I think this tension is also in many ways implicit in your description of the early Liberal Jewish attitudes to Zionism.

For many American Jewish leaders of the nineteenth century, the answer was straightforward: Zionism simply was not compatible with universalist values of modern Judaism. In 1885, the Pittsburgh Platform of the Central Conference of American Rabbis testified:

> We recognize, in the modern era of universal culture of heart and intellect, the approaching of the realization of Israel's great Messianic hope for the establishment of the kingdom of truth, justice, and peace among all men. We consider ourselves no longer a nation, but a religious community, and therefore expect neither a return to Palestine, nor a sacrificial worship under the sons of Aaron, nor the restoration of any of the laws concerning the Jewish state.[3]

After decades of modern Zionist activity, this earlier rejection of belonging to a Jewish nation sounds radical to our ears, but in truth the Pittsburgh Platform was an accurate barometer of the Jews of its age. Its authors' main agenda was to be as authentically American as their neighbors, and surely emigrating to Palestine was an anxiety-provoking pipe dream.

With the passage of time, we can observe a sea change in Zionist attitudes among American Jews. Half a century after the Pittsburgh Platform, Reform rabbis assembled in Columbus, Ohio, to issue another statement of principles. In 1937 they could declare:

> In the rehabilitation of Palestine, the land hallowed by memories and hopes, we behold the promise of renewed life for many of our brethren. We affirm the obligation of all Jewry to aid in its upbuilding as a Jewish homeland by endeavoring to make it not only a haven of refuge for the oppressed, but also a center of Jewish culture and spiritual life.[4]

Still, this is pride from afar. Despite the heroic and eloquent exemplars of early and mid-twentieth-century Zionism—Stephen S. Wise, Louis Brandeis, and Abba Hillel Silver come to mind—even in the 1950s, the establishment of Israel was a source of pride and a target of philanthropy, but it was not the main preoccupation of American Jews.

The story of the growth of Zionist institutions in America is best told elsewhere. What is useful to note here is that American Zionism was *always different* from other Zionist movements around the world in one very significant way. Unlike most other Zionist communities, American Zionism was not predicated on *aliyah* as a necessary expression of Zionism. Quite the opposite: American Zionism, from its inception through today, was certain that Americans could be good Zionists—from *over here.*[5]

CB: I would say that this attitude has always been assumed within a Liberal Jewish framework; the difference is perhaps that we in the UK have not had the self-confidence to articulate it so clearly. As North American Jews it is arguable that the numerical size of your constituency has warranted you a power and self-assurance we could never muster.

NG: I think this is true. One famous illustration of this is in the historic "agreement" that was negotiated between David Ben-Gurion and Jacob Blaustein, the powerful mid-century president of the American Jewish Committee. In 1950, Ben-Gurion agreed to tone down his public insistence on the *aliyah* of American Jews and his rhetoric of negating the Jewish life of the Diaspora. In return, the mainstream Jewish organizations became wholeheartedly Zionist in their outlooks and priorities.[6]

The tipping point was the Six-Day War in 1967. After Israel's unexpectedly swift victory, American Jews began to look upon Israel with liberal pride and determination. And this coincided with the rise of other ethnic pride movements in the United States, most notably Black Power. Israel was no longer the home of the poor cousins overseas, but a source of self-esteem for Jews everywhere; they were perceived as vigorous Jews who could defend themselves against the enemies of our people. At this time begins the phenomenon of the American Jew's first instinct in the morning: to reach for the newspaper to investigate, with no small measure of anxiety, what is happening in Israel.

CB: I think that is also true for many UK Progressive Jews. But in many ways the early 1990s until the early millennial years were the strongest for UK Progressive Jewish engagement with Israel. The confidence and optimism of the Oslo Accords and a consistent positive discourse about Israel within congregations and youth movements ensured that many in our communities felt they could articulate a pride in their relationship with Israel in a way that they had not been able to before. However, with the breakdown of the peace accords, the rise of social media, the introduction of university fees,[7] and reduction of subsidies for Israel trips, as well as a move away from centrist and left-wing governments in Israel to a harder right rule, attitudes began once again to change dramatically.

In 1995 Jewish Policy Research [JPR] published a report on Social Attitudes (as quoted in a later 2010 report) where they predicted that almost across the communal board of British Jewry the relationship with Israel was changing and that, unless something significant was done, positive engagement would decline.[8] This trend was identified as being the strongest in those Jews they defined as secular or having no religious affiliation and next in those they defined as Progressive. The trend they identified was that an individual's relationship to Israel was moving from an ideological and emotional one to one linked to religiosity and experience. This was combined with an internal national religious narrative within Israel whose main opposition was secularism and consumerism, which the Progressive world could not offer up as a positive ideology for its members, old or young. One line in their conclusion appears almost prophetic: "Whereas Israel once appealed to radicals and later to all denominations in the community, as time passes it looks as if increasingly it will appeal more to Traditional and Orthodox Jews than to others."[9]

This prediction has arguably come to fruition. In their latest report on this issue JPR points to long-term programming in Israel as being the only means by which people end up having a significant and lasting relationship with Israel.[10] It is a simplistic explanation, and one that deserves greater analysis and an articulation of the nuances, but as our numbers on long-term programming decrease, so too does the idea that Zionism is a central tenet of our religious identity.

In addition, one cannot underestimate the impact of the fairly recent Gaza War and the increased prevalence of anti-Semitism. While not on the levels one has seen in France and other areas of Europe, the topic has surfaced, at least in the political arena, in a way not seen for many years. In some segments of the Jewish community it could be argued that this increases an affiliation with Israel and a reminder of why the Land of Israel is so central. However, at least anecdotally, we have seen an increase in the desire for Progressive Jews to separate their religious and ethnic or national identities. If one faces an anti-Zionism that seems to merge into anti-Semitism, it is easier to desire separation at best, and at worst to walk away from both. We have not done well at creating an articulated Zionism or the educational resources to support it that creates an emotional and religious connection to the Land, while allowing for the space to criticize the government of Israel. Engagement with Israel has become exhausting for many, and without the personal connection there is little to hold people in relationship.

NG: I agree with your observations about the significance of Jewish youth movements. I do not think that we can overstate their significance for molding Zionist education throughout the second half of the twentieth century. Jewish summer camps, including those with an especially Zionist focus, shaped a generation of American Jews. They also, perhaps controversially, conveyed a certain idealization about the State of Israel: it was presented as a young and romantic place, where by day soldiers patrolled Israel's borders against her enemies, and by night they sang *"Hafinjan"* and danced in circles around campfires!

By the mid-1990s, the Reform Jewish Movement alone was

sending over fifteen hundred high school students annually on NFTY's summer-in-Israel programs. Movement leaders were able to articulate a goal of sending *every* Jewish student to Israel for a summer or more before graduating high school.

Unfortunately, the Second Intifada changed all that. From the peak years of the 1990s, participants in high school trips to Israel dropped dramatically. During the intifada years, American Jewish leaders rightly worried that an entire generation of young people would come of age without any personal firsthand experience of Israel. Partially in response to this concern, prominent Jewish philanthropists created Birthright Israel. Birthright's primary mission was straightforward: to send young Jewish adults on a free trip to Israel in their college and post-college years. In this regard, Birthright has succeeded dramatically: now over five hundred thousand young people from around the world, primarily from the United States, have participated in its programs. This has undoubtedly altered a generation's attitudes toward Israel.

In a similar way to what you describe in the UK, the rise of anti-Semitism and anti-Israel activity on college campuses has also shaped Zionist identities. Many Jewish teenagers arrive at college unprepared for the full-on attacks of the BDS (Boycott, Divestment, Sanctions) movement and other anti-Israel activists, occasionally fomented or supported by faculty members. Many Jewish students find themselves unprepared for the attacks they face from the left when they arrive on campus—especially from affinity groups and social-justice-minded organizations with whom they generally would be inclined to partner. Naturally enough, some of these students find their Jewish/Zionist identities invigorated, others choose to retreat, and a significant number report "Israel fatigue" from constantly facing these battles.

In a more positive vein, study after study of the Jewish community demonstrates there is one factor that is a reliable indicator of a strong Zionist identity, and that is having a *strong Jewish identity*. In other words, there is a strong correlation between Jewish religious commitments and literacy (including Hebrew literacy) and feeling emotionally attached to the State of Israel.[11] Investing in Jewish life, synagogue communities, day schools, and summer camps where Jewish education is a prime mission are proven, reliable ways to ensure positive connections to Israel.

CB: What is the relationship of the Reform Movement to other Jewish and Zionist organizations in the United States?

NG: Within organizations such as AIPAC [American Israel Public Affairs Committee], the Jewish Federations of North America, and the Council of Presidents of Major Jewish Organizations, the Reform Movement typically commands an important left-of-center voice. The CCAR and the Union for Reform Judaism and its affiliates, especially ARZA [Association of Reform Zionists of America], reliably voice concerns about settlement activity, human rights, and religious pluralism in Israel at the Zionist table.

The World Zionist Congress elections of 2015 demonstrated that the Reform Movement holds a commanding voice in the American Zionist community. ARZA claimed 56 of 145 American seats at the congress—more than any other North American faction, and more than the second- and third-place factions combined. True, only a very small fraction of American Jews voted in the WZC elections in 2015 (and most U.S. Jews—even those who feel a strong affinity for Israel—probably still don't know what the congress does). Nonetheless, the strong showing of ARZA in the election is a resounding statement that liberal Jews can claim their authentic place at the Zionist table.

Is there a similar story in the UK?

CB: Unlike the States we are not the largest Jewish movement in the UK. We often represent the minority voice, one that is consistently perceived as representing a more left-wing stance than the mainstream Jewish community.

Another way that Britain is unique is that it has two movements both affiliated and active within the World Union for Progressive

Judaism: The Movement for Reform Judaism, and Liberal Judaism. While these days there is little ritually or ideologically to separate them, their relationship to Israel has not always taken the same path either in reality or perception. Yet today they are in the initial stages of forming the first joint UK Progressive Israel Desk, funded by both movements as well as by the Israeli Progressive Movement and the UK's Zionist Movement for Progressive Judaism—Pro-Zion. This desk is a recognition that both movements have to address their relationship with Israel; neither can make an assumption that individual congregants or congregations will automatically have a relationship with Israel but that it has to be nurtured, supported, and most importantly reformulated. The desk aims to reinvigorate the communities' relationship with Israel, seeking a model of mutuality—not one where Israel is placed on a pedestal and is expected to adhere to a morality beyond that which they expect of themselves, but rather one where there is shared learning and a recognition that both communities have skills they can share and help develop.

It is hoped that the resources provided by the desk will ensure that we can support our communities in having confidence in the relationship they have with Israel. One of its first tasks will be to articulate what Zionism means for this modern community, ensuring that it has a religious foundation and reminding us of the centrality of our connection with Israel.

NG: Do you think that, given the differing dynamics of our individual communities' relationship to Progressive Zionism, there is anything we can learn from each other?

CB: While there may be differences between North American Progressive Jewry and that of the UK, we must be able to agree that we have always recognized the tensions among particularism and universalism, nationalism, our ethnic Jewish identity, and the boundaries of our religious identity. This is made all the more poignant when we discuss Israel and Zionism. However, for British Progressive Jewry, not only are we the minority as Jews in a nominally Christian country, but we are the minority within the Jewish community. Perhaps we punch above our weight in terms of media coverage and the breadth of our voice; nevertheless, internally we are still the smaller sibling. There has been a dominant narrative that has affected many of our members, and perhaps most of all our youth, that to criticize Israel is to be disloyal—and even worse, an anti-Semitic Jew. We do not have the numbers to significantly combat this narrative. It also means that we have to fight harder for our voice to be recognized by cross-communal organizations and within the internal and external media.

There must therefore be a strong argument for affiliating ourselves more closely with our American cousins. It can only help us in feeling that we are part of a larger movement and that we do not stand alone in asking and answering the questions of what it means to be a Progressive Jewish Zionist.

NG: I could not agree more. Clearly, there are dynamic differences between British Zionists and American Zionists. Their Jewish histories and the experiences that brought the respective communities to the Zionist agenda are distinct from one another. They work with different institutions and a different set of cultural dynamics.

But there is a crucial question to ask together: what, exactly, does Jewish peoplehood mean in the twenty-first century? At a time when the bonds that bind Jews together amidst multicultural communities are dissolving, and when community boundaries are so porous, what exactly does a Jew in Boston have in common with a Jew from London (or Berlin, Moscow, Delhi, Buenos Aires, Paris, or Haifa)? For that matter what do secular, liberal, Orthodox, and *Haredi* Jews share with one another that makes them part of a collective unity called *Am Yisrael*?

A Conclusion and a Beginning

It is our belief that dialogues such as this can be beneficial for Jewish communities around the globe. Both of us are active participants in liberal Jewish institutions with long histories of supporting the State of Israel. Yet as our conversation has revealed, British and American Jews enter into the Zionist discussion from different starting points (although not necessarily the ones we perceived them to be prior to our discussion). The Zionist education of our youth groups, the standing of the Progressive movements in our respective countries' Zionist infrastructure, and our communities' perspective on the Israel-Diaspora relationship are all quite different.

Furthermore, the present condition of the world brings a whole host of new questions. As we watch the reverberations of globalism—including economies that rise or fall together, the rise in international anti-Semitism, and the tragedy of the Muslim refugee situation—old questions arise. Should we be placing more emphasis on *aliyah*? How confident are we about our futures in our host countries? The World Union for Progressive Judaism, the international umbrella of Reform and Progressive Jewish congregations, and ARZENU, the network of Reform and Progressive Zionist communities, would be natural places to develop this international conversation.

As scholar Noam Pianko has pointed out, only a few decades ago *Jewish nationhood* was not necessarily synonymous with *Jewish statehood*.[12] A variety of twentieth-century thinkers offered alternative ways of understanding the ties that bind Jews around the world together. Ultimately, the State of Israel won the right to be synonymous with the "Jewish nation." Still, a transatlantic dialogue would be valuable to help figure out what, exactly, being part of the Jewish nation means today for Jews who love Israel but do not plan on emigrating from their Diasporas any time soon.

NOTES

1. Toby Greene and Yossi Shain, "The Israelization of British Jewry: Balancing Between Home and Homeland," *British Journal of Politics and International Relations* 18, no. 4 (November 2016): 848–65.

2. For a history of the emergence of Liberal Judaism and its difference from Reform Judaism in the UK, see Lawrence Rigal and Rosita Rosenberg, *Liberal Judaism: The First Hundred Years* (London: Liberal Judaism, 2004).

3. Central Conference of American Rabbis, "Declaration of Principles," 1885 Pittsburgh Conference, http://ccarnet.org/rabbis-speak/platforms/declaration-principles/.

4. Central Conference of American Rabbis, "The Guiding Principles of Reform Judaism," The Columbus Platform—1937, http://ccarnet.org/rabbis-speak/platforms/guiding-principles-reform-judaism/.

5. Steven T. Rosenthal, *Irreconcilable Differences? The Waning of the American Jewish Love Affair with Israel* (Hanover, NH: Brandeis University Press, 2001), 12.

6. Jonathan Sarna, *American Judaism* (New Haven, CT: Yale University Press, 2004), 334–35.

7. Until 1998 universities in England did not charge tuition fees; its introduction has meant a decline in those students willing or able to take a gap year before university.

8. David Graham and Jonathan Boyd, *Committed, Concerned and Conciliatory: The Attitudes of Jews in Britain towards Israel* JPR Report (London: Institute for Jewish Policy Research, July 2010).

9. Ibid.

10. David Graham, *Strengthening Jewish Identity: What Works?*, JPR Report (London: Institute for Jewish Policy Research, September 2014).

11. Pew Research Center's Religion & Public Life Project, "A Study of Jewish Americans," chapter 5 in *A Portrait of Jewish Americans* (Washington, DC: Pew Research Center, 2013), http://www.pewforum.org/2013/10/01/chapter-5-connection-with-and-attitudes-towards-israel/.

12. Noam Pianko, *Zionism and the Roads Not Taken* (Bloomington: Indiana University Press, 2010).

Zionism, Liturgy, and Theology

Zion and Zionism in Reform Prayer Books

RABBI DALIA MARX, PhD

THROUGHOUT THE GENERATIONS, Jews have expressed their beliefs, anxieties, and aspirations through their prayers. More than theological or halachic treatises, prayer books have embodied the most refined expressions of their editors' world and consciousness, and through these prayer books Jews attached meaning (for themselves and their surroundings) to the reality in which they lived and to their experiences. This is particularly true in the case of the Reform Movement, since its leaders actively chose to omit, add, and modify prayers to adapt them to their religious beliefs and sensibilities. Accordingly, discussion of the attitude to Zion and Zionism in Reform prayer books—a discussion that touches on a series of fundamental questions of principle relating to the attitude to nationalism, the attitude to peoplehood, and the tension between particularism and universalism in Judaism—can serve as an interesting case study illustrating the ideological and theological developments in this movement.

When we discuss the attitude of Reform prayer books toward Zion and Zionism and the changes that occurred in this respect, it is important to distinguish between two matters: on the one hand, the attitude toward the memory of Zion as the cradle of the Jewish people and, on the other hand, petitions to return to Zion, with all these entailed. The petitions to return to Zion can themselves be divided into two key types: first, petitions relating to the classic narrative of redemption—return to Zion, the establishment of Jewish dominion, the reconstruction of the Temple, the reinstatement of the sacrifices, and the coming of the Messiah; and second, what we refer to as a national-Zionist narrative embodying a worldview on Jewish life in Israel and the State of Israel. While the former type was almost totally rejected in Reform prayer books since the beginning and until now, a higher level of variance is found regarding the second.

Any international, multicultural, and multigenerational movement shows a measure of theoretical and textual diversity. This is particularly true in the case of Reform Judaism, which was founded some two centuries ago. Its communities operate on five continents, from North America to Israel and from South Africa to Hong Kong. Moreover, its very essence is a desire to confront and respond to local and contemporary needs, which axiomatically change over the generations. For reasons of brevity, I will begin by reviewing the principal developments in Reform liturgy in Germany, and later in the North America, before comparing these to the situation in the Israeli Reform Movement. Our review will describe the dramatic transformations that have occurred in the Reform response to these questions.

Zion and Zionism in Early and Classical Reform Liturgy

The alienation experienced by the editors of prayer books as they faced the multiple petitions in the traditional prayers for the return to Zion, the rebuilding of the Temple in Jerusalem, and the reinstatement of the sacrifices was one of the factors that led to the emergence of Reform Judaism. "Such pleas [for the return to Zion, etc.] no longer 'rang true' when uttered by the 'German of the Mosaic Persuasion, who had no wish to be uprooted from his German fatherland.'"[1] In keeping with their perception of Judaism as a religious community, rather than a national collective, the editors of early and classical Reform prayer books omitted the petitions for the ingathering of the exiles and the return to Zion.

Indeed, these anti-nationalist approaches predated Zionism by many decades. A very early and particularly forthright expression of the belief that prayers for the rebuilding of Jerusalem and the return to Zion were no longer meaningful or valuable can be found in comments made by the banker, writer, and communal leader David Friedländer in 1812—the year when the Jews of Prussia were granted emancipation:

Indeed, it requires no special mental effort, only rectitude of soul, for the religious Israelite to say to himself: "Here I stand before God. I pray for blessing and success for my king, for my fellow-citizens, for myself and for my family—not for the return to Jerusalem, not for the restoration of the Temple and the sacrifices. Such wishes I do not have in my heart. Their fulfillment would not make me happy. My mouth shall not utter them."[2]

Friedländer's far-reaching call was not implemented immediately. Petitions relating to Zion and the return to Zion were omitted in a relatively gradual manner and to different degrees in different prayer books. However, prior to the Second World War, the dominant approach rejected the inclusion of such petitions in Reform liturgy.

In the introduction to the first edition of his prayer book, published in 1854, Rabbi Abraham Geiger (1810–1874), the most prominent and influential rabbi in European Reform,[3] explained the changes he had made regarding the petitions for a return to Zion as follows:

Jerusalem and Zion are places from which instruction went forth, and memories are attached. But as a whole, they are to be celebrated more as a spiritual idea—as the nursery of the Kingdom of God—than as a certain geographical locale connected with a special divine providence for all times.[4]

Geiger's approach was not universally adopted in Reform circles, and a significant measure of variance can be seen. Rabbi Manuel Joël (1826–1890), Geiger's successor in his congregation in Breslau, adopted a more traditional approach, emphasizing the importance of Zion and Jerusalem as part of the Jewish people's historical past and memory. Joël claimed that the denial of these aspects would be the self-denial of the Jewish past. He distinguished between expressions conveying the consolation of Jerusalem and the hope of personal return. The former are "harmless," while he said of the latter, "Modern consciousness is unable to make this wish its own; and it is this point against which protest is made."[5] Geiger responded forcefully to Joël's position, arguing that any change that includes a greater

presence of Zion than that included in his own prayer book is evil;
Jerusalem is only a city of ruins and is no more the focus of longing
than modern-day Athens.[6] As an example of this approach during
the early days of Reform, we can compare the traditional wording
of the tenth blessing of the *Amidah*, Ingathering of the Exiles (*Kibutz
Galuyot*), with the version included in Geiger's prayer book:

TRADITIONAL ASHKENAZI VERSION:	GEIGER'S VERSION (1854):
תְּקַע בְּשׁוֹפָר גָּדוֹל לְחֵרוּתֵנוּ **וְשָׂא נֵס לְקַבֵּץ** גָּלְיוֹתֵינוּ וְקַבְּצֵנוּ יַחַד **מֵאַרְבַּע** כַּנְפוֹת הָאָרֶץ. בָּרוּךְ [...], **מְקַבֵּץ נִדְחֵי** עַמּוֹ יִשְׂרָאֵל.	תְּקַע בְּשׁוֹפָר גָּדוֹל לְחֵרוּתֵנוּ **וְהוֹשַׁע** ה׳ אֶת עַמְּךָ אֶת שְׁאֵרִית יִשְׂרָאֵל. **בְּאַרְבַּע** כַּנְפוֹת הָאָרֶץ. בָּרוּךְ . . . **מוֹשִׁיעַ שְׁאֵרִית** עַמּוֹ יִשְׂרָאֵל.
Sound a great horn for our freedom	Sound a great horn for our freedom
And **raise a banner to gather** our exiles	And **save**, Lord, Your people
And unite us together **from the four corners** of the earth.	The remnant of Israel **in the four corners** of the earth.
Blessed . . . who **regathers the scattered** of His people Israel.	Blessed . . . who **saves the remnant** of His people Israel.

Geiger maintained the structure of the blessing and its key phrases,
but the apparently minor changes replace the traditional petition to
ingather the exiles with a petition to save the Jewish people wherever
they may be—"**in the four corners** of the earth" (Jeremiah 31:6).

   In the second edition of his prayer book, published in 1872, Geiger adopted a more radical approach to the deletion of references to
Jerusalem and Zion. By way of example, the section quoted above
from the blessing Ingathering of the Exiles was omitted in its entirety. On the other hand, in the same year, Joël published his prayer
book in the Breslau congregation that was formerly led by Geiger,

restoring certain references to the rebuilding of Jerusalem that his predecessor had deleted.

The variations in the manifestations of Reform in Germany were at most of degree rather than of kind.[7] This was due, in part, to the organizational structure of the congregations in this country. The unified community (*Einheitsgemeinde*) included highly traditional synagogues alongside liberal ones. In the United States, by contrast, where community affiliation was voluntary, Reform Judaism developed separately from more traditional tendencies.[8] Here, the ideas of Reform could be manifested in a more explicit and resolute form.

The American Reform prayer books indeed included ideological expressions in a clear and explicit manner. The blessing for the Ingathering of the Exiles, as discussed above, was imbued with a slightly different character from the German version, perhaps under the influence of the American ethos. It was transformed into a petition for peace and liberty for all, removing all references not only to the Land of Israel but also to the Jewish people. The following is the version of the blessing in *Minhag America*, the prayer book of Rabbi Isaac Mayer Wise (1872):[9]

Let resound the great trumpet for the liberty all nations;	תְּקַע בְּשׁוֹפָר גָּדוֹל לְחֵרוּת כָּל הָעַמִּים
Lift up the banner to unite them in the covenant of peace,	וְשָׂא נֵס לְיַחֲדָם בִּבְרִית שָׁלוֹם וְקָרְבֵם אֵלֶיךָ לְעָבְדְּךָ בֶּאֱמֶת.
And bring them nigh unto Thee, to worship Thee in truth.	בָּרוּךְ אַתָּה ה׳ חוֹבֵב עֲדַת לְאוּמִים.
Blessed be thou who lovest the community of nations.	

In his more radical prayer book *Olat Tamid* (1896), Rabbi David Einhorn combined all the blessings in the *Amidah* relating to the redemption narrative into a single blessing on the subject of social justice.[10] The *Union Prayer Book*, the first official prayer book of the Reform Movement in the United States, which was published in two volumes and three editions, and was used in the American Reform Movement for eight decades, adopted a similar approach.[11]

This prayer book, which was strongly influenced by Einhorn, also omits the blessing Ingathering of the Exiles entirely from the *Amidah*. Together with the other blessings relating to the traditional manifestations of ritual in Zion and the redemption narrative, these sections are replaced by a single blessing focusing on justice and truth. In the 1892 version, the blessing was referenced in two rather vague words in the Hebrew (meaning "and gather in the scattered ones"). These words were not represented in the English translation in the prayer book.

In conclusion, it is apparent that the editors of the early and classical Reform prayer books generally showed an unsympathetic approach toward references to Zion, though some were more willing to regard it as the birthplace of the Jewish people. Conversely, explicit hostility was apparent toward expressions in the prayers referring to the role of Zion in the future of the Jewish people. The starkest manifestation of this approach is provided in the first platform of the American Reform Movement, known as the Pittsburgh Platform (1885):

> We consider ourselves no longer a nation, but a religious community, and therefore expect neither a return to Palestine, nor a sacrificial worship under the sons of Aaron, nor the restoration of any of the laws concerning the Jewish state.[12]

Winds of Change: The Attitude to Zion and Zionism from the Mid-Twentieth Century

The scholar of prayer Jacob Petuchowski proposed ten principles of Reform liturgy, one of which is "the deletion of the petitions for the ingathering of the exiles and the return to Zion."[13] However, Petuchowski's list was published in 1967, when this position was in a gradual but significant state of decline. The optimism and the positivist approach of the early Reformers, who believed that humanity was on the verge of a messianic brave new world of universal enlightenment and justice, gradually receded over the course of the twentieth century with the rise of Nazism, the Second World War, and the Holocaust. The result was a renewed recognition of the importance of Jewish peoplehood and nationhood.[14] The establishment of the State of Israel in 1948 and the Six-Day War of 1967 constituted important milestones in the developing attitude toward Zion and Zionism. The earliest expression of a new approach came in the 1937 Columbus Platform and in the newly revised edition of the *Union Prayer Book* (1940, 1945), which showed a more positive attitude toward Zion and Zionism. This position was reflected even more overtly in the movement's platform adopted in 1976 and known as the San Francisco Platform, which declared:

> We are privileged to live in an extraordinary time, one in which a third Jewish commonwealth has been established in our people's ancient homeland. We are bound to that land and to the newly reborn State of Israel by innumerable religious and ethnic ties. We have been enriched by its culture and ennobled by its indomitable spirit. We see it providing unique opportunities for Jewish self-expression. We have both a stake and a responsibility in building the State of Israel, assuring its security, and defining its Jewish character. We encourage *aliyah* for those who wish to find maximum personal fulfillment in the cause of Zion.[15]

This changing approach led to the compilation and publication of the *Gates of Prayer* prayer book (1975), which not only restored references to Zion, but also added liturgical references to the State of Israel. By way of example, the closing section of the Blessing of Worship (*Avodah*), which anticipates the reinstatement of the Divine Presence in Zion, was restored in certain services, though not all of them (see the appendix on this aspect). In other respects, however, this prayer book maintained the cautious approach to Zionism. *Gates of Prayer* transformed the blessing Ingathering of the Exiles, which we discussed above and which includes an explicit petition to return to Zion, into a call for social justice and universal freedom:

Sound the great horn to proclaim freedom,	תְּקַע בְּשׁוֹפָר גָּדוֹל לְחֵרוּתֵנוּ
Inspire us to strive for the liberation of the oppressed,	וְשָׂא נֵס לִפְדוֹת עֲשׁוּקֵינוּ

And let the song of liberty be
  heard in the four corners of
  the earth.
Blessed is the Lord, Redeemer
  of the oppressed.[16]

וְקוֹל דְּרוֹר יִשָּׁמַע בְּאַרְבַּע
כַּנְפוֹת הָאָרֶץ.
בָּרוּךְ אַתָּה ה' פּוֹדֶה עֲשׁוּקִים.

The proportion of Hebrew, which had already increased in the later editions of the *Union Prayer Book*, was again increased substantially. In additional to traditional prayers presented in Hebrew, *Gates of Prayer* also included a number of Israeli songs in Hebrew and English. In addition, a special prayer was added for Israel Independence Day,[17] together with extensive suggested readings, including the following excerpt, in which the rebuilding of Jerusalem forms part of the path of redemption from torment to repair and building:

A long road, full of torment, from the fall of Jerusalem to its rebuilding. A long road from Jerusalem rebuilt, the building of God's kingdom.... We stand before You in pain and need, remembering our martyrs and heroes, praising the Source of life, from whom we come, to whom we return.

אֲרֻכָּה הַדֶּרֶךְ וּמַכְאִיבָה מֵחֻרְבַּן
יְרוּשָׁלַיִם וְעַד בִּנְיָנָהּ, וּמִבִּנְיַן
יְרוּשָׁלַיִם וְעַד תִּקּוּן כָּל עוֹלָם
בְּמַלְכוּתֶךָ [...] בְּזָכְרֵנוּ אֶת
קְדוֹשֵׁינוּ וְאֶת גִּבּוֹרֵינוּ שֶׁצָּפוּ
לִגְאוּלָה וְנִלְחֲמוּ בַּעֲדָהּ, נְהַלֵּל
אֶת מְקוֹר הַחַיִּים שֶׁמִּמֶּנּוּ בָּאוּ
וְשֶׁאֵלָיו שָׁבוּ.

New Reform: Full Adoption of Zion and the State of Israel

Rabbi Herbert Bronstein shows that each of the American Reform prayer books was published in close proximity to the adoption of the movement's various platforms, as if to realize in practice the directions adopted by way of resolution.[19] Just as the first *Union Prayer Book* echoed the spirit of the Pittsburgh Platform (see p. 257), and *Gates of Prayer* the San Francisco Platform of 1976 (see p. 265), so the new American Reform prayer book *Mishkan T'filah* (2007) embodies the spirit behind "A Statement of Principles for Reform

Judaism," known as the Pittsburgh Principles (1999) (See p. 277). This document is marked by full adoption of Zionism and appreciation for those who choose to live in Israel, alongside recognition of the value of Diaspora Judaism as a legitimate life choice. Here is the opening paragraph from the 1999 Statement of Principles regarding Zionism:

> We are committed to מדינת ישראל (*Medinat Yisrael*), the State of Israel, and rejoice in its accomplishments. We affirm the unique qualities of living in ארץ ישראל (*Eretz Yisrael*), the land of Israel, and encourage עליה (*aliyah*), immigration to Israel.[20]

Mishkan T'filah[21] marks the completion of the process that began with *Gates of Prayer*. Acceptance of Zionism and of the State of Israel, with Modern Hebrew as its language, is manifest in both symbolic and overt dimensions. This is the first prayer book of the American Reform Movement that has only a Hebrew name. All the traditional prayers included in the prayer book appear in Hebrew, as well as in transliteration and in English translation. While the reinstatement of forms of prayer referring to Zion is a restorative act, the addition of prayers relating to the State of Israel is an act of liturgical creativity.

Mishkan T'filah includes a service for Israel Independence Day (Yom HaAtzma-ut) and for Israeli Memorial Day (Yom Ha-Zikaron). Both are presented as autonomous services, rather than immersed in the regular prayers, as was the case in *Gates of Prayer*. The ceremony for Israel Independence Day is based on the paragraphs of Israel's Declaration of Independence, which divide the ceremony into sections with titles such as "For the Beauty of the Land," "For the Ingathering of the Exiles," and so forth. This contrasts with *Gates of Prayer*, which mainly provided additional texts to accompany the regular service. *Mishkan T'filah* also includes an abridged form of the Prayer for the State of Israel,[22] as well as a selection of canonical modern Israeli poetry, such as excerpts from Lea Goldberg's poems (in Hebrew and in Penina Peli's English translation). An equally important point to note is that prayers originally written in English are translated into Hebrew.[23]

The process that came to maturation in *Mishkan T'filah* is manifested even more explicitly in the *machzor* for the Days of Awe *Mishkan HaNefesh* (2015).[24] The machzor includes numerous poems by Israeli poets, some relating to contemporary Israeli reality. Yehuda Amichai's poems on the subject of Jerusalem are particularly prominent. The editors sought to present numerous Israeli voices and to ensure that Israeli reality is present in the *machzor*. By way of example, the Prayer for the State of Israel is accompanied by Ehud Manor's song "I Have No Other Country."[25] However, the editors of the *machzor* evidently sought to strengthen the bond to Israel on an even deeper level. The *Avodah* service for Yom Kippur is organized in some fifteen sections under the general title "*Masa el HaK'dushah*: A Journey to Holiness," paralleling the fifteen steps that led to the Jerusalem Temple. The authors explain the reference to the fifteen "Songs of Ascent" (Psalms 120–134), before adding: "Our Sages used to teach: Fifteen steps led up to the holy Temple in Jerusalem. And on these steps, the Levites stood with trumpets and drums: an orchestra of holiness for the singers of David's psalms."[26] Thus the entire service is structured as an entrance into holiness and into the Temple, mking Jerusalem and its Temple vividly present in the service.[27]

Zion in Reform Prayer Books from Zion

In the Israeli Reform realm, no reservations have ever been apparent regarding Jewish nationhood or the centrality of Zion in the Jewish experience, past and present. The overtly Zionist approach is evident in the fact that *HaAvodah SheBaLev* (1982), the first prayer book of the Israeli Reform Movement, includes all the traditional references to Zion as the cradle of the Jewish people. This prayer book adopts a relatively consistent approach, whereby references to the messianic narrative and petitions for the rebuilding of the Temple are replaced by petitions to complete the building of Jerusalem, namely modern Jerusalem.

The petition "build Jerusalem, the holy city" in *Birkat HaMazon*, for example, was changed to "complete the building of Jerusalem," reflecting recognition that Jerusalem is indeed being built as the capital of the State of Israel and that it is *this* building for which we pray, and not that of the Temple or the reinstatement of the sacrifices.

Other changes reflect the fact that the Jewish people dwells in its Land. In *HaAvodah SheBaLev*, for example, the traditional petition "bring **us** in peace from the four corners of the earth" is replaced by "and ingather **our exiles** from the four corners of the earth." The meaning of this petition is that *we* are already in Israel and hope the Diaspora Jews will join. In the "redemption" blessing recited during the *Sh'ma* liturgy, alternative (or complementary) wordings are suggested in which the idea of the return to Zion is framed against the memory of the Holocaust:

ARVIT	*SHACHARIT*
הַמְזָרֶה יִשְׂרָאֵל בֵּין הַגּוֹיִם וּמְקַבֵּץ נְדָחָיו כְּרוֹעֶה עֶדְרוֹ. גַּם כִּי הָלְכוּ בְּגֵיא צַלְמָוֶת, שֵׁשׁ מֵאוֹת רִבּוֹא בְּתִמְרוֹת עָשָׁן, פָּקַד אֶת שְׁאֵרִית פְּלֵטָתָם, רֵאשִׁית גְּאוּלָתוֹ הֶרְאָה לָהֶם וַיְבִיאֵם וַיִּטָּעֵם בְּהַר נַחֲלָתוֹ.	מִמִּצְרַיִם גְּאַלְתָּנוּ [...], שְׂרִידֵי חֶרֶב הִצַּלְתָּ, וּפְלִיטֵי חֶנֶק מִלַּטְתָּ, נְדָחִים אָסַפְתָּ וּנְפוּצוֹת קִבַּצְתָּ וְשָׁבוּ בָנִים לִגְבוּלָם.
He who spreads Israel among the nations and gathers His rejected ones like His flock. Even if six million walked in the valley of the shadow of death in columns of smoke, He guarded the remnant of their survivors, showed them the beginning of redemption, and brought them to be planted on the mount of His inheritance.	You redeemed us from Egypt... You saved the remnants of the sword and rescued the survivors of asphyxiation, You gathered the dispersed ones and brought together those scattered. And so the beloved have praised and exalted God.

The *chatimah*, the closing words of this blessing, were shifted from the past tense, "Blessed are You, Adonai who **redeemed** (*ga'al*) Israel," to the present, "Blessed are You, Adonai who **redeems** (*goel*) Israel." The change emphasizes that the reality of life in the Land of Israel forms part of the redemption plan. Among other factors, the strong emphasis on Zionism and on the importance of Israel may reflect a desire on the part of the leaders of the Israeli Reform Movement to distance themselves from the anti-Zionist overtones of the Diaspora Reform prayer books of the past and its reputation that lingered on much after they ceased to exist.

Israeli Reform liturgy also grants a special status to modern-day Israeli reality. In addition to the prayers for the Memorial Day for Fallen IDF Soldiers, Israel Independence Day, and Jerusalem Day, which are included in *HaAvodah SheBaLev*, the movement's congregations have in recent years added a special service for the Memorial Day for Prime Minister Yitzhak Rabin. Prayers for the State of Israel and for IDF soldiers are recited every Shabbat, and a special prayer has been added for those about to embark on their military service.

The guiding principles for *HaAvodah SheBaLev* state that the prayer book seeks "to grapple with the reality of the emerging life of the Jewish people, so that the worshiper will see their prayer not only as the continuation of a sacred tradition, but also as a faithful manifestation of contemporary mores (introduction)."

The new Israeli Reform prayer book, which is currently in the editing process, continues and indeed accentuates this approach. One way in which it does so is by reflecting the presence of different Jewish communities that live in Israel, as well as different parts of the country, in order to create an inclusive and multi-vocal Israeli voice. The draft version of the service for Friday night includes a section entitled "Welcoming Shabbat Up and Down the Land." The section includes poems and songs relating to the Sabbath experience in specific parts of the country, such as Yehoshua Rabinov's "Shabbat Has Come," Nathan Alterman's "Song of the Valley," and Gilad Meiri's "Sabbath Evening Walk in Katamon."

Today, alongside clear and explicit expressions of Reform Jewish

life in the sovereign State of Israel, there are those who are calling
for a more measured tone regarding Zionism. By way of example,
in *Birkat HaMazon* in the *Haggadah for These Times*, the words *l'ma'an
t'hei* (that it may be) was added in brackets in the petition for the
State of Israel: "*HaRachaman* will bless the State of Israel [that it
may be] the beginning of the flowering of our redemption."[28] This
suggestion has been the subject of extensive arguments; in any case,
however, its purpose is not to diminish the commitment to the value
of life in Israel, but to note stress that much work lies ahead in order
to make Israel "the beginning of the flowering of our redemption,"
and we cannot afford to rest on our laurels.

The Israeli Reform liturgy expresses a desire for the ingathering
of the people of Israel to Zion but does it in a much more moderate
and restrained manner than in the traditional prayer books. See,
for example, the paragraph that deals with the Diaspora Jews in the
Prayer for the State of Israel:

Remember favorably	פְּקׇד־נָא לִבְרָכָה
our kinfolk of the house of Israel	אֶת אַחֵינוּ בֵּית יִשְׂרָאֵל
throughout the lands of their dispersion.	בְּכׇל אַרְצוֹת פְּזוּרֵיהֶם.
	טַע בְּלִבָּם אַהֲבַת צִיּוֹן,
Plant the love of Zion within their hearts,	וּמִי בָהֶם מִכׇּל עַמֶּנוּ יְהִי
	אֱלֹהָיו עִמּוֹ
and may there be those among them—may God be with them—	וְיַעַל לִירוּשָׁלַיִם עִירְךָ,
who shall come to Jerusalem,	אֲשֶׁר נִקְרָא שִׁמְךָ עָלֶיהָ.
Your city, that bears Your name.[29]	

The prayer first expresses care and solidarity with the Jews in the Diaspora and then encourages "those among them" who may consider
living in Israel. Embedded in this statement is the understanding
that life in the Diaspora is legitimate and that life outside Israel is
not sinful or an expression of divine punishment. This rather lenient
approach in the Israeli Reform liturgy is especially conspicuous
when compared with the official version of the Israeli chief rabbinate, which explicitly requests the ingathering of "all exiles."[30]

Needless to say that questions relating to Zion and Zionism in Israel are much more present (and pressing) than in the Diaspora. For Israelis, the State of Israel is their actual homeland, and therefore it is more present in their liturgy. In fact the attitude to Zion as actual home is one of the things that sets the Israeli Reform liturgy apart from its sister in the Diaspora.

Conclusion

The early and classical Reform prayer books were characterized not only by the omission or obscuring of the petitions for a return to Zion and the ingathering of the exiles, but also sometimes by a reduction in the number of references to Zion as the cradle and spiritual center of the Jewish people. In the case of the American *Union Prayer Book*, these petitions were completely omitted. From the 1930s onward, however, a gradual change can be seen in the attitude of Reform Judaism toward Zionism. The horrors of the Holocaust, on the one hand, and conversely the establishment of the State of Israel, followed by the existential anxieties of the young state during the period before the Six-Day War and the ensuing sense of relief, all led to significant developments in prayer. Many liturgical sections that had previously been omitted were reinstated in the prayer book.

Prayer in the Reform Movement in Israel is a distinct issue, since this movement never questioned the importance of Zion and Zionism and never omitted from its prayer books references to the centrality of Zion. The perception of Israel as the national home of the Jewish people is even more explicit, in some places, in Israeli Reform prayer books than in traditional ones. The appendix to this chapter discusses the evolution and development of the *chatimah* (conclusion) of the Blessing of Worship by way of a test case for the liturgical manifestations of the ideological and theological changes that have occurred in the Reform Movement in the Diaspora and in Israel.

The Mishnah instructs us, albeit indirectly, to face Jerusalem in prayer; the Talmud adds, "If one is in the east, they should turn their face to the west; if in the west, they should turn their face to the east; if in the south, they should turn their face to the north; if in the north, they should turn their face to the south. In this way, all Israel will be turning their hearts toward one place" (BT *B'rachot* 30a). This passage teaches that we do not necessarily have to physically be in Jerusalem; perhaps we cannot all be there. But as long as we direct ourselves—physically, and consequently also mentally and emotionally—toward it, we are all virtually in the same place. And maybe this is the lesson that we can learn regarding the role of Zion in the Reform Movement: there are many ways to be in Zion or to be connected and committed to it. Its connecting role will continue to connect us together in spite of our different life experiences, diverse ideologies, political approaches, and even bitter disagreements, provided that we do not give it up!

APPENDIX
A Test Case: The Evolution of the *Chatimah* of the "Blessing of Worship"

The traditional version of the Blessing of Worship (*Avodah*), the seventeenth blessing in the *Amidah*, the central prayer in Jewish worship, relates to the reinstatement of the sacrifices in Jerusalem, on the one hand, together with a petition that the sacrifices be found acceptable, on the other. The editors of Reform prayer books modified the language of this blessing, in many cases completely rewriting it. In traditional prayer books, the blessing ends with the *chatimah* "Blessed . . . **who returns His Divine Presence to Zion.**" This phrase, which has its origins in the Babylonian prayer books, was replaced in most Reform prayer books by "Blessed . . . **whom alone we serve in reverence.**"[31] This is the ancient *chatimah* once current in the Land of Israel and known to the Reform editors from the Ashkenazi rite for festivals.[32] This *chatimah* was better suited to Reform prayer, since it constituted a purified expression of ethical monotheism, as distinct from the petition in the Babylonian Talmud that the *Shechinah*, the Divine Presence, return to Zion. The following table presents the evolution of the *chatimah* to the Blessing of Worship in American Reform prayer books:

PRAYER BOOK	CHATIMAH
Union Prayer Book (1894, 1922, 1940)	״שֶׁאוֹתְךָ לְבַדְּךָ בְּיִרְאָה נַעֲבוֹד״ "whom alone we serve in reverence"
Gates of Prayer (1975)	Sometimes ״שֶׁאוֹתְךָ לְבַדְּךָ בְּיִרְאָה נַעֲבוֹד״ "whom alone we serve in reverence" Sometimes ״הַמַּחֲזִיר שְׁכִינָתוֹ לְצִיּוֹן״ "who returns His Divine Presence to Zion"; euphemistically translated "whose presence gives life to Zion and all Israel"; sometimes without any reference to Zion[33]
Mishkan T'filah (2007)	Sometimes ״הַמַּחֲזִיר שְׁכִינָתוֹ לְצִיּוֹן״ translated literally: "whose Presence returns to Zion" Sometimes, as an alternative form: ״שֶׁאוֹתְךָ לְבַדְּךָ בְּיִרְאָה נַעֲבוֹד״ "whom alone we serve in reverence"
Mishkan HaNefesh (machzor, 2015)	״הַמַּחֲזִיר שְׁכִינָתוֹ לְצִיּוֹן״ "whose Divine Presence is felt again in Zion"

As noted, Israeli Reform liturgy never omitted references to Zion petition or petitions for the ingathering of the exiles, though it did exclude petitions for the rebuilding of the Temple and the reinstatement of the sacrifices. The following example illustrates the comment made above that the Israeli Reform prayer book sometimes reflects a more overtly Zionist attitude than its traditional counterparts.

In the *Har-El* congregational prayer book,[34] the first Reform prayer book published in Israel, the blessing ends with the *chatimah* "who returns **His people** to Zion" (instead of "who returns **His**

Divine Presence to Zion"). Thus the editors chose to express explicitly the idea of the return to Zion. The IMPJ prayer book *HaAvodah SheBaLev*, which was published in 1982, adopted a wording that combines the traditional *chatimah* with that of *Har-El*: "who returns **His Divine Presence and His people** to Zion."

Today, some in the Israeli Reform Movement are proposing the reinstatement of the Land of Israel *chatimah*, "**whom alone we serve in reverence**," alongside the traditional Babylonian format. The reasons for the proposed change differ from the classical Reform desire to obscure the centrality of Zion. Currently, the proposal reflects a desire to showcase the ancient form of prayer formulated in the Land of Israel, which does not include the suggestion that the Divine Presence has supposedly left the Land of Israel. Others prefer to keep the text as it is in *HaAvodah SheBaLev*, and others still prefer the commonly accepted format in contemporary prayer books, "who returns **His Divine Presence** to Zion," without adding "and His people," which is alluded to in the traditional version. The draft version of the new Reform prayer book currently being prepared in Israel proposed a compromise solution: "who returns **His Divine Presence [and His people] to Zion**" and suggests the old *Eretz Yisrael* text "Whom alone we serve in reverence" as an alternative.

NOTES

I thank Professor Michael Meyer for his helpful comments on this article and Shaul Vardi for its translation from the original Hebrew.

1. Jakob J. Petuchowski, *Prayerbook Reform in Europe: The Liturgy of European Liberal and Reform Judaism* (New York: World Union for Progressive Judaism, 1968), 277.
2. Cited from ibid., 133.
3. Michael A. Meyer, *Response to Modernity: A History of the Reform Movement in Judaism* (New York: Oxford University Press, 1988), 88–99.
4. Abraham Geiger, *Israelitisches Gebetbuch* (Breslau, 1854), vi, cited from Petuchowski, *Prayerbook*, 278–79.
5. Manuel Joël, *Zur Orientierung in der Cultusfrage* (Breslau, 1969), cited from Petuchowski, *Prayerbook Reform*, 279. See Meyer, *Response*, 187. Regarding

Joël as a religious leader and thinker, see Michael Meyer, "The Career of a Meditator: Manuel Joël, Conservative Liberal," *Transversal: Journal for Jewish Studies* 14, no. 2 (Dec. 2016): 56–64.

6. The response appears in Petuchowski, *Prayerbook*, 279–81.

7. David H. Ellenson, *After Emancipation: Jewish Religious Responses to Modernity* (Cincinnati: HUC Press, 2004), 220.

8. Michael A. Meyer, "Our Collective Identity as Reform Jews," in *Platforms and Prayer Books*, ed. Dana Kaplan (Lanham, MD: Rowman & Littlefield, 2002), 93–94; Meyer, *Response*, 225–95.

9. Isaac Mayer Wise, *Minhag America Prayer-Book* (Cincinnati, 1857), 44–45.

10. David Einhorn, *Olat Tamid: Book of Prayers* (Chicago, 1856).

11. *The Union Prayer-Book for Jewish Worship for Shabbat and Weekdays* was printed in 1892 (and replaced in 1895); the revised version was published in 1918, and the newly revised edition was published in 1940.

12. Cited from Meyer, *Response*, 265–70, 388.

13. Jacob J. Petuchowski, *Guide to the Prayerbook* (Cincinnati, 1967), 44–45.

14. Meyer, *Response*, 326–34.

15. Cited from ibid., 393.

16. Chaim Stern, ed., *Gates of Prayer: The New Union Prayerbook* (New York: CCAR Press, 1975), 41. This blessing appears in only one of the four weekday services. In the other services a short petition replaces all the intermediate blessings of the *Amidah*. For explanation of this liturgical choice, which is based on Joël's prayer book, see Lawrence A. Hofman, ed., *Gates of Understanding* (New York: CCAR Press, 1977), vol. 1, 190, n. 69.

17. In *Gates of Understanding*, the companion book to *Gates of Prayer*, the following explanation is provided regarding this prayer: "The State of Israel came into being on 14 May 1948, 5 Iyar 5708. Because of the great importance of this event for world Jewry, the annual commemoration of Israel Independence Day (יום העצמאות) has become widely established among Jewish communities everywhere. The CCAR has proclaimed this day to be a festival, and our service reflects it" (248).

18. *Gates of Prayer*, 610.

19. Herbert Bronstein, "Platforms and Prayer Books: From Exclusivity to Inclusivity in Reform Judaism," in Kaplan, *Platforms and Prayer Books*, 25–39.

20. All the American Reform platforms are cited from the CCAR website (ccarnet.org/rabbis-speak/platforms/).

21. *Mishkan T'filah: A Reform Siddur* (New York: CCAR Press, 2007).

22. Dalia Marx, "Particularism and Universalism in the Prayer for the State of Israel," in Lawrence Hoffman, ed., *All the World: Universalism and Particularism in the High Holidays* (Woodstock, VT: Jewish Lights, 2014), 49–76.

23. An example of this is the revised version of the abridged version of the *Amidah*, written by Rabbi Judith Abrams on the basis of the Jerusalem Talmud (*B'rachot* 4:3; 8a). This prayer was translated into Hebrew by Yechiel Hayoun (102).

24. *Mishkan HaNefesh: Machzor for the Days of Awe*, 2 vols. (New York: CCAR Press, 2015).

25. Ibid., vol. 2, 289–90.

26. Ibid., vol. 2, 450. The page in the *machzor* opposite the introduction features Psalm 122, known as "A Pilgrimage Song."

27. The awareness that the prayers replaced the sacrifices is, of course, nothing new and is mentioned in the writings of the Sages. See Dalia Marx, "The Missing Temple: The Status of the Temple in Jewish Culture following Its Destruction," *European Judaism* 13, no. 2 (2013): 61–78. However, the explicit design of the service in *Mishkan HaNefesh* as a pilgrimage and an entrance to the Temple is certainly innovative in the Reform liturgical context.

28. *Haggadah for Our Time: The Passover Haggadah of the Movement of Progressive Judaism in Israel*, Yehoyadah Amir, Yehoram Mazor, and Dalia Marx (eds.), Tel Aviv 2009, https://www.academia.edu/6747145/Haggadah_for_Our_Times_Yehoram_Mazor_Yehoyadah_Amir_and_Dalia_Marx_eds._in_Hebrew. To the best of my knowledge, this idea was first raised by Rabbi Aharon Soloveitchik and was mentioned in Avi Weiss's article "Open Orthodoxy! A Modern Orthodox Rabbi's Creed," *Judaism: A Journal of Jewish Life & Thought* 46, no. 4 (Fall 1997): 409–21.

29. *HaAvodah ShebaLev* (Jerusalem, Israel Movement for Progressive Judaism, 1982), 129. For discussion of the ideology and theology of this document, including its attitude toward non-Jews, see Marx, "Particularism and Universalism," 58–62.

30. The official (Orthodox) prayer text on this matter is as follows: "Remember favorably our kinfolk of Israel throughout the lands of their dispersion, and lead them quickly and upright to Zion, Your city, and Jerusalem, the dwelling place of Your name, as it is written in the Torah of Moshe Your servant: 'If any of you that are dispersed be in the uttermost parts of heaven, from thence will Adonai your God gather you, and from there will He take you' (Deuteronomy 30:4–5)."

31. The Land of Israel *chatimah* first appeared in Reform prayers in the 1841 edition of the Hamburg Temple prayer book (the 1819 edition maintained the traditional version). In support of their change, the editors quoted Rashi's comments on BT *B'rachot* 11b (beginning "And worship"). See Ellenson, *After Emancipation*, 200–201.

32. See Uri Ehrlich, *The Weekday Amidah in Cairo Genizah Prayerbooks* [in

Hebrew] (Jerusalem: Yad Ben-Zvi Press, 2013), 219–38.

33. As, for example, in the *chatimah* of a creative version of the blessing celebrating their ingathering of the exiles, i.e., of the Jews in the Land of Israel. The paragraph ends: "Their peace is our hope; their freedom is our joy; their creation is our pride. Together may we become a light to the nations" (*Gates of Prayer*, 361).

34. Shalom Ben-Chorin, Penina Naveh, and Y. L. Ben-Or, eds., *Siddur Har-El* (Jerusalem: 5722).

I Have No Other Country
From an Israeli Rabbi Living in the United States

RABBI DAVID ARIEL-JOEL

As ZIONISTS we are not neutral observers; we should speak about Israel from a place of loyalty and love. These feelings of devotion may also reflect our pain: an ache caused by the direction Israeli society is leaning; anguish from watching Israeli society far removed from the aspirations of its founders and from our own sense of the values the country should embrace.

As a Zionist, I believe in our right to possess a Jewish state. We earned the right not because of God's promise to Abraham and not for the reason that it was declared in the Bible, but rather as a consequence of our sustained history and what happened to our people as a result of not controlling our own lands, our own destiny, and our own state.

The essence of Israel's Declaration of Independence, reflecting the vision of the founders of Israel, is of a Jewish state that expresses our right to self-determination, our right to protect our lives, and a safeguard of our heritage. Such a state would respect the rights of all its citizens, allow a free society to flourish, and ensure a political setting where every child born will live in dignity as a member of the free world.

This founding vision is vanishing. Perhaps it is already abandoned or lost, as, according to surveys and research, the image is no longer supported by the vast majority of Israeli Jews. The Jewish and democratic Israel envisioned by its founders does not exist anymore.[1]

I Have No Other Country

I have no other country[2]
even if my land is burning
Just a word in Hebrew pierces
my veins, penetrates my soul
With a body that hurts,
with a heart that is hungry
here is my home.

I will not be silent, when my country
      has changed her face
I will not give in to her,
I will remind her
And I will sing here in her ears
until she has opened her eyes.[3]
                              —EHUD MANOR

אֵין לִי אֶרֶץ אַחֶרֶת
גַּם אִם אַדְמָתִי בּוֹעֶרֶת,
רַק מִלָּה בְּעִבְרִית חוֹדֶרֶת
אֶל עוֹרְקַי אֶל נִשְׁמָתִי.
בְּגוּף כּוֹאֵב,
בְּלֵב רָעֵב,
כָּאן הוּא בֵּיתִי.

לֹא אֶשְׁתֹּק כִּי אַרְצִי
שִׁנְּתָה אֶת פָּנֶיהָ,
לֹא אֲוַתֵּר לָהּ,
אַזְכִּיר לָהּ,
וְאָשִׁיר כָּאן בְּאָזְנֶיהָ,
עַד שֶׁתִּפְקַח אֶת עֵינֶיהָ.

"I Have No Other Country" was written by Ehud Manor, one of the most popular songwriters in Israel's history. He wrote the lyrics in memory of his beloved brother, killed during the War of Attrition in 1968. The song reflects on the senseless death of Israeli soldiers. A popular success, it was extremely admired in Israel, seen as condemning the war in Lebanon and quickly adopted by social and political movements.

Since it was first published in 1986, the song has been embraced by the entire political spectrum in Israel. The right employed it to protest the disengagement from Gaza, and the liberal left appropriated the line "I will not be silent, when my country has changed her face" as a slogan critical of the policies of the Netanyahu governments.

It is a very important song; Ehud Manor, an Israeli icon, presents his critical voice. While the song demonstrates a total commitment to Israel, it is also an outcry of the deep pain rising from the awareness that Israeli society is changing. It expresses disapproval against a society that is disintegrating morally and calls for Israel to fulfill its obligations.

It is a critique that comes from love—love for the country and the people—an analysis that comes from loyalty to a beloved country. While not giving up on Israel, the verses call on us not to be silent or silenced. Manor asks the questions we should all be posing: What do we expect from the State of Israel? What should be our contribution to shaping Israeli society?

A generation ago, the late Rabbi Pinchas Hacohen Peli wrote, "If someone asks me whether prayer is real, I have an answer to show them: the State of Israel is a prayer that has become real."[4] A sovereign Jewish state is truly a prayer that has come true, a dream of many generations that at long last materialized. However, the hopes and ideals are clashing with our modern reality and creating a deep sense of disappointment. Many Israelis, feeling desperation with regard to politicians and government, claim an almost physical ache and grief when watching the direction toward which Israeli society is moving.

"The State of Israel will ensure complete equality of social and political rights to all its inhabitants without distinction of religion, race, and sex"[5]

The Pew Research Center survey examining trends in Israeli society, completed in 2015, was the largest of its kind ever facilitated in Israel.[6] The result of the study confirms Manor's statement "my country has changed her face" and validates statements made by President Rivlin: half of Israel's citizens are not Zionist, and a quarter of the citizenship is not Jewish.[7] The most worrying discovery is that the majority of Israeli Jews are not committed to the democratic nature of Israel.

The Pew survey illustrates that half of Israeli Jews support deportation of Arab citizens from Israel and that 79 percent of Israeli Jews think that Israeli Jews should be favored by the government over Israelis who are not Jewish.

These findings correspond to and are consistent with a similar survey presented by the Israel Democracy Institute, one of Israel's leading research institutes, whose studies are utilized by the Knesset and government bodies. The survey reveals that 62 percent of Israeli Jews believe that the right to vote in Knesset elections should be conditional upon a declaration of loyalty to Israel as a democratic, Jewish, and Zionist state. In other words, the majority of the Jewish public seeks to change the laws applied to Israel's Arab citizens in an attempt to exclude Israeli Arabs from the political arena. The research also finds that 86 percent of the Jewish public believes a Jewish majority should determine critical decisions for the state.

The editor of the survey, Professor Tamar Hermann, regards these results as a very serious matter. "This is a terrible statement," she claims, "and a type of exclusion that cannot be accepted by any democracy. These are citizens—not foreigners or immigrants. The implication is that any Jew who arrives here can exert an influence the day after arriving, but Israeli Arab citizens cannot."

In other findings, 70 percent of the respondents oppose the inclusion of Arab parties and ministers in government. "Arabs are not perceived as part of the collective that is relevant in the context of political deliberation," Professor Hermann explains, "they are excluded and viewed as a fifth column." She concludes, "People say things today that they once would have been embarrassed to admit. It has become legitimate to make comments that were once only whispered in certain circles."[8]

These surveys indicate that some thoughts and statements once considered politically incorrect are now turning into actions. Many Jews in Israel are displaying loathing toward minorities and non-Jews, sometimes resulting in hate crimes. Meanwhile, Israel's leadership, instead of expressing the need for calm and peace, is arousing incitement against Israeli Arabs and adding fuel to the fire.

In recent years, and emerging from many circles of Israeli society, it is more frequent to hear hate-filled speech rallied against Israeli Arabs and Palestinians and to learn of attacks on mosques and churches. Provocative and racist remarks pour directly from Prime Minister Bibi Netanyahu and many of his coalition members. Unfortunately, there are on average four hundred hate crimes committed by Jews toward non-Jews in Israel every year. This represents more per capita hate crimes than anti-Semitic acts toward Jews in any single country in the world.[9]

There are many voices in Israel calling on the Israeli public in the name of democracy, equality, and reason. One special one, and a beacon of light, is President Rivlin. A non-elected official, he was selected by the Knesset members to hold the position. At a rally against hate crimes, he shared the following words: "Friends, the flames are spreading in our land, flames of violence, flames of hatred, flames of false, distorted, and twisted beliefs. Flames which permit the shedding of blood, in the name of the Torah, in the name of Jewish law, in the name of morality, in the name of a love for the land of Israel.... We must put out the flames, the incitement, before they destroy us all . . . a Jewish and democratic Israel needs a wake-up call today."[10]

As Jews, we are at our best when our Jewish American community, a small minority, acts with the mind-set of a majority—thinking of the good and welfare of others. For most American Jews, "justice" compels us to ask ourselves how to help those in need, including oppressed minorities in our midst. During the twentieth century, it is well documented that Jews in the United States were at the forefront of many significant social battles, fighting for the rights of others.

We are far from attaining our aspirations when those representing the Israeli government act with the mind-set of a minority—only for the good and welfare of their own political base. It is embarrassing when the government of Israel, the only place in the world where Jews are a ruling majority, is introducing legislation to oppress its minorities. The administration and many Israeli Jews approach this issue viewing justice as "What can I do for my own ethnicity . . . , even . . . at the expense of minorities?" This growing concept needs to change, not just be accepted or defended. The democratic values of equality are exactly what President Rivlin is fighting for, and he needs our help.

As liberal American Jews, we can no longer afford to ignore these clear social trends of preserving rights for only the Jewish majority. Those who dream of a Zion that is "what it could and should be" face tremendous challenges due to the changed demographics of the country. The results include the Israeli actions of protracted occupation and confiscation of land belonging to non-Jewish citizens; low value attached to Arab lives and rights, in the Occupied Territories or in Israel; ongoing exclusion of Arab citizens and systemic discrimination against them; lack of land usage plans in Arab communities; and, in general, the Arab community's removal from the benefits of life in Israel.

The Reform Movement and Israel to Date

An examination of the attitude toward Israel on the part of the American Reform Movement shows that, in general, it has focused on an effort to influence the Jewish character of the state, fighting for acceptance of more than only Orthodox standards.[11] The movement works to create governmental acceptance and support for Reform rabbis and members of Reform synagogues and seeks to shape government positions, such as acknowledging egalitarian practices. The movement has chosen to concentrate on issues relating to Jewish pluralism in Israel, rather than on aspects that test Israel's democratic character.

During the period in which I served as associate director and then as executive director of the Israeli Reform Movement, we frequently commented that the early Zionists adopted the biblical message "House of Jacob, come and let us walk" but had neglected the following words—"in the light of God" (Isaiah 2:5). We saw our mission in Israel as a possibility to add the dimension of Torah (from a progressive Jewish perspective) to the Zionist endeavor. We tried—and continue working—to show that one manifestation of the revolutionary significance of a Jewish state is to enable diverse Jewish cultures to flourish while maintaining a commitment to the destiny of the people. The Israeli Reform Movement continues to see its American counterpart as a full partner in the effort to secure legitimacy for egalitarian and progressive Judaism in Israel.

This is a holy task, and the Israeli Reform Movement is making enormous efforts in spiritual and educational spheres as well as communal activities and social action projects. The movement has an influence on Israeli society with impact far beyond its size and budget. Those involved deserve great praise for their efforts and achievements. Indeed, the Reform Movements in North America and Israel have worked diligently to protect the right of the Israeli Reform Movement to convert non-Jews, to receive government funding for educational activities, to enjoy financial support from municipalities and local councils for synagogues, and for many other struggles that shape the pluralistic Jewish character of the State of Israel. The most challenging and significant efforts concern the struggle to secure the recognition of the State of Israel for conversions at which we officiate in North America. The Israeli Reform Movement and the Israel Religious Action Center have won substantial achievements, with the immeasurable assistance of the North American movement.

The measures to create positive change are certainly important but only reflect a primary concern for our own rights as partners in determining the Jewish character of the State of Israel. In this context, we would do well to take heed of a comment made in multiple public addresses by Rabbi Dow Marmur that "we are strongest when we advocate beyond our own concerns."[12]

So What Should We Do?

The State of Israel is a strong and prosperous country. During the critical decades needed for the growing success of the state and for its emergence as a modern nation, American Jews provided almost unconditional support. However, I believe the time has now come to change direction—certainly here in North America, but also in our small sister movement in the Holy Land. American Jewry in general, and the liberal American Jewish movements in particular, must stop evading controversial issues. Jews living outside of Israel have a right and a responsibility to boldly express views on broader issues relating to human and civil rights.

It is time for us to take a good look at ourselves and question our agreement with the current agenda promoted in Israel. Do we really concur with what Israeli democracy has become and where it is leading to in the future? Israel is a very dynamic society, constantly changing and reinventing itself. Israelis who left the country twenty years ago or more remember a society that has long since disappeared. This shifting character requires us to consider where Israel is heading and whether the country is losing the essence of a Jewish and democratic state. Are we letting the extremists in our midst define the course our beloved homeland is taking?

When we speculate as to Israel's potential risk as a democracy, it is imperative to support positive agents of change such as the Israeli Reform Movement or Tag Meir—the largest grassroots organization fighting hate crimes—as well as Rabbis for Human Rights. All can take pride in Israel's president and have faith that his unprecedented popularity indicates Israelis are an inherently decent people who value a moral and honorable politician. To help ensure an optimistic future, as Americans we must insist that our Federation dollars designated for Israel are directed to progressive social projects and not to irrelevant institutions that represent a past that no longer exists.

At a conference in the Bedouin city of Rahat, speaking to young Israelis—Jews and Arabs, who work collectively to create a better Israeli society—President Rivlin proclaimed, "When I look at these wonderful young people volunteering together for a better Israel, I believe in our ability to build a common future. The beauty of Israeli society lies in its diversity and in its multi-faceted components. A heterogeneous society is always richer than a homogeneous one. All citizens, Jews and non-Jews, are equal before the law. I call upon all the Jews and Muslims to respect each other's faith; do not be tempted to incitement and evil voices." [13]

"I Have No Other Country" by Ehud Manor does not just speak to those who live in Israel; it must also embolden us to support a democratic Israeli society and become true partners in the *tikkun*, to establish the change and repair Israel so desperately needs.

NOTES

1. In his Herzliya speech of June 7, 2015, Israel's president, Mr. Ruby Rivlin, spoke of the "new Israeli order." He described Israeli society as four different "tribes" that do not speak to one another, do not attend the same school systems, do not serve together in the army, and do not know or acknowledge one another. He suggested that the new Israeli order has completely changed the secular, liberal Zionist character of Israel and is threatening the entire Zionist endeavor. In Rivlin's words, "We must ask ourselves honestly, what is common to all these population sectors? Do we have a shared civil language, a shared ethos? Do we share a common denominator of values with the power to link all these sectors together in the Jewish and democratic State of Israel? . . . Are we, the members of the Zionist population, able to accept the fact that two significant groups, a half of the future population of Israel, do not define themselves as Zionists?" (http://www.president.gov.il/ English/ThePresident/Speeches/Pages/news_070615_01.aspx).

2. In Hebrew, ארץ (alef-reish-tzadi) could mean "land," "country," "state," or "earth."

3. The poem "I Have No Other Country" is now part of our liturgy, as it is published in the new Reform machzor *Mishkan Hanefesh: Machzor for the Days of Awe*, vol. 2, *Yom Kippur* (New York: CCAR Press, 2015), 289.

4. As quoted in Dr. Aviad Hacohen, "Zeh hayom asah Hashem nagilah venismechah bo," 1 Iyar 5765; the article appears on the website Kipa, http://www. kipa.co.il/holidays/show.asp?id=5502.

5. Israel's Declaration of Independence, 5 Iyar 5708 (May 14, 1948).

6. Pew Research Center's Religion & Public Life Project, *Israel's Religiously Divided Society* (Washington, DC: Pew Research Center, March 8, 2016), http://www.pewforum.org/2016/03/08/israels-religiously-divided-society/.

7. In this article, I choose to ignore the Palestinian residents of the Occupied Territories. If including those Palestinians under Israel's authority, we might conclude that Israel is no longer a Jewish or a democratic state. A state in which more than half its residents are not Jewish cannot be labeled Jewish, especially if it forces its Jewishness. A state where more than half its residents are either allowed no civil rights or are discriminated against is not a democratic state.

8. Asher Arian et al., *Auditing Israeli Democracy—2010: Democratic Values in Practice* (Jerusalem: Israel Democracy Institute, November 2010), https://www.idi.org.il/media/4849/madad_2010_eng_abstract.pdf.

9. The numbers of hate crimes in Israel are based on the official annual reports of the Israeli police for the years 2009–2014, the annual reports of OCHA

(UN agency) for the years 2009 and 2010, and the Israel police report to the Knesset Interior Committee on June 2013.

10. President Reuven Rivlin address at solidarity rally in Jerusalem's Zion Square against violence and promoting tolerance (August 1, 2015).

11. Examples would be the battle for egalitarian prayers at the Kotel, for the right of Reform rabbis to perform weddings, or for recognition of Reform conversions.

12. Cited in Lawrence A. Englander, "Progressive Religious Zionism: From Ideology to Practice," *CCAR Journal* (Fall 2011): 67.

13. http://president.gov.il/Presidential_Activities/Press_Releases/Pages/news_080915_02.aspx

Israel: Projection, Potential, and Self-Actualization

Rabbi David Z. Vaisberg

WE OFTEN PREACH that human beings are created *b'tzelem Elohim*—in God's image (Genesis 1:27)—and we Reform Jews typically invoke this concept in the context of treating other human beings with justice and kindness. This axiomatic belief in being created in God's image also helps, though, when we consider the breadth and depth of human potential—specifically Jewish potential. When we consider what it truly means for human beings to be made in God's image, one option is to understand that it is the psyche—the human mind—that makes us godlike; it is our knowledge, our ability to understand, discern, learn, and judge, that makes us resemblances of the Divine.[1]

If the human mind and its potential are the starting point of holiness in human beings, then, when we try to determine the holy purpose, if there is one, of the establishment and continued existence of the State of Israel, it may be worthwhile to begin the conversation not with the state but with the human beings who sought it, created it, built it, and prayed for it: the Jewish people.

I operate from the premise that the State of Israel is the national projection of the Jewish people, designed to fulfill needs we cannot fulfill elsewhere. To determine which Jewish needs in fact must be fulfilled (and therefore what is the ultimate sacred potential of the Jewish state), we must first examine what the Jewish people's divinely created needs may be.[2] While it is most certainly worthwhile to turn to Torah for perspective, so too may it be worthwhile, for an investigation into the divine workings of the mind, to turn to psychology, and specifically its subfield of motivational psychology.

The human mind is driven, according to motivational theory, by needs. (For more on this idea, see discussion below.) All our thoughts and actions are driven by needs. When there's a lack in our lives, we act. We're hungry, so we eat. We lack energy, so we sleep. We need connection, so we find others, and we find God. These needs are known as motivational drives.

In his 1943 paper "A Theory of Human Motivation," Abraham H. Maslow explores the categories of needs that guide human behavior, and he posits that these needs, or motivations, are hierarchical. In Maslow's words, "The appearance of one need usually rests on the prior satisfaction of another, more prepotent need."[3] These needs, in order of lowest (or most fundamental) to highest, often pictured as a layered triangle, are (1) basic physiological needs, (2) safety, (3) love, (4), esteem, and (5) self-actualization.

If human beings are divinely created, then all aspects of us, and most certainly our higher, less animalistic parts, may be treated as divinely connected, influenced, or even designed. What could be higher in us and more a reflection of the Divine than the psyche? And if we understand the psyche to be divinely formed, then it would logically follow that the forces that motivate us (part of the inner workings of our mind) are also divinely formed. I can only guess that these motivational drives were created to ensure that we survive and thrive. So if we are created with our motivational drives, and with the understanding that as human beings we will behave according to these drives, then we could conclude that what Maslow calls motivations the religious person could call divine expectations. After all, these five motivations can all be linked, to greater or lesser extent, to mitzvot. Physiological needs? *Pikuach nefesh*. To keep a life safe, we must violate almost any other commandment if necessary. Safety? The same. Love? *P'ru ur'vu*—be fruitful and multiply; and *v'ahavta l'rei-acha kamocha*—loving our neighbors as ourselves. This drive is covered through multiple mitzvot. Esteem, a little less clear than its supporting drives, refers to our need for self-respect and confidence. It seems clear to me that our divine account, the Torah, demands of us that we lead lives worthy of respect and esteem, as one of the stated results of our mission as explained by Torah is that we will be held in esteem by those who encounter us. The Torah states, "Observe them faithfully, for that will be proof of your wisdom and discernment to other peoples, who on hearing of all these laws will say, 'Surely, that great nation is a wise and discerning people'" (Deuteronomy 4:6). Fulfilling mitzvot will lead to respect from others, and thus our drive for esteem could be a built-in reward system for mitzvah observance.

As for self-actualization, it may be the most sacred drive of them all. Maslow describes self-actualization as the fulfillment of a person's total potential. "A musician must make music, an artist must paint, a poet must write, if he is to be ultimately happy. What a man can be, he must be."[4] And the human being must connect with God. For the Jewish human being, this means bringing God into this world, and partnering with God in whatever capacity one can, to complete, fix, and perfect this world.

Understanding these drives to be divine in origin and purposefully part of us and that to fulfill these drives is to fulfill mitzvot, then we can assert that these five stages of motivation reflect five stages of divine expectation for humanity. And while all human beings have these built-in drives and maps for sacred behavior, the Jewish people as a whole, through the Torah, have a particular way of doing it—of fulfilling what we understand as mitzvot, of connecting with God, and of doing God's work in this world. As a collective of human beings with a particular way of understanding God's will and our purpose in this world, we together have become a particular body with particular needs.

This brings us to Israel. The Land of Israel, under Jewish sovereignty, is the only place where the Jewish people as a collective, in relationship with God, can self-actualize and realize their full potential. It is the only place where a people in relationship with God can operate as a holy people, a kingdom of priests, and a true light unto the nations, as the Torah commands. Any individual Jew can achieve self-actualization any place in the world, but for an entire people to work together to bring about change in this world, not only to do mitzvot but to use our entire system of holy and constructive

behaviors, ethics, and morals, we require (1) a primarily Jewish environment, clear of the threats, temptations, and influences foreign
majority cultures pose to Jews who might assimilate to some degree,
thus causing their identity to be partly Jewish and partly something
else; (2) the national resources—the legal system, the military,
health care, the religiously national culture—that allow us to do
sacred work for ourselves, our neighbors, and other nations in the
world; and (3) the challenge of having our own nation to run, forcing
us to apply Jewish values and laws to all aspects of life.

Let us be clear. Many—including some of the Zionist founders—have argued that the State of Israel exists for Maslow's lower
stages. Herzl, for example, did not work toward a state for Jewish
self-actualization. He sought Jewish safety and security. He would
have been content for Israel to be a nation similar to all the others.
Many Israelis and Jews still understand Israel to be their safe haven.

But the Jewish people do not need Israel to fulfill those lower four
stages.

Safety is a very legitimate concern. We have been persecuted and
attacked in almost every place we have lived. But most of us, particularly here in North America, live in great safety. In the wake of the
2016 American election, that feeling of safety has been rocked by a
resurgence in xenophobia, prejudice, and acts of hate, which logically leads to a sense that Israel may once again be a safer place. But
we could also make the argument that under Israel's current leadership, with its virtual abandonment of the two-state solution and
the frustration it is causing Palestinians in the territories, violence
once again may rear its head. That means that in the wake of our
shaken sense of security in North America, the argument that Israel
is still a safer place for Jews may be inaccurate, as there may be more
acute threats in Israel than here in North America. Also, despite
attempted and successful threats to our existence throughout history, as a collective nation we always survived in the Diaspora, with
a will as strong as it has always been. And the existence of the State
of Israel unfortunately has not changed the fact that there still are
those who seek to kill us. Having our own state has simply changed

things in establishing that with national sovereignty, the Jewish people has far more control over our security than ever before.

Love is something we all seek—as individuals, from others, and as
the people of Israel, from God. Israel, for all its beauty and spiritual
importance, is not a requirement for God's love. Our covenant—our
b'rit, not so different in my mind from a *ketubah*, a marital contract—
was given to us not within the boundaries of the nation, but in the
unclaimed wilderness. And when we left for exile in Babylon, after
having had our land, the prophet Ezekiel comforted us with his description of a divine chariot. God has a vehicle, he said, and would
come to us wherever we are. Having a palpable connection with God
and being able to express and feel love, according to Ezekiel, is not
dependent upon being in the Land of Israel.

Esteem can come through Torah and sacred observance. Deuteronomy (Deut. 4:6) tells us that when the other nations hear the laws
of Torah, they will think of Israel as a great nation.

Self-actualization, the fifth and final level, is different. Jews and
Jewish communities throughout the world most certainly can live
spectacularly meaningful and Jewishly creative lives. All you have to
do is note that the Talmud was edited in Babylon, think about the
richness of literature that came out of Spain, France, Germany, and
Eastern Europe, or mark the intensity and vibrancy of Jewish life
in places like New York City, Los Angeles, Chicago, Toronto, and
London. But these spurts of creativity all are limited. The Babylonian Talmud refrained from any extended application of halachah
to agriculture, as its compilers were not in their own land. Medieval
Judeo-Spanish literature is in many ways comparable to contempo-
raneous Muslim works of science, philosophy, and art. And for all
the vibrancy of New York Jewish living, it still is a Jewish life painted
on a multicultural/assimilated American canvas, where individuals
can opt in or out of Jewish activities depending on the needs of the
hour. It is still a place where synagogue offices close for Christmas
and Easter. It is still a place where as a young parent I repeat my
parents' efforts as I try to ensure that my children's Jewish needs
are respected and fulfilled by teachers who are well-intentioned but

believe egg dyeing and ornament decorating to be nonreligious activities. And it is still that place where school and work events may
be scheduled on a Friday night or Saturday morning. We ought not
disparage Jewish living in the Diaspora. It is often beautiful and fulfilling. It gives us the opportunity to truly interact with non-Jews,
build ties, and be that light unto the nations. But it is limiting and
still sometimes works against our efforts at higher Jewish practice
and creativity.

Additionally, being in the Diaspora means that while we will apply
Judaism to prophetically mandated issues of social justice, we do
not consider how Judaism approaches mundane issues, like traffic
or banking or even defense. To do so would be simply a theoretical
exercise. A Jewish state in Israel, on the other hand, gives us the challenge of applying Jewish ethics, values, and laws to every single walk
of life. And the State of Israel puts our views to the test, forcing us
to deal not in idealism and platitudes but in realpolitik. Rabbi David
Hartman, z″l, observed:

> Israel, however, not only allows us to give expression to what is
> most noble in Jewish tradition, but it also readily exposes moral
> and spiritual inadequacies in that tradition. Israel therefore
> provides unique conditions for a serious critique of Judaism
> as it is practiced by committed halakhic Jews. In Israel there
> is no external non-Jewish world to inhibit the tradition's full
> self-expression. Moral attitudes that one never expected to
> characterize Jewish behavior can surface in this uninhibited,
> passionate, and complex Jewish reality. Triumphalist national-
> ism, lack of tolerance for other faith communities, indifference,
> and often an open disregard for the liberal values of freedom of
> the individual, human dignity, and freedom of conscience can
> be found articulated by would-be religious leaders in Israeli
> society.[5]

Having a state not only forces us to implement mitzvot at all societal
levels, it also makes blatant the results of any inconsistencies or problems created by halachah, ethics, and values. Having a state forces us
to apply Jewish tradition to laws in connection to business, property,

and agriculture. It requires that we consider in a Jewish manner, at all levels, what it means to need to deal with nations with spotty records in human rights and justice that we still need on our side at the United Nations; or how we deal with those in our midst who incite violence and hate in the name of our own people; or how we address minorities living among us or other human beings who also have their own legitimate claims to our land (i.e., the Palestinians).[6]

We most certainly have not yet achieved full self-actualization in Israel. There is too much discontent, disagreement, and vitriol among the different demographic entities—the Jewish people and non-Jews in Israel and the territories. But progress is being made. Many Jews and Israelis experiment with all possibilities that halachah and Jewish values offer in the realms of health, science, arts, literature, and society, to the point where the whole world is influenced and helped by Jewish ingenuity and creativity.

We do not always approach these challenges correctly on the first, second, or fifth time around. But we try, and sometimes we will succeed. True artistry requires not just masterpieces but rejected canvases, realized to be poor refractions of the truth in the artist's eye. A state creates for Jews the possibility of honing our skills to a sharpness unavailable elsewhere. Our own state, like an artist's studio, gives us room, and freedom, for experimentation, for creating masterpieces and deciding that certain works would be better off erased. Having a state allows us the intensity and unadulterated Jewishness to improve, focus, and expand our skill of being holy, so that eventually we can fulfill the mandates of Torah and partner with God in completing this world.

Personally, I crave the opportunity for this deep level of connection and the potential for being part of our people's self-actualization in the Land of Israel. As a rabbi, I find my work and my community's work, with the Jewish community and the non-Jewish community, to be meaningful, engaging, and of a high Jewish standard, and I most certainly understand that as long as there are Jews in the Diaspora, there is important Jewish-actualizing work to be done in the Diaspora. I think it is a good thing, in fact, that there are Jews outside of Israel working with countries and communities for the betterment of humankind and our planet, much in the way the Religious Action Center does here in the United States. But I still feel religiously limited outside of Israel's primarily Jewish environment in what I can experience and accomplish and with whom I can work to do so. I miss from my time spent living in Israel the nationwide celebrations of Purim and Lag BaOmer, the way everything stopped for remembrance on Yom HaShoah and Yom HaZikaron; the way public schools make knowledge of Hebrew, *Tanach*, and Jewish history ubiquitous; the fact that there can be institutions like the secular yeshivot that seem secular from an Israeli standpoint but wholly Jewish from the Diaspora; the diversity of our own people from all over the world; the political divides that are as much Jewish as they are political conversations; the soldiers who all have official army *Tanachim* and are guided by Jewish ethics in their decision-making; and the sense that Jews now have the responsibility for looking after, caring for, and coexisting with non-Jews, some of them hostile, in our communities, and that the onus for figuring it out is finally on us. Israel enables and requires Judaism to go down so many more varied venues of Jewish engagement than is possible in the Diaspora.

So you might ask me why, if I care so much, don't I make *aliyah*? The answer for me is quite simple—family. The vast majority of my family lives in New York, New Jersey, Montreal, or Toronto, and as much as I yearn for Israel, I could not be so far away from those I love. And fortunately, as a Jew and a congregational rabbi, my Jewish life, while not at an Israeli level, is still tremendously rich and fulfilling.

Above, I likened the Torah to the *ketubah*—the marital contract between God and the people Israel. A marriage exists wherever the partners find themselves. When love is strong, it carries and sustains us, whether we are together or apart, at home or abroad. But marriage requires the creation of a home—a place where the marriage is manifest. A place where the partners can be together in the environment they make, with their own photos, projects, keepsakes, and creations; where they can host friends, cook meals, and laugh and cry together in intimacy; where they pay their bills and balance their budgets; and where they dream of what they might accomplish together in the years ahead.

The home is where partners in relationship actualize their full potential, and Israel is very much the home for the Jewish people. What does God want from the people Israel? For us to self-actualize. Thankfully, we have a land in which to do so.

NOTES

1. We human beings were kicked out of *Gan Eden* after eating the fruit from the Tree of All Knowledge, after which God shared, "Here, the human being has become like one of us, in knowing good and evil" (Genesis 3:22, translation Everett Fox). Adam and Chava, while made in the divine image in the first Genesis Creation account, only took on this status in the second Creation account once they partook from the Tree of All Knowledge. Our being able to consider and analyze, and specifically here, evaluate the difference between what is good and what is not, is the part of us that emulates the original divine model. (For more, see Ovadiah Sforno's commentary on Genesis 1:27 and 3:22.)

2. Presuming, of course, that human beings were in fact created, or even designed, by God, as per Genesis 1:26–28. Even if we do not take this belief literally, if we presume human beings to be made in the image of God, enough for purposes of *tikkun olam*, it is not a far jump to attribute at least some divinity to the human mind, and specifically here, to psychological drives. If uncomfortable with stating that God deliberately made them, we can still treat internal drives in a manner that understands them as part of the greater religious-spiritual-halachic framework of humanity and motivation. One example of a recurring treatment of psychological drives from Rabbinic literature is that of *yetzer hatov and yetzer hara* (the good inclination and evil inclination). These are treated as created elements within us that drive us toward certain behaviors, and to these inclinations in our textual tradition, there is a religious response: halachic discussions of why we actually need both, halachic suggestions of how to manage and balance them, and aggadic descriptions of times that these inclinations were out of balance. A study of the Rabbinic tradition's treatment of human inclination toward good and evil is an example of a religious effort to understand motivational drives, and that this is part of our religious-halachic canon shows that we

believe there to be something divine in the presence of motivational drives and/or our response to them. My read on the tradition is that there is precedence for explorations of the human psyche as a religious study of a divine product.

3. Abraham Maslow, "A Theory of Human Motivation," in *Classics in the History of Psychology*, ed. Christopher D. Green, http://psychclassics.yorku.ca/Maslow/motivation.htm, section I.7.

4. Ibid., section II.

5. David Hartman, "The Third Jewish Commonwealth," in *Contemporary Jewish Theology: A Reader*, ed. Elliot N. Dorff and Louis E. Newman (New York: Oxford, 1999), 445.

6. I understand Palestinian claims to the Land of Israel to be valid as per their historical narratives and their people's history living in the Land of Israel.

Zionism and Tikkun

Restoring Tikkun Olam
to Liberal Religious Zionist Activism

RABBI NOA SATTATH

THE FIRST PROPHETS and leaders of Zionism envisioned a future state that would rest on firm principles of justice, equality,
and peace. Herzl's utopian vision was of a model, prosperous society, built on pillars of solidarity, support for the weakest members,
equality, and morality—a testament of faith in the human spirit.[1]

Achad HaAm spoke about the critical *moral* role of prophetic truth
and justice in the salvation of Jews through Zionism, a cause that
would promote the most exalted and supreme moral values.[2] In his
letter "Zionism and *Tikkun Olam*," Achad HaAm articulated the need
for Zionism to solve not only the "Jewish" question but, by doing so,
to also resolve the major social and economic questions for all. Universal *tikkun olam*, he claims, is central to the Zionist question.[3]

The Reform Movement, loyal to our values of justice, equality, and
inclusivity, has been inspired particularly by these elements of the
Zionist vision. For eighty years now, we have integrated the dream
of peace and justice into our Zionist commitment and identity. The
Columbus Platform, adopted in 1937 by the Central Conference of
American Rabbis (see p. 261), includes the first official expression of
support for Zionism by the Reform Movement. In this platform the
movement embraced the Zionist enterprise as part of the effort to
establish "the kingdom of God, of universal brotherhood, Justice,
truth and peace on earth."

The CCAR's Miami Platform on Reform Zionism, adopted in
1997 (see p. 271), reiterates and expands on that commitment. It
details a vision of Israel:

The Jewish State is therefore unlike all other states. Its obligation is to strive towards the attainment of the Jewish people's
highest moral ideals to be a *mamlechet kohanim* [a kingdom of
priests], a *goy kadosh* [a holy people], and *l'or goyim* [a light unto
the nations] . . . the kind of society in which full civil, human,
and religious rights exist for all its citizens. Ultimately, *Medinat
Yisrael* will be judged not on its military might but on its character. . . . We express the fervent hope that *Medinat Yisrael*, living
in peace with its neighbors, will hasten the redemption of *Am
Yisrael*, and the fulfillment of our messianic dream of universal
peace under the sovereignty of God.

In light of this inspiring and moving vision, we find ourselves faced
not only with political challenges but with a crisis of faith as well.
Twenty years after the Miami Platform was adopted we are further
than ever from that vision: fifty years into the military occupation
of the West Bank and Gaza (and with no end in sight); with the domestic democratic sphere shrinking and facing constant threats;
with growing religious extremism in Israel affecting women and the
LGBTQ community; with alarming racist militias violently targeting
Arab citizens and residents; and with growing economic inequality.

When we discuss Israeli politics, we often elaborate on the progress that is constantly being made: more equality for the LGBTQ
community, growing strength and recognition of Progressive Judaism, and technological and environmental innovation. This progress is indeed significant and encouraging. However, despite all this,
we need to recognize our current point of crisis.

Contemporary Israel is not the fulfillment of our Zionist vision
when measured against our aspirational values of justice, peace, and
brotherhood. Quite the opposite—on many moral questions the
current situation in Israel is a profound disappointment.

As a religious movement, we need to provide the spiritual as well
as the intellectual answers to how we cope with confronting this disappointment and find the strength to keep recruiting all of our creativity, energy, and faith in the struggle to fulfill our vision. We need
to build our stamina as a movement for a long-term commitment to

a struggle that may take decades to complete and that will include multiple challenges even as we achieve certain successes.

In light of all this, I would like to suggest that the concept of *tikkun olam* is vitally necessary for us as a religious Zionist community. The concept of *tikkun olam* recognizes both the brokenness of our world and the fact that our role as partners with God in making the world more just is constant and ongoing. We are no longer envisioning a perfect moral society, but a society that is constantly (or at least for the foreseeable future) in need of urgent repair. Our role is not to eliminate deeply embedded problems, but to be constant partners in an ongoing work to improve an imperfect situation. I believe that this theological framework will work best to adapt our vision and build our capacity to deal with questions of justice in Israel.

The current discourse around Israel within Jewish communities around the world is dominated by two conflicting narratives: either a discourse that is promoted by the Israeli government that justifies every behavior and every policy with convoluted reasoning, or a discourse that recognizes a profound moral crisis in Israel and offers a response in the form of boycott.

We, as a movement that is rooted both in Israel and around the world and that holds the concept of *tikkun olam* as a foundation of our faith can offer a third narrative: we recognize the profound moral crisis with all its intensity, but the response we offer is to engage more intensively with the issues. Our movement—with powerful connections between Diaspora progressive Jews and Israeli progressive Jews—can put the emphasis on both understanding the issues *and* supporting change on the ground to address issues of justice and equality for all Israelis and for Palestinians.

The Israel Religious Action Center (IRAC) is a prime example of this kind of important work promoting *tikkun olam*. This response to the situation in contemporary Israel is exemplified in the stories of six leaders of our Israeli Reform Movement who work for *tikkun olam*. The work that they do for social justice ties directly into their identity as Reform Jews.

Suzanne Cannon, a member of Congregation Kol Haneshama in

Jerusalem, works for Bizchut—Israel's human rights center for people with disabilities. Bizchut was set up in 1992 as a special project for the Association for Civil Rights in Israel (ACRI). When Cannon began working there in 2001, it was a small organization with only six staff members; it has now grown to fourteen.

> It is a real *z'chut* [privilege] to be involved in an organization that is continuously at the forefront of changing the lives of people with disabilities in Israel. In contrast to other social issues, this is one where you can really succeed, where you can't with other human rights issues.

She described three anchors in her life: family, community, and the work that she does. She has high expectations of people and organizations around her. There are some values she takes for granted as a member of the Kol Haneshama community and has grown to expect them from other people. The Kol Haneshama community is egalitarian and inclusive and believes in mutual responsibility.

Professor Galia Tsabar is the president of the Rupin Academic Center. She is extraordinary both in her academic achievements and in her leadership in the field of social change in Israel. She is a member of Congregation Beit Daniel in Tel Aviv and sits on the public council of the Israeli Reform Movement. She is on the board of the Hotline for Refugees and Migrant Workers and was very active in Jerusalem's Project AIDS, which built culturally sensitive programs for the prevention of HIV among Ethiopians, as well as for refugees and asylum seekers.

Professor Tsabar began working with Ethiopian Jews in Ethiopia in the 1980s, during which she learned about the many faces of the Jewish people.

> The Jewish experience I had then was different from anything I had known before. Their deep connection to Judaism, to Zion and Jerusalem, was so different from any Jewish experience I had ever encountered. Their journey was full of hope and difficulty on the one hand, and on the other hand a feeling of religious connection. For me, this was a formative experience in developing my pluralistic view, which is so meaningful in

the Reform world. The voices I heard from Ethiopia were new voices that joined the different voices in the range of Judaism.

During her work with Ethiopian *olim* (immigrants) in Israel, she first encountered opacity, racism, and contempt—things that did not resonate with her at all within Judaism, the Zionist identity, or the State of Israel. When she saw the price the *olim* paid in Ethiopia and then the attitudes they encountered in Israel, she was shaken and her ties to Reform Judaism were strengthened.

This led her to research the religious space of refugees and migrants.

> As a Reform woman, I come with the view that the spiritual and religious experience is meaningful to one's daily conduct. With this view I encountered African migrants and asylum seekers in Israel. I felt a strong connection to them. The fact that I knew how to identify these points of strength opened many doors for me that were closed for other researchers. Reform Judaism allowed the eye-to-eye connection (equal connection), a connection that every person knows. I invited many of my friends and members of the asylum-seeking community to Bet Daniel—there we had the opportunity to celebrate together, as equals, and share our religious-spiritual experience.

Rabbi Tamir Nir founded the Achva BaKerem (in Beit HaKerem, Jerusalem) congregation about a decade ago to do *tikkun*—to fix— the neighborhood socially, culturally, and physically. As time passed, these goals broadened to include people making changes in their lives, as well as a focus on the environment. His activities reached the people of the neighborhood, who subsequently became more active in city activities (including helping to elect him to the municipal government as the deputy mayor of Jerusalem). Today, because of this pattern of cooperation, there are over seventy community gardens throughout Jerusalem.

> What is beautiful about community gardens is that they are a neutral space. Everyone who lives in the area is welcome to take part. The people who come create not only a garden, but also community leadership. It is a space not just for growing

vegetables, but also for developing relationships and providing support to the community.

It was from there that Rabbi Nir was elected to the city council and then served as deputy mayor in charge of transportation in Jerusalem.

In Israel, the tendency has been toward private cars, and Rabbi Nir believes that this is a basic mistake.

> We are on our way to a catastrophe, with traffic jams threatening the environment, freedom, and equality. To whom do the streets belong? And public space? How can we ensure that the streets are in fact for everyone? How do we ensure that public space is open to everyone equally, to those who can have five cars and those who have none?

In order to promote equality, he envisions stricter regulation of parking, encouraging bike riding, creating spaces that are off-limits for cars, and expanding public transportation.

> I think that I am motivated/influenced by the Jewish values that are important to me: freedom, equality, responsibility, connection to and excitement from the world, prayer. Everything is expressed in action.

Rabbi Nir imagines an Israel in which Judaism is expressed in every aspect of society—not limited to separate religious spheres, but present in everything that we do, including the way we speak and create policy around the environment, transportation, and socio-economic gaps.

Professor Rafi Walden is the deputy director of the Sheba Medical Center, the largest hospital in Israel. He is an active member of Congregation Beit Daniel in Tel Aviv and sits on the Public Committee of the Reform Movement in Israel. He is the chairperson of Physicians for Human Rights in Israel, an organization of health professionals committed to ensuring adequate medical services to all, including prisoners, the poor, the elderly, refugees and asylum seekers, Bedouin communities, and Palestinians in the Occupied Territories. Physicians for Human Rights provides essential medical services to tens of thousands of people annually.

He sees his pioneering work as rooted both in the Socratic oath and in Jewish values.

> In Judaism there is the obligation to treat the enemy's injured; as Maimonides says, we must treat everyone, so it is a Jewish obligation to treat and help all. My work is inspired by the Jewish value of life, and respect to all, as those apply in the medical world in Israel. We are responsible as Jews to not just help ourselves, but to help others, our neighbors in the area—that is *tikkun olam.*

Sarah Bernstein is also a member of Congregation Kol Haneshama. She serves as the director of the Rossing Center for Education and Dialogue and before that worked at the Interreligious Council. She has been working in the field of interfaith relations in Israel/Palestine for fifteen years. The Rossing Center mainly focuses on educational work. Jewish-Christian relations are different in Israel than in the West because Israel is the only place in the world with a Jewish majority, and since the Christians here are also Arabs, the Israeli-Palestinian conflict plays into it. Recently the JCJCR has begun to do more work around different religions and anti-racism work.

> We live in a situation of violent conflict, which creates its own dynamic of scarring and trauma. If we don't address this reality, we won't be able to move forward. The conflict becomes more intractable, and we now have generations of people who have never known peace, which affects the way we think of ourselves and of others. If we don't address and challenge our core beliefs, we are destined to many more years of violent conflict. It is not that the conflict is religious; it is political, but religion plays a more and more important role. Each side is bringing religious motifs to the conflict, and we are in danger that there could be a serious escalation of the conflict. It is extremely important to begin to address this conflict by working closely with various religious groupings and to take advantage of the influence that various religions can bring to bear to ease the tensions and to transform the conflict. We must learn to live together before the conflict evolves into a religious war.

Sarah Bernstein has stated:

> Over time my work has become my religious identity. I have
> come to believe that if we can't do this right, if we can't stop
> killing each other, none of the rest of it matters. I don't believe
> in a God that cares if I eat milk and meat together while we are
> killing each other. We have to learn to live with each other. This
> work very much ties in with everything that I do.

It also has very much impacted her prayer life. She changed some of
the wording of the prayers that she struggles with, so that those texts
are better integrated into her Jewish and community life.

> For me it's not for *tikkun olam*—it's more than that. It is the es-
> sence of what Zionism is about—I don't believe in the Jewish
> state just for the sake of having a Jewish state. I believe in having
> a Jewish state because the world is organized by nation-states
> and we need one too, as long as it serves the purpose of social
> justice and wider issues. It [*tikkun olam*] is right at the core of my
> Zionism—what it's all about. If Zionism isn't about that, then
> in my eyes there is no worth to it.

Each of the interviews above describes how individuals have focused
on a specific cause within Israeli society and invested years, if not
decades, in the effort to improve the conditions around the cause,
viewing that as an ultimate expression of their liberal Judaism and
an attempt to bring Jewish values to Israeli society.

In addition to the inspiring work of multiple Reform congregants
toward *tikkun olam*, the Israel Religious Action Center is the body
representing the Israeli movement, as well as all the Progressive and
Reform Movements around the world in our political and legal work
to make Israel live up to our Progressive Zionist values.

IRAC works on issues of society and religion: advocating for the
end of the Orthodox monopoly on religious life in Israel, for gender
equality, and against racism and Islamophobia. We believe our work
is laying the essential foundations for our Progressive Zionist vision.
It is crucial that we do this work as part of a Jewish religious movement (not only as human rights and civil liberties activists), because
it expands the discourse on Progressive Jewish values in Israel.

In his writings, Herzl builds a detailed vision for welfare, education, health, and employment. Dr. Uri Zilbersheid, a political philosophy scholar from the University of Haifa, describes the two layers of Herzl's vision for a just socioeconomic society. The initial stage is a realistic implementation of current conditions of society and economy, based on the principles of a modern welfare state. The seeds for the second, utopian stage are planted in the first applicable stage, and they move the society to a higher state of development that can sustain the ultimate justice for all citizens.[4]

This is the expression of our Reform Zionism that is relevant for today: we must hold on to the ultimate vision for a just society as we diligently do the work on the details of the first stage—building the foundations on which the just society of our redemption can grow.

Notes

1. Uri Zilbersheid, "The Utopia of Theodor Herzl," *Israel Studies* 9, no. 3 (2004): 80–114, http://in.bgu.ac.il/bgi/iyunim/10/19.pdf, 634–38 (in Hebrew).

2. Achad HaAm, "The First Zionist Congress," *HaShiloah* 2, no. 6 (Elul 1897), http://benyehuda.org/ginzberg/Gnz042.html.

3. Achad HaAm, "Zionism and Repair of the World," *HaShiloah* 11, no. 4 (Nissan 1903), http://benyehuda.org/ginzberg/Gnz065.html.

4. Uri Zilbersheid, "The Utopia of Theodor Herzl," *Israel Studies* 9, no. 3 (2004): 80–114, http://in.bgu.ac.il/bgi/iyunim/10/19.pdf, 613–14.

The Land's Still Small Voice Beckons Us All
Preserving a Collective, Zionist Environmental Ethic

PROFESSOR ALON TAL, PhD

ZIONISM has always been focused on meeting needs of the Jewish people as a collective entity.[1] The Land of Israel and its environmental health were part of the common cause to which private interests were expected to yield. The needs of individual Jews were secondary. Indeed, for most of the past century, Zionism was synonymous with sacrificing for this greater good.

Sacrifice was surely required. During the first half of the twentieth century, Palestine was a hard sell, even to an oppressed and restless Eastern European Jewry that suddenly found it had options.[2] The universal vision of Trotsky and a new classless, Soviet society surely had appeal for young idealists. The American "Golden Medina," or even the Canadian, Australian, and Argentinian versions, offered unprecedented economic opportunities for the more pragmatic or materialistic.

And then there was Palestine, with an "attractive" package that included malaria, violent Arab attacks, abject poverty, Tel Aviv summers without air-conditioning, and absolutely no guarantee that anything would come of the Jewish people's nascent national aspirations. It is little wonder, therefore, that only about 3 percent of the Jews who emigrated from Europe during this period purchased tickets to the Jaffa port. And sooner than later, most of this intrepid cohort found the challenge to be too much. David Ben-Gurion may have been exaggerating when he noted that 90 percent of his peers in the second *aliyah* eventually left.[3] Nonetheless, disillusionment among immigrants has always been a prevalent phenomenon.

What the Zionist idea could offer, however, was an inspirational ideology of the collective. For the first seventy-five years of the twentieth century, the kibbutz movement wielded a disproportionately powerful influence, expecting its members—and its country—to "take according to their needs and to give according to their abilities." Regardless of the ideological camp, Zionist thinkers—from the pragmatic politics of Herzl to the selfless socialism of Borochov to the religious mysticism of Rabbi Kook—all called for casting one's lot "all in" with the national revival of the Jewish people. Even Revisionist-Zionist leader Ze'ev Jabotinksy, who is often presented as an advocate of radical individualism and capitalism,[4] in fact also appealed to a sense of collective Jewish responsibility. He argued that at the very least, a Jewish state was duty bound to ensure the "elementary" needs of all citizens: "food, housing, clothing, education, and health."[5]

Environmental stewardship was a common denominator among these disparate, principled, Zionist visions of collective responsibility. The Land of Israel, neglected and exploited for almost two millennia, awaited an ecological makeover. Zionism expected its agents to be partners in this transformation, contributing to both the renewal of the Land's ecological identity and the Jewish people's renewed identity as an indigenous people in a Promised Land.[6]

IN 1904, at age forty-eight, Aaron David Gordon left his comfortable life as an estate manager in Russia and moved to Palestine, where he began to espouse Romantic philosophy about the meaning of a Zionist identity. His was a secular spiritualism with a strong ecological passion that called for an organic harmony between Jews and their rediscovered homeland. It was a green spiritualism that captured the hearts and minds of the young pioneers. In an entire monograph dedicated to "The Human and Nature" he wrote:

> Moreover, the more man develops and the more his emotions and awareness become deeper and broader, and his knowledge becomes richer, he is in greater need of direct attachment inside of nature. To suckle directly from this vast global experience. . . .

And you shall learn Torah from the mouth of nature, the Torah of building and creating. And you shall learn to do as nature does in all you build and in all you create. And so in your ways and in your life, you will learn to become a partner in creation.[7]

Such views were not merely philosophical musings. They also were quickly translated into operational public policy in the *Yishuv*. The Jewish National Fund / Keren Kayemet L'Yisrael (JNF/KKL) first articulated Zionism's land ethic, later adopted by the State of Israel, in 1901. Its refusal to ever sell the lands it acquired in Zion became axiomatic, informed by the prohibition appearing in Leviticus 25:23: "The land must not be sold permanently." This was not so much a religious ethos that assumed that environmental responsibility was a divine obligation, but rather that ultimate ownership of all land belongs to God. The traditional Jewish view that "the earth is the Eternal's" is not unlike the assumptions of Native American tribes. But the Zionist ethic was steeped in a devotion to the Jewish peoplehood. These were "national lands" that belonged to the nation. They were only to be utilized for the benefit of the Jewish people and the creatures with which it shared the land.[8] Much as the first Zionists gave little thought to the national aspirations of the Arabs living in Palestine during the early twentieth century, neither did local land practices and land ethics warrant meaningful attention. Theirs was a decidedly European, Romantic ideology that prioritized national and ecological restoration.

As the Zionist movement came to assume a significant presence in Palestine, additional environmental manifestations of this commitment to the collective emerged. Exceptional programs in afforestation, land reclamation, malaria eradication, and agriculture were part of a higher collective purpose and love of homeland. The craving of the young Zionist settlers for intimacy with Israel's natural world and vistas was extraordinary.[9] A high value was placed on "knowing the land"—with all the biblical double entendre intended. This was not an individual aspiration but part of a renewed, national culture that provided a meaningful—and for many, a transformative—outdoor experience in return for the tribulations that the Land of Israel imposed on immigrants.

Even the ecological follies of the nascent Jewish state were performed in pursuit of collective visions rather than individual enrichment. The Huleh Lake and its magical ecosystem were drained in the 1950s with the high-minded (albeit misguided) goal of creating fertile, arable land for new immigrant farmers. Israeli novelist Meir Shalev shares a story—which may well be apocryphal—that reflects Zionism's deep faith in the insuperable capacity of Jewish communal effort: Dutch consultants had come to advise the JNF/KKL engineers as they began to plan the massive drainage project. After evaluating the soils, the visiting engineers concluded that once deprived of dampness from the wetlands, the underlying peat soils in the valley would combust and collapse, undermining any anticipated agricultural production. But the JNF professionals were indignant, insisting that such a scenario was unthinkable: "Our peat is Zionist peat. Our peat will not cause damage," they railed. "As is known, the Dutch have much experience in the reclamation of land. But even they had not yet met land with a political conscience."[10]

Other environmental crimes and misdemeanors were committed without thought of personal gain by the polluters. For instance, in the 1960s, Israel's government insisted on expanding Tel Aviv's Redding polluting power plant. The motivation behind a project that was already recognized to be a public health insult involved energy supply for the local economy that had to grow rapidly in order to meet the needs of a burgeoning population.[11] Indeed, cities and factories were allowed to dump their wastes into the public sphere because their economic resources were so limited, domestic and international environmental standards were still low, and the needs for jobs and a reasonably viable economy in a new nation were so great. Indeed, the major polluters in Israel for the country's first forty years were government corporations: Israel Chemicals, the Israel Oil Refineries, the Israel Electric Company, and the Eilat-Ashkelon Pipeline.[12] For Israel's early governments, worrying about environmental damage was a luxury that simply needed to wait.

The collateral damage that the zeal for national development left behind did not go entirely unrecognized by the general public. By the 1960s, the Society for Protection of Nature in Israel (SPNI), a conservation and educational NGO, emerged as the country's largest nonprofit organization of any kind. The SPNI began to draw attention to the loss of ecosystems and landscapes, conducting innumerable successful campaigns during its first decades of work.[13] When they were successful, it was because their arguments appealed to the shared, societal love of the Land of Israel and its commons.

The year 1977 brought with it the first Israeli government that was not driven by a socialist economic orientation. The free-market reforms instituted by the Begin administrations unleashed the power of the profit motive as an engine of economic growth. After decades of austerity and a tax system that produced the world's lowest Gini coefficient (or highest level of society equality), it was now possible to become rich in Israel. It would not take long before the entrepreneurial genius of Israelis became an international sensation and the "start-up nation" phenomenon was born.

Slowly but surely, within mainstream Israeli society, the focus on individuality became pervasive. In the past, it was something of an ideal to study for careers in agriculture or engineering, professions so important to nation building. In the new economy, MBAs, law programs, and accounting programs produced a glut of managers, attorneys, and accountants who opted for the lucrative incomes offered by less productive professions. The kibbutzim, once a beacon to idealistic Israeli youth as well as to young volunteers from around the world, became increasingly privatized. Members preferred personal freedom and pursuing individual affluence to embracing national challenges. Even Israeli museums, which had traditionally been a forum for presenting communal treasures or customs, began to reflect the narratives of individual heroes,[14] with Yitzhak Rabin and Menachem Begin lionized in museums that blurred the lines between history and hagiography.

Israel's new culture of prosperity and individual self-actualization began to redefine the financial aspirations of citizens, along with the societal perceptions of material comfort and economic opportunity. It should not be surprising that the country's environmental dynamics dramatically reflected these changes. Air pollution was now an externality, which a reasonable company might try to impose on society as its CEO sought to maximize the corporation's profits. Developers identified previously unimaginable bonanzas associated with construction projects that primarily benefited the wealthy on scenic, open spaces. Proposals to build marinas and coastal resorts flooded the country's planning commissions. Top local (and in certain cases, international) environmental experts were brought in as consultants to help rationalize projects with environmentally destructive outcomes.

Frequently outgunned and always underfunded, Israel's Ministry of Environment sought to assume a new identity as a regulator of private enterprises and their environmentally destructive activities —rather than a partner, working in sync with government corporations. As the range of environmental insults expanded, Israel's local environmental community became more aggressive, sophisticated, and diverse: over a hundred environmental active organizations, local and national, along with local and national green parties fought for an alternative, sustainable paradigm. The power wielded by Israel's environmental movement was due to the tremendous public backing it enjoyed.

This support suggests that the new era of Israeli individualism and entrepreneurial creativity has not entirely eliminated Israel's Zionist communal ethos. A deeply engrained concern for the commons remains a central theme in the remarkable culture and education of the country's many youth movements and an increasingly green public school curriculum. The high percentage of Israeli high school graduates who volunteer for a gap year of national service and then seek to complete their mandatory service in combat military units reflects a selfless ethos. The best and the brightest continue to dedicate "the best years of the life" to their country's defense and well-being.

When there are terrorist attacks, Israelis continue to line up to donate blood. Rocket fire from the Gaza Strip only strengthens citizens' resolve. And this idealism goes beyond solidarity in time of existential threats. The social-protest movement of summer 2011 was a reminder that a majority of Israelis still expect their country to be a paragon of social justice. The country's general solidarity with environmental campaigns suggests that environmental justice is part of this modern vision for a healthier State of Israel. Whether you call it that or not, it is a very Zionist vision.

So it seems that Zionism's long-held collective orientation is hardly irrelevant in Israeli society today, even as the country venerates its eighteen billionaires and ninety thousand millionaires.[15] The Zionist ideal, that all Jews pitch in for the greater good of the Jewish people, is still quite valid and not only in hours of crisis. It resonates in small acts of patriotism—from paying enormously high taxes (along with growing donations to Israel's charities and civil society) to a culture of volunteering—a culture that is celebrated by tens of thousands of citizens involved in environmental activism.

The truth is that Israel does not need to go back to a time when its citizens were asked to forgo personal ambitions and endlessly sacrifice for the country's greater good. Those days are probably better left in the past.

To be sure, the discipline imposed on the *Yishuv* and then Israeli society during the early years of Zionism may have been necessary, given the extraordinary exigencies facing the incipient nation. Without a selfless national ethos, the young country would not have been able to meet such a formidable array of challenges; it would not have built an incredible water infrastructure, absorbed over three million immigrants, and established world-class universities, while withstanding constant attacks from its neighbors. Today, however, those expectations are unnecessary. Zionism's success means that the country need not live according to a Spartan code of ethics that suffocates individual creativity and initiative.

The challenge for Zionism is finding the balance between an ideology that expects totally self-abnegation and the nihilistic self-indulgence that can be found in some of the greedier pockets of Israel today. There is nothing new about such a balance. Indeed, it is simply a societal application of Hillel's famous adage from the Mishnah's "Ethics of the Fathers": "*If I am not for myself*, who will be for me? But if I am only for myself, who am I?" (*Pirkei Avot* 1:14).

As an extreme example of a multicultural society, it is no small challenge to maintain a shared sense of purpose within Israel. The environment is probably the most natural area for galvanizing all sectors in Israel to work together, providing the kind of higher, common purpose that was a unifying force in the country's earlier years. There is ample empirical experience that supports this notion. One invariably finds meaningful cooperation and friendships when Arab and Jewish, secular and Orthodox, urban and rural environmental organizations join together to protect a common natural resource.

Israel's environmental laws are not perfect, but they are sufficient to give the environment a fighting chance when facing competing interests. The courts have shown time and again that Israel's legal system creates an even playing field in which public interests can successfully compete with private revenues. The environment can come out a winner if there is a righteous cause and an unwavering effort.

Just like the early Zionists found spiritual sustenance in the local natural world, when Israel's secular Jews today seek a consequential, modern, Jewish identity, their environmental heritage offers one salient area of meaning. From its laws about Sabbatical years to the prohibition on wasteful consumption, for the most part Judaism and environmentalism are synonymous. The Bible offers a rich treasure chest of environmentally inspirational legends—from the biodiversity conserved in Noah's ark, to when Abraham's sensitivity to overgrazing and carrying capacity with his herds competed with those of his nephew Lot. But Judaism also gave rise to a tradition of laws that reflect environmental ethics. For instance, as Israel finally begins to face the ecological implications of its consumer culture, the ancient Jewish proscription on wasting contained in the precepts of *bal tashchit* offers a wonderful starting place. It is an inspirational place where their Israeli and Jewish roots overlap.

If Zionism is to claim a modern environmental identity, however, it will have to show the kind of open-mindedness and nimble thinking that allowed it to evolve over the years to meet the ever-changing reality and challenges facing the Jewish people. That means that it might not make sense any longer to focus on maximum agricultural production, but rather prefer to leave more public lands as habitats and natural parks. It means that the government no longer needs to obsessively subsidize large families or immigration programs when the country's population is already exceeding its carrying capacity; rather, demographic stability needs to be a paramount Zionist goal in order to ensure that population density in the Land of Israel does not destroy quality of life and ecological services.

At the same time Zionism needs to double down on its historical commitment to public land ownership and prioritization of the commons. Zionism always sought to heal the land. But for too long this impulse was overshadowed by the country's zeal to build a robust economy. This neglect created toxic brownfields, anaerobic streams, and decimated inventories of mammals, birds, reptiles, and amphibians. Israel still faces the enormous task of becoming a true ecological restoration movement that can transform the Jewish people's tiny corner of the planet into a Garden of Eden. It will need to redefine its priorities and return to its historical commitment to collective solidarity with the Land of Israel and its natural resources.

For Jews living around the world, the call for ecological harmony with the homeland offers a challenge and a vision for the future. To truly understand our past and the heritage of the Bible, we should all look more intently to the Land of Israel, which for millennia has provided inspiration to prophets and pilgrims. People seeking meaning in the ancient narratives that inform Jewish life will most easily find it when they bring their hearts and heritage to the very land that produced the Jewish people. If you listen closely, a still small voice whispers that the dream of returning to the homeland is still germane. The Land of Israel beckons, reminding us that making the Zionist dream a sustainable one still requires a collective effort.

NOTES

1. Anita Shapira and Derek Jonathan Penslar, *Israeli Historical Revisionism: From Left to Right* (London: Routledge, Abington, 2002), 37.

2. Judith Shuval and Elazar Leshem, "The Sociology of Migration in Israel: A Critical View," in *Immigration to Israel, Sociological Perspectives*, ed. Elazar Leshem and Judith Shuval (New Brunswick, NJ: Transaction Publishers, 1998).

3. David Ben-Gurion, "At the Half-Jubilee Celebration" [in Hebrew], in Bracha Habas, ed., Sefer Ha-Aliyah HaShniyah (Tel Aviv: Am Oved, 1947). ברכה חבס (עורכת) (בהשתתפות אליעזר שוחט), ספר העלייה השנייה, תל אביב: הוצאת עם עובד, תש"ז-1947, 17–18, as quoted in Gur Alroey, "The Jewish Emigration from Palestine in the Early Twentieth Century," *Journal of Modern Jewish Studies* 2, no. 2 (2003): footnote 44.

4. Ezra Mendelsohn, *Studies in Contemporary Jewry*, vol. 12 (New York: Oxford University Press, 2003), 47.

5. Ze'ev Jabotinsky, *The Social Redemption* (Warsaw: D'ar Mament, 1934), 297–98.

6. Alon Tal, *Pollution in a Promised Land: An Environmental History of Israel* (Berkeley: University of California Press, 2002).

7. Aaron David Gordon (tr.: Frances Burnce), *Selected Essays* (New York: Arno Press, 1973).

8. Tal, *Pollution in a Promised Land*.

9. Oz Almog, *The Sabra: A Profile* [in Hebrew] (Tel Aviv: Am Oved, 1997), 255–59.

10. Meir Shalev, *Primarily about Love* [in Hebrew] (Tel Aviv: Am Oved, 1991), 34.

11. Richard Laster, "Reading D: Planning and Building or Building and then Planning," *Israel Law Review* 8 (1973): 480.

12. Tal, *Pollution in a Promised Land*.

13. Ofer Regev, *Forty Years of Blossoming* (Tel Aviv: Society for the Protection of Nature in Israel, 1993).

14. Michael Hollander, personal communication, October 31, 2016.

15. Roee Bergman, "Israel in 2015: 17 Billionaires, over 88,000 Millionaires," *Ynet*, October 14, 2015, http://www.ynetnews.com/articles/0,7340,L-4711244,00.html.

Is There a Common Ground?

Rabbi Joshua Weinberg

O N THE OCCASION of Israel's eighth anniversary Rav Joseph Soloveitchik gave a landmark lecture called "*Kol Dodi Dofek*," or "The Voice of My Beloved Knocks," that quickly became a seminal document in the canon of Religious (Orthodox) Zionism, which examines clear manifestations of God's presence in modern historical events. This visionary rabbi—tasked with the mission to rebuild the Orthodox community in a post-Shoah reality—realized that merely eight years after the establishment of the State of Israel we were already seeing a drifting apart between the two largest Jewish communities in the world, Israel and North America. His hope was that these two communities would operate as one body with two heads.[1] Soloveitchik's argument boiled down to a basic *tocheichah* (rebuke) of Israeli and American Jewish life—accusing Israelis of being too centered on peoplehood and relatively weak on Torah values of mitzvah and scholarship; and American Jews for being weak on peoplehood and mutual responsibility while being overly focused on religion. His is a statement claiming that the early development of these two polarities could set a course of distancing one from the other, creating an insurmountable values-driven distance between the two communities.

Six decades later we do see a trend of distancing and a widening rift. For many liberal Jews in the twenty-first century, the State of Israel's existence is a given and also provides a strong sense of inspiration from which to build and strengthen Jewish identity. There's no question that it is also a source of contention and of serious concern. Before we deal with some of the specific movement-based programs or the philosophies of particular leaders, let us touch on the very fundamental basis of this potential rift: Zionism.

If we define Zionism simply as the Jewish nationalist movement
to establish a sovereign state in the Land of Israel, it is understood
that a Zionist is one who would live in Israel. Most Zionist movements around the world had as their foremost aspiration the goal
of *aliyah*, to leave one's birthplace to go and live in the Jewish state.
This was the case for almost every Zionist movement from religious
to secular, from socialist to revisionist, with considerable exception
for the varieties of American Zionism. While there were notable
sub-movements of American Zionists who encouraged *aliyah*, by
and large the mainstream American Jewish population was never
going to embark on mass immigration to Israel.

While many American Zionist movements and organizations see
Israel as a central redemptive, moral, and spiritual link to the meaning of being Jewish in America, this form of Zionism is unique in its
characteristics—both in a supporting role to ensure Israel's security
and well-being and as a source of spiritual and cultural nourishment,
without the notion of fulfillment being *aliyah* to Israel.[2] In 1915
Judge Louis Brandeis articulated the following claim, that American
Zionism

> is not a movement to remove all the Jews of the world compul-
> sorily to Palestine. . . . It is essentially a movement to give to the
> Jew more, not less freedom . . . to live at their option either in
> the land of their fathers or in some other country. . . . Zionism
> seeks to establish in Palestine, for such Jews as choose to go and
> remain there, and for their descendants, a legally secured home,
> where they may live together and lead a Jewish life, where they
> may expect ultimately to constitute a majority of the popula-
> tion, and may look forward to what we should call home rule.[3]

From this speech one might see little difference between Brandeis
and other well-known contemporary Zionists such as David
Ben-Gurion or Berl Katznelson, who made similar claims before
different audiences. However, it became clear over time that the
American discussion had to take a different approach.

Brandeis understood that Zionism in America needed to be
defined and defended in language that would resonate with the

American ethos. *Sh'lilat hagolah*, "repudiation of the Diaspora," could not possibly win adherents in America, he knew, and as a result, he completely discarded that facet of Zionist ideology. Nor did he talk much about *aliyah*—recognizing, I suspect, that most American Jews would not ultimately make *aliyah*. Instead, he defined Zionism in terms of America's own history and ideals, speaking of the early *chalutzim* as Jewish "pilgrim fathers" and associating Zionism with American Progressivism and the spread of American ideals.

"By battling for the Zionist cause," Brandeis explained to delegates of a 1915 Zionist convention, "the American ideal of democracy, of social justice, and of liberty will be given wider expression." "Democracy, social justice, and a longing for righteousness," he argued, formed the essence both of Judaism and of Americanism. For that reason, he famously declared that "to be good Americans we must be better Jews and to be better Jews we must become Zionists."[4]

But what did that mean? Surely he did not intend to imply that good Americans would leave the United States to pursue the actualization and fulfillment of the Zionist ideal, but rather to espouse specific overlapping values that linked Americanism with Zionism. In fact, Brandeis had no intention of living in Israel and saw his support largely as financial. In his many discussions with Israel's first president, Dr. Chaim Weizmann, Weizmann noted the following:

> Brandeis's stay in Palestine did not exceed a fortnight, and could not possibly permit a thorough survey of conditions. When he returned, he was obliged to generalize on the basis of the scanty facts he had been able to collect; his views, however correct theoretically, squared badly with realities. He was for instance definitely of the opinion that unless a large-scale "sanitation" of the country were first undertaken it would be wrong to encourage immigration. He supposed that the Government's first act would be to drain the marshes, clear the swamps, build new roads, not realizing that no one in authority had the slightest intention of starting these operations. He repeatedly stated— this was thirty years ago—that Zionist political work had come to a close, that nothing remained but the economic task. These views pointed to a coming conflict between Brandeis and

myself, as also between the majority of European Zionists and a powerful group of our American friends. In America itself they were to lead to a breach with the Zionist Organization which was not to be healed for many years.[5]

In the role of quintessential American Zionist, Brandeis talked the talk and inspired generations to take a pro-Israel stance. However, he did not cast his lot with the fate of the Zionist movement, nor did it ever occur to him to actually spend significant time or make a life in Israel.

Almost a century later, Brandeis's words resonated for me personally. Having grown up in the Reform Movement, been educated in its camps, and been a product of its youth movement, I came to understand that those *olim* (immigrants) who made the fateful decision to leave the United States for Israel were few and far between. "Israel is very important to us, and will always be a place to visit, take groups, and create educational materials," explained a prominent Reform Movement educator to me as I was exploring my career options, "but we live here."

"Are Your Brothers to Go to War While You Stay Here?" (Numbers 32:6)

For American Jews, there seems to be a limitation and almost an expectation that Zionism and love for Israel is and will remain based in America. We are for the most part long past the days of *sh'lilat hagolah*[6] whereby Israelis look down on Jewish life and existence outside the State of Israel and provide no room for a legitimate voice from the Jewish family abroad save for the necessary financial support. However, there is a difference between those who put their lives on the line for the State of Israel and those who do not. It is no longer politically correct to say so, but I dare pen these words out of a strong feeling that many American Jews do not fully comprehend the sacrifice and commitment that is made by those who serve and those who send their children to fight and defend the country. At the end of the day, one can be for Jewish settlement beyond the Green Line or against it, in favor of a two-state solution or against it, and either agree or disagree on any number of central controversial issues, but for one demographic it is largely hypothetical and at best emotional, and for the other it is potentially a matter of life and death. There is a fundamental difference between liberal Jews who live in Israel and work to implement their values through the Israeli political system and Diaspora Jews, for whom attachment and connection to Israel is itself the litmus test.

In a recent conversation with an American Jewish journalist, I learned that she had spent several years in Israel, speaks Hebrew, and is in frequent contact with Israelis. As it turned out, she had not visited Israel in over a decade. "I just don't feel comfortable going now, as I struggle with the reality that is the Occupation. I couldn't imagine sitting at a Jerusalem café and enjoying myself, while I knew that down the road are the horrors of the Occupation. I just need to keep my distance from it for a little while. Don't get me wrong," she insisted, "I love it so much, it's just too difficult for me right now."

How Do We Compare?

It is often the case that when arguing about the impact of Reform Jews and Reform Judaism on Israeli society that those seeking to belittle said impact or to perpetuate the seemingly hopeless situation are quick to quip that "when one million Reform Jews make *aliyah*, then you'll be influential." The example is then quickly drawn to the 1990s and the significant societal effect the mass immigration of Jews from the former Soviet Union had on Israel. Just look at the 1999 Israeli election, some would say. Everything was in Russian, and we saw the rise of the Russian-speaking parties. When will Reform Jews from North American internalize that?

North American Liberal Zionists can learn, from the Woody Allen outlook on life, that 80 percent of life is just showing up. The Israel Movement for Reform and Progressive Judaism (IMPJ) realized several years ago that providing religious services, life-cycle events, and ceremonial duties was not enough. It became clear that to be a movement, they needed to permeate Israeli society in a way that had real impact and could be a tangible marker on society as a whole, not just for "members." The Reform Movement in Israel has several organizations and institutions that go beyond the focus on members. The Israel Religious Action Center (IRAC) of the IMPJ focuses on issues of freedom and equality, specifically surrounding religion and state, exposing racism and discrimination, and helping immigrants navigate the system with its legal aid center. In addition, the IMPJ runs a humanitarian wing, a pre-army preparatory program, and now a social justice year of service in Israeli urban environments. This is in addition to the growing number of congregations that will well exceed fifty by the year 2020, with the goal of establishing at least one Reform congregation in every city in Israel.[7]

The goal is to transform Israeli society and to contribute to it being a pluralistic and democratic Jewish state. The Reform Movement holds the spirit of the Declaration of Independence of the State of Israel to the highest degree and champions its message as one of egalitarianism, equality, and freedom for Jews and non-Jews alike.[8]

If American Jews are serious about developing our relationship with Israel, I would suggest several things. First of all, we have to be there. We have to be there in critical numbers both for Israel's sake and for the sake of our community and Jewish identity.[9] As previously discussed, the concept of *aliyah* has never been a serious force in American Jewish life. Yes, there are many American Jews who have moved to Israel and become citizens; however, those who do so are still the minority and even the anomaly in their communities. In total, there have been roughly between 140,000 and 145,000 immigrants to Israel from the United States since 1948.[10] While numerically higher than most countries (except for the former Soviet Union, which has seen roughly 1.2 million immigrants), it is percentage-wise much lower. This figure has never been higher than the low four digits per year, and statistics show that in each year the majority of immigrants stem from the American Orthodox communities. In the 1970s and 1980s a small movement called Garin Arava was started, which successfully established two Reform kibbutzim, Yahel and Lotan, but did not have the sweeping effect that many of its participants had hoped, nor did it retain many of the early founders.[11]

There are many reasons, explanations, and historical factors that led to this phenomenon, which may be a topic for another essay, but for now suffice it to say that American Jews have not come to Israel on *aliyah* in droves, and the force of the American Jewish impact on Israel remains at its strongest from abroad.

I would also argue that we in the Reform Movement, despite our platforms, have not made Zionism or Israel to be a significant part of Jewish identity for American Jews. Only a minority of U.S. Jews have visited Israel, and few feel that Israel plays a meaningful role in their lives.

Per the Pew study of 2013: "Orthodox Jews are more likely than American Jews of any other denomination to have traveled to Israel; 77% have done so, followed by 56% of Conservative Jews, 40% of Reform Jews and 26% of those who have no denominational affiliation."[12]

In beginning to track the numbers of participants in Reform Movement Israel programs since the year 2000, we have seen a relatively low turnout. There are five areas from which to track participation, which does not take into account Reform Jewish participation on programs outside of the Reform Movement. In general, Reform Jews travel to Israel through congregational trips, NFTY in Israel summer trips, NFTY-EIE High School in Israel, Kesher Birthright Israel, and Masa Israel (long-term post–high school programs).[13]

It is difficult to pinpoint the numbers on congregational trips (or individual trips and visits), and we do not have sufficient data on Masa long-term programs, but the numbers on summer and semester experiences project that just a minority of Reform Jews travel to Israel in an organized educational experience.

Since the year 2000, when roughly 1,500 participants were coming to Israel with NFTY, we have seen a steady level of participation at roughly only 500 participants a year,[14] leading to a total of approximately 6,000 Reform Jews. The NFTY-EIE Semester in High School program (now called URJ Heller High) has seen approximately 1,800 students over the past seventeen years, and Kesher Birthright has seen between 20,000 and 25,000 (this is of course not counting the Reform Jews who participate in Birthright Israel through non–Reform Movement trip organizers).[15]

This is in stark contrast to what has happened in American Orthodoxy, in which "full time Torah study in a yeshiva in Israel, once considered an exotic experience for a modern Orthodox high school graduate, is now a commonplace phenomenon in North American Jewish education."[16] For many a Reform Jew, the central question of "Why Israel?" still needs answering.

> Israel is the place where Jewish spiritual and social possibilities are endless. The relevance of Jewish teachings and values can be tested on a national front. Through our relationship with Israel, we are able to dream about what an ideal, Jewishly based society would look like and then explore that vision. The idealism and inherent optimism that Israel can represent to our children, and especially our teenagers—most clearly manifest by a visit—are characteristics that will serve them well in life.[17]

Of course, that vision and hopeful optimism cannot be achieved without the initial fundamental relationship, which is difficult—even impossible—to attain without spending significant time there.

We in the Reform Movement often make the claim that we are the largest movement in Jewish life worldwide and in order to really make our impact felt it is upon us to show up in serious numbers to Israel and instill the centrality of Israel to American Reform Jewish identity. As I see it, there are two direct ways to make an impact on Israeli society. The first way that we as the Reform Movement are going to make an impact on Israeli society commensurate with our numbers is through spending significant time there. If every Reform teenager were to spend a semester or year in Israel before the age of twenty-two, our movement would look very different. *Aliyah* is important, and mass *aliyah* from North America would significantly impact our reality. Sadly, this is not realistic. Nevertheless, widespread long-term programming in Israel will influence both Israeli society and meaningfully affect North American Jewish life in the long term.

The second is financial. Just like political action committees

(PACs) work to finance the candidates that uphold their values and support their political success, we can also use our capital in North America to support our values in Israel. That means a joint and movement-wide effort toward investment in growing our movement in Israel. With significant financial backing, we could quickly expand exponentially the number of congregations and communities throughout Israel and increase the reach of our legal advocacy wing, IRAC. If we act as a PAC and see the Israeli Reform movement as our agent for societal change, then we can clearly articulate the vision and method for implementing our values in Israel and from abroad.

Love of Israel Is Conditional

A major disconnect between liberal Jews in the Diaspora and liberal Jews in Israel is the sense of conditionality. Although the far left in the Diaspora is largely composed of those who might identify as anti- or non-Zionists, it generally agrees on the need to challenge the contemporary form of Zionism that prevails within both Israel and the mainstream American Jewish community.[18] In contrast, the less politicized masses of liberal religious Jews (Reform, Conservative, and Reconstructionist) often tend to shy away from involvement with or affinity toward Israel. With increasing recognition that the Occupation of the Palestinian people is no longer a passing phenomenon, or at all temporary, combined with the tendency toward right-wing politics and Israel's display of disdain for liberal Judaism, many American Jews would rather have little to do with the Jewish state. Ours is an era where universalism needs no particularistic balance in the free marketplace of ideas, and the refusal to check one's liberalism at the door when it comes to a remote place with which one does not feel any particular affinity makes the choice not very difficult at all.

All this is to say that the very notion of unconditional attachment to the State of Israel is the source of a major, and even often unmentioned, rift between the liberal religious Jewish communities in Israel and abroad. For Israelis, as critical and often upset as they are at any one of the many issues that plague Israeli society—the seemingly unending Occupation, expansion of West Bank settlements, increasing religious extremism, racism, and right-wing rule—they continue to live there, report for active reserve duty, send their children to the army, and work toward change from within.[19] As much as we often spout words of praise of partnership and undeniable bonds between Diaspora and Israeli Jews, we do see a difference between one another that touches on the core notion of authenticity, commitment, and support.

In a recent Facebook post, American-born Israeli journalist Calev Ben-David touched on the core issue at hand:

> Israel is not a morality play being acted out for the Diaspora Jews of the world; it's a real country, a flawed democracy trying to survive in a particularly dangerous corner of the world. The piece was part in response to the growing outcry I heard from many progressive Jews in the U.S. (and some here) that Israel was "losing" them, that they were "done with Israel" due to the actions of the Netanyahu government—an attitude that is of no help to either their politically like-minded brethren in Israel, or for that matter, the Palestinians. You don't "give up" on a country you feel a special bond with just because of the actions of a specific government—and if you do, your support and connection wasn't worth all that much anyway.[20]

Some may hear this message as more of the same typical rhetoric from Israelis to Diaspora Jews, but I hear it clarifying an important point. It is easy to be pessimistic, and it is also, while sometimes painful, tempting to simply stop caring and ignore what happens in Israel. More and more North American Jews have simply turned off, "focused on other things," and lost patience with Israel as the trends veer in a direction that makes them uncomfortable.

Now, as we unravel the extremely important connections[21] and unbreakable bonds between Israel and the Jewish communities abroad, we must say that there are endless possibilities and opportunities to strengthen one another and that we must not abandon the cause for fear of futility.

Common Ground
There is, in fact, a great deal of common ground between the liberal religious Zionists of the Diaspora and those in Israel, and that is our shared vision of what the State of Israel can and should be. Both groups recognize that the inherent system of religion in Israel no longer works, and the polarizing dichotomy between (what is commonly understood to be) "religious" and "secular" no longer answers the needs of the mainstream. They realize that for so long Israel has justifiably worried about its existence or its "body" that it hasn't had the opportunity to worry about its "soul." Liberal Jewish Zionists—both in Israel and abroad—are committed to reinventing what it means to be Jewish in the Jewish state and doing so through the building of a vibrant liberal and Progressive Jewish movement in Israel. Reform Judaism in North American has come a very long way in a relatively short time. A century ago it might have been unthinkable that the movement would have its own Zionist organization whose responsibility it would be to represent the movement in the Zionist political arena, to work to build the movement in Israel, and to create a love for and connection to Israel for North American Reform Jews.

This must also go both ways.

Done with "Diaspora"
Are we, in fact, done with the notion of Diaspora? Few non-Orthodox Jews outside of Israel see themselves as living in exile, nor do they see themselves as having been dispersed from a center point. Rather, they see themselves as nationals of their host country and also Jewish. This concept, a product of the Enlightenment, could potentially leave little room for a Zionist existence or mentality, and it is upon our generation to alter the model.

> Strongly influenced by postmodernism . . . the geography of Judaism can no longer be viewed as Israel standing in the center surrounded by Jewish communities everywhere else; indeed, they question whether the term *diaspora* makes any sense at all now that Jews have taken their place in a global melting pot. . . .

The Diaspora hasn't disappeared but, rather, all Jews increasingly live within it, including those who have made Israel their home. [22]

Babylon and Jerusalem

If "Israel versus Diaspora" is an increasingly anachronistic concept, then we must look to *alt-neu* models as we continue to reinvent Jewish life and lay the groundwork for future success. The philosopher Simon Rawidowicz radically developed the reinsertion of the ancient polarity between Babylonia and Jerusalem to provide a potential model for today's reality:

> Twenty years ago I began to speak about a "partnership" between the *Land of Israel* and the *Diaspora of Israel*. Instead of Achad HaAm's prevailing conception of a center and a circumference, of a circle and with one focus, I attempted to develop a conception of the people of Israel as a whole as an ellipse with two foci, the Land of Israel and the Diaspora of Israel. Later, I tried to develop this system further under the symbolic title of "Israel Is One": the Land of Israel and the Diaspora of Israel, two that are one.[23]

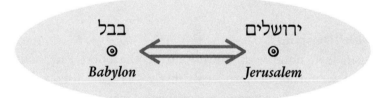

Rawidowicz makes the following two points:

- Babylon-and-Jerusalem signifies the unflinching and unbending battle of [the people of] Israel for her survival, a dauntless struggle for her life and ideals. Many are the garbs in which Israel in Babylon has appeared since the end of the First Commonwealth. It is our duty to ensure that every garb in which Babylon clothes itself—now and in the future—be woven into the texture of Israel, of Babylon-and-Jerusalem, that it fit the very soul of Israel and not be a mere cloak on a mannequin.

- "Two that are One," however, must not be understood as a one-sided obligation; each must mutually recognize the other. The Diaspora of Israel must build the State of Israel with all its strength, even more than it has in the past seventy years, and the State must recognize the Diaspora as of equal value, and an equally responsible co-builder and co-creator of all Jewish life.[24]

I have heard no stronger a point made than to advocate for Diaspora[25] Jews' obligation to support and have a strong and intimate relationship with the State of Israel, while also realizing that the support and relationships must be mutual.

There have been unparalleled successes in Israel seen in the growing numbers of openly identified Reform Jews,[26] and what is known as the larger phenomenon of Jewish renewal[27] has taken off and is growing exponentially, attracting more and more young Israelis—both from the "secular" world and from the more traditional. Israeli Jews are increasingly inspired by what they find while visiting Jewish communities abroad, and many Diaspora Jewish communities are welcoming the creativity and contributions of Israeli text, liturgy, music, art, literature, and language into their communities. These developments will only to continue to grow, inspire, and create a newer version of Judaism if they are nurtured and supported from both Israel and the Diaspora and are recognized as the continuation and reinvention of Zionism in today's world.

What Can We Do?

This is all well and good in theory, but in practice we need a general game plan. I encourage us, Jews in North America, to approach change in the following way.

I am proposing a radical change in North American Jewish culture. It is a shift that embraces Jewish peoplehood and takes pride in our identity as an *am*, a nation. It means being unequivocally supportive of the State of Israel while being unabashedly critical. Our commitment should be visible in every movement institution—our synagogues, schools, offices, and movement gatherings. We want to create a culture in which the norm is for every Reform Jew to spend significant time in Israel and for firsthand knowledge and experience in Israel to become an essential component of one's identity and Jewish education.

In North America, by and large, we have successfully created a thriving Jewish community. We have built thriving synagogues and congregations, large and far-reaching organizations, and meaningful institutions—all in a privatized economy where (with minor exception) we receive no government funding. We have countless organizations that deal with Israel, from educational institutions to political support organizations, and have even given away free trips to over half a million young people.

Now, I call on the largest movement in North American Jewish life to shift gears in its commitment to the State of Israel, to our movement there, and to the development of a sense of peoplehood among our members here. This change of culture will be multifaceted and will play out on different levels.

In order to change our culture, to build a pluralistic, Jewish, and democratic state, and to be built by it, we must not rest until we do the following:

- Send tens of thousands of Reform Jews to Israel each
  year to our youth programs and long-term experiences.
  Imagine how our world would be different if every Reform
  Jew had a relationship both with Israel and with Israelis.
  This will have a significant impact on Jewish life both for
  North American Jews and for Israelis.
- Make the impossible possible: invest in the Hebrew
  language and revive it as a real living language for North
  American Reform Jews. Language is a carrier of culture
  and a connector of communities. Hebrew is the tool to
  unlock the Jewish past and to ensure a Jewish future.

- Support our movement financially. As the largest movement in North America we have the ability to be a game
  changer on the Israeli scene. We desperately need our
  movement to thrive and to have a significant presence in
  every community in Israel. This requires sacred resources,
  and they are ours to provide.

I believe firmly that these challenges are indeed surmountable,
and even though it is a narrow bridge to cross, we must not be afraid.
We can develop skills of civil discourse and must find creative and
exciting opportunities to engage our constituencies.
The more our leaders and professionals commit, the sooner it will
happen. And last, at its inception the Zionist movement was to create a universalistic exemplary society built upon justice, freedom,
and democratic values. If we are concerned about the future of these
values—in Israel *and* abroad—then we must do everything we can to
ensure their viability.

אל תגידו יום יבוא הביאו את היום כי לא חלום הוא.

Don't say the day will arrive, bring the day! For it is not a dream.[28]

Notes

1. *Shared suffering*: A logical, and natural, consequence of the awareness of a
   shared predicament would be a commonality of anguish; the sharing by all
   Jews of each other's suffering. To illustrate this point, Rav Soloveitchik uti-
   lizes a midrash based upon the discussion of the legacy to which a man with
   two heads is entitled (based on a parable in BT *M'nachot* 37a). The situation
   poses the question whether he should receive two shares or just one; does
   he constitute two separate entities inhabiting the same body or just a single
   entity with diverse appearances? Answer: The answer is to have boiling water poured on one of the heads. If it alone cries out in pain, then it is truly
   separate from the other; if both experience the agony, however, then there
   is but one entity.
2. There are of course movements within the American Jewish scene that have
   clearly outlined an aspirational program for *aliyah*, such as Habonim Dror,
   HaShomer HaTzair, and others. However, generally speaking, this was not
   the case in large numbers, as it was in Eastern Europe or South America.

3. *Brandeis on Zionism: A Collection of Address and Statements by Louis D. Brandeis* (Washington, DC: Zionist Organization of America, 1942), 24, from an address delivered to the Conference of Eastern Council of Reform Rabbis, New York City, June 1915, entitled "The Jewish Problem: How to Solve It."

4. Excerpted from a speech given by Professor Jonathan Sarna to the WZO Zionist National Council, November 2016.

5. Chaim Weizmann, *Trial and Error: The Autobiography of Chaim Weizmann* (Philadelphia: Jewish Publication Society, 1949), 248–50.

6. It is important to note that there are scholars who differentiate between *sh'lilat hagolah*, a negation of life outside of Israel, and *sh'lilat hagalut*, a negation of the mind-set of exile. The Israeli author A. B. Yehoshua goes to great lengths to make the point that those who live outside of Israel are only "partial" Jews. He often accuses Diaspora Jews of holding Judaism as a coat that can be taken on and off, while for Israelis it is their skin.

7. For all intents and purposes we define Israel by the mainstream definition of Israel, and the IMPJ has not established any congregations in Jewish settlements beyond the Green Line.

8. Paragraph 13 of the Declaration of Independence states the following: "THE STATE OF ISRAEL will be open for Jewish immigration and for the Ingathering of the Exiles; it will foster the development of the country for the benefit of all its inhabitants; it will be based on freedom, justice and peace as envisaged by the prophets of Israel; it will ensure complete equality of social and political rights to all its inhabitants irrespective of religion, race or sex; it will guarantee freedom of religion, conscience, language, education and culture; it will safeguard the Holy Places of all religions; and it will be faithful to the principles of the Charter of the United Nations."

9. The 1997 Miami Platform on Reform Zionism adopted by the CCAR considers *aliyah* to be a mitzvah.

10. Source: Israel Central Bureau of Statistics.

11. There will be many readers of this statement who will insist on greater explanation and analysis of this important movement, and I am not giving it its due place here. For more on the topic, please see the following two books: Gidon Elad, *Light in the Arava? Yahel—Dialogue and a Joint Undertaking between the Kibbutz Movement and the Reform Movement* (Kibbutz Lotan: Tzell Hatamar, 2008); and William F. S. Miles, *Zion in the Desert: American Jews in Israel's Reform Kibbutzim* (Albany: State University of New York Press, 2007). There are many who also encourage ARZA to reestablish and reinvent the concept of a Reform *garin* for group *aliyah*. While this is certainly an admirable and aspirational goal, it has yet to be determined if this would be an effective initiative in today's American Jewish community.

12. Pew Research Center's Religion and Public Life Project, "Connection with and Attitudes toward Israel," chapter 5 in *A Portrait of Jewish Americans* (Washington, DC: Pew Research Center, 2013). I will add that among the 40 percent of Reform Jews, it is safe to say that that number has doubled as a result of the Birthright Israel program since the year 1999. This means that, despite the efforts, it is still only a minority of Reform Jews who have ever been to Israel.

13. As a point of reference, there were other long-term programs that provided opportunities for youth in Israel, such as Machon Greenberg, the College Academic Year, a short-lived initiative to create a liberal *beit midrash* in Israel.

14. The years 2001–2003 showed one group or less, leading to count these statistics from 2004. This is, as per the author's historical interpretation, largely due to the cancellation of the program during the summer of 2001 and the subsequent security situation that prevented significant participation.

15. Statistics provided through an interview with Paul Reichenbach, director of Camping and Israel Programs, Union for Reform Judaism, August 2016. Commentary is by the author.

16. Shalom Berger, "A Year of Study in an Israeli Yeshiva Program: Before and After" (doctoral dissertation, Yeshiva University, January 1997).

17. Yosef I. Abramowitz, Susan Silverman, and Elie Wiesel, *Jewish Family and Life: Traditions, Holidays, and Values for Today's Parents and Children* (New York: Macmillan, 1998), 200.

18. Dov Waxman, *Trouble in the Tribe: The American Jewish Conflict over Israel* (Princeton, NJ: Princeton University Press, 2016), 106.

19. I am sure we are all familiar with individual cases who decide to leave Israel over dissatisfaction with the situation there, and we can cite news articles about the growing trend of Israelis flocking to destinations such as Berlin. But by and large most liberal Israelis do not leave, and we have seen record-high turnouts for reserve duty (especially during times of war) and increased tendency toward activism and NGO work.

20. Facebook posting by Israeli journalist Calev Ben-David based on a previous column in *JWeekly*, http://www.jweekly.com/article/full/77591/the-column-israel-is-not-a-jewish-morality-play-mr.-chabon/.

21. The word for "connection" in Hebrew, *kesher*, also means "knot."

22. Alan Wolfe, *At Home in Exile: Why Diaspora Is Good for the Jews* (Boston: Beacon Press, 2014), 150.

23. Simon Rawidowicz, *State of Israel, Diaspora, and Jewish Continuity: Essays on the "Ever Dying People"* (Hanover, NH: University Press of New England, 1998).

24. Ibid.

25. Despite the aforementioned point regarding the cessation of use of the term (which one could argue is a different kind of "repudiation of the Diaspora"), I continue to use it in this chapter for convenience purposes.

26. Guttman–AVI CHAI report, *A Portrait of Israeli Jews: Beliefs, Observance, and Values of Israeli Jews*, 2009, http://en.idi.org.il/events/conferences-and-seminars/findings-of-the-third-guttman-avi-chai-report/.

27. This is a reference to what is known as in Israel התחדשות יהודית and not to be confused or associated with the American-based Renewal movement.

28. Yaakov Rotblit, "Shir L'Shalom" (A Song of Peace), 1969.

To Love and to Criticize

Diaspora Reform Zionists Must Make Our Voices Heard

RABBI JOHN L. ROSOVE

In 2005, I spoke by phone with Benny Begin as I was preparing to bring a group of twenty-five congregants to Israel and invited him to address my group on the pending Gaza disengagement. I was stunned by his response: "This is none of your business. I'd be happy to discuss other matters with your group, but the Gaza disengagement is an internal Israeli matter."

Ten years later, I questioned Avraham Burg at a Los Angeles living room discussion sponsored by the New Israel Fund. Burg is the former chairman of the Jewish Agency for Israel (JAFI), whose "mission is to inspire Jews throughout the world to connect with their people, heritage, and land, and empower them to build a thriving Jewish future and a strong Israel,"[1] and so I was stunned again when he said, "What happens in Israel is Israel's business and none of your affair. I understand that you have concerns about Israel. I have concerns about the United States, but as non-Israeli citizens your concerns are irrelevant just as mine are irrelevant in the United States when you debate issues of critical importance."

We Diaspora Jews are not Israeli citizens. We don't pay Israeli taxes nor do we serve in the IDF. I appreciate that when it comes to making the decisions confronting Israel, it is the Israelis who bear the direct consequences of what they decide. However, I disagree with Begin and Burg that existential issues confronting Israel are none of our business as Diaspora Jews or that being concerned bystanders constitutes the limit of our involvement in what Israel is and does, because how Israel behaves affects Jews everywhere. The character of Israel, its democracy, stability, strength, security, cohesiveness, diversity, and ethics impact upon the nature of Jewish life as practiced around the world. Israel influences the character of Diaspora Jewish identity and affects our standing as minority communities in our nations.

I respect Benny Begin and Avraham Burg as principled Israeli thought leaders and public servants, but I disagree with what I regard as their narrow attitude about the role Diaspora Jews must play vis-à-vis the nation-state of the Jewish people. We American Jews in particular have a unique role to play because of our ability to influence the American government's relationship with and support for Israel. As American Reform Zionists who love and care about what happens to Israel and her citizens, just as we love and care about what happens to our own families, we have a natural, familial, and special duty to support Israel and criticize decisions she takes that we believe are not in her own best interests or ours.

In January 1926, Chaim Nachman Bialik prepared to tour the United States to raise money for the Jewish settlement in Palestine. He acknowledged the important link between Jews in Palestine and Jews around the world. Before departing Tel Aviv he said:

> Everything depends on how we live in our land and how we behave here. Our brethren in the Diaspora want to see here what is missing there in the cultural and spiritual and moral life of Galut. . . . If they do not feel that our values here are unwavering we will not find a path to their hearts. . . . Eretz Yisrael must give the Diaspora something more than Jews of any other country can give: something with a spirit of holiness, above and beyond the usual and commonplace.[2]

Bialik spoke these words in the pre-state period, but they are applicable still after Israel became a sovereign nation, and the nation-state of the Jewish people must do everything possible, especially in the context of power and sovereignty, to protect Jewish culture, diversity of religious expression, and moral and ethical values relative to all Israeli citizens and to Jewish residents in all lands.

Though Bialik's generation knew persecution, nothing compared to what was to come during the Shoah. That singular experience, coupled with the numerous wars Israel has had to fight and terror-ism against which it has had to protect itself since it was established, has powerfully influenced Jewish and Israeli perceptions of its place in the region and world. For many Israelis and Diaspora Jews, the need for security has challenged traditional Jewish values developed during the Rabbinic period in the context of exile and vulnerability. In this sense, the State of Israel was born out of crisis.

I was born a year after the State of Israel was established. I was raised on "the crisis narrative" of Jewish history. The Holocaust hov-ered over my childhood and formative years and has been a defining experience affecting the postwar Jewish psyche. The Shoah taught Jews everywhere that when we are powerless we risk destruction and that the State of Israel is our surest protection against forces that would destroy us.

By the time I was seventeen Israel had fought three wars. When I was twenty-three and living in Jerusalem, Israel was nearly overtaken in the Yom Kippur War. I understood that Israel could not lose a sin-gle war on the battlefield, that her security and survival must be the number one priority for Israelis and world Jewry, and that to ignore the real threats to the Jewish people is never an option. However, as Israel has grown more powerful militarily, economically, politically, and culturally, it is shortsighted for Jews everywhere to worry about Israel's security to the exclusion of other cultural challenges.

Dr. Tal Becker, an associate at the Washington Institute for Near East Policy and a fellow at the Shalom Hartman Institute in Jeru-salem, has written of the contemporary challenge facing Israel and world Jewry:

> [The] conventional [crisis-based] narrative is both narrow and
> shallow. Narrow, in that its focus is on the physical existence
> of the Jewish people in their homeland, not on the breadth of
> what this sovereign project might offer for the collective Jew-
> ish experience. Shallow, in that it pursues Jewish survival for
> its own sake but tells no deeper story as to why that survival is
> important and worth fighting for.[3]

Dr. Becker argued for a values-based conversation about Israel that differs from the crisis narrative that has dominated the past six-plus decades since the state was founded. A values-based conversation asks what it will take to address Israel's challenges and build a moral and just society reflecting in policies, politics, and culture our Jewish values, tradition, and experience as a people. This conversation is not only about Israelis but about the Jewish people as a whole. Whereas it is understandable that Israelis are often consumed with self-protection and from fear and experience want a "strong-man" government and approach to crisis, Diaspora Jewry is schooled in the necessity of accommodation as a minority living in lands governed by non-Jewish majorities. Especially for those of us living in Western democracies, our modus operandi is to find the right balance between our tribal, national Jewish concerns and our wider universal, democratic concerns. Consequently, the conversation about the nature of Israeli culture, religion, and society requires that Israeli Jews and Diaspora Jews become closer partners in the building of the future of the Jewish people in the State of Israel and around the world. In this, Israeli citizens and Diaspora Jews have much to offer each other for reasons of enlightened self-interest. On the one hand, per Bialik's aspirational emphasis, it is our nation-state's duty to maintain the liberal, democratic, and prophetic values upon which it was founded and that are articulated in the Declaration of Independence; and on the other, it is our people's duty wherever we live, in Israel and around the world, to embrace our national identity and share our common concerns about the security and well-being of the State of Israel and Diaspora communities.

FOR THOSE operating strictly out of the crisis mind-set, Jewish unity is defined narrowly by common threats. A values narrative defines Jewish unity in terms of a common moral engagement that we share—not because we agree or because the one overriding issue confronting us is survival, but based on our shared commitment to engage in a complicated, divisive, agonizing, and exhilarating process of writing together the next chapter of Jewish history in a way that is worthy of our tradition and historical experience.

If the conversation were to shift out of crisis mode to a values mode, a new Zionist paradigm would emerge that reflects a new stage in Zionist, Israeli, and Jewish history. We have had Theodor Herzl's political Zionism, Achad HaAm's cultural Zionism, Chaim Weizmann's practical Zionism, David Ben-Gurion's Labor Zionism, Rav Abraham Isaac Kook's religious Zionism, Vladimir Jabotinsky's and Menachem Begin's revisionist Zionism, and now right-wing extremist anti-democratic nationalist Zionism. This new stage could be called, per Dr. Becker, "aspirational Zionism." Already, the values mode is a motivating impulse at the heart of the Israel Movement for Reform and Progressive Judaism (IMPJ), the Israel Religious Action Center (IRAC), the Association of Reform Zionists of America (ARZA), the Zionist arm of the Union for Reform Judaism (URJ), and ARZENU, the international Reform Zionist movement.

This kind of Zionism (aspirational Zionism) asks other questions: How do Jewish values augment Israel's democratic, diverse, and pluralistic society? How do the moral aspirations of the biblical prophets and the compassionate impulse of the Talmudic Rabbis interface with contemporary ethical challenges? How do Jews in Israel and around the world fight together against the sinister intentions of our enemies without sacrificing our Jewish moral sensibilities and democratic values? How do we as a people genuinely pursue peace as a moral and quintessentially Jewish obligation in spite of the threat of terror and war? And how do we Diaspora Reform Zionists support our Israeli Reform and Progressive brothers and sisters and Israelis generally while advocating on behalf of democracy and the equal rights and dignity of Israel's minorities?

We in the Progressive Zionist community are increasingly alarmed by the anti-democratic trends in Israeli society and the ascent of anti-democratic politicians into mainstream Israeli politics, as reflected in a number of bills that have been submitted to the Knesset in recent years to limit free speech and the press, to control Israeli NGOs and human rights organizations, to restrict Arab Knesset members, to exclude the rights of non-Orthodox Jewry, to maintain second-class citizenship of non-Jewish Arab Israelis, and to promote a one-state solution to the Israeli-Palestinian conflict without regard for the legitimate national rights and yearnings of the Palestinian people living in the Occupied Territories of the West Bank and East Jerusalem.

For too long most of the organized American Jewish community has argued that we American Jews who love Israel should not publicly criticize her leaders, policies, and actions when we believe that they are not acting according to the democratic principles articulated in Israel's Declaration of Independence:

> THE STATE OF ISRAEL . . . will foster the development of the country for the benefit of all its inhabitants; it will be based on freedom, justice and peace as envisaged by the prophets of Israel; it will ensure complete equality of social and political rights to all its inhabitants irrespective of religion, race or sex; it will guarantee freedom of religion, conscience, language, education and culture; it will safeguard the Holy Places of all religions; and it will be faithful to the principles of the Charter of the United Nations.

These American Jewish leaders remain quiet while Israel's democratic traditions are threatened by its government, saying that we American Jews are here to support the State of Israel unconditionally, not to criticize openly or second-guess her government's policies and actions. They have told us that being outspoken and critical will divide American Jewish support for Israel and thereby weaken support for Israel among American political and governmental leadership while giving succor to Israel's enemies, who will use our criticisms as a bludgeon against the State of Israel. Even if what we Diaspora Zionists say is a mirror of the criticism that Israelis themselves make of their leadership and policy choices, we are told, as non-Israeli citizens, to keep our mouths shut and to mind our own business, per Begin and Burg.

I became conscious of history in the late 1950s and 1960s during the American civil rights movement and the Vietnam War. Al Vorspan, a former vice president of social justice for America's Reform

Movement, used to say that "the highest form of patriotism is criticism from love." As I grew into young adulthood and fell in love with the land, people, and state of Israel, with the Hebrew language, with the Jerusalem light and its ancient memories, with the forward-looking Tel Aviv culture, with the sounds, smells, vistas, and sensibilities of the Land of Israel, I recalled Al's teaching about the importance of criticism from love in my relationship with Israel and the Jewish people as a whole. Winston Churchill put it another way: "Criticism may not be agreeable, but it is necessary. It fulfills the same function as pain to the human body. It calls attention to an unhealthy state of things."[4]

American Jews, I believe, are making a serious mistake by remaining silent when the Israeli government violates democratic norms. There are so many actions that require us to protest, including the following:

- The government's support for the expansion of West Bank settlements and unilateral nationalization of privately owned Palestinian land.
- The military administration's undemocratic and often harsh treatment of Palestinians living in East Jerusalem and the West Bank.
- The demolition of Palestinian homes and orchards in the West Bank for any reason.
- The growing hegemony of Israel's ultra-Orthodox political parties over the lives of Israeli Jewish citizens.
- The lack of equal rights and governmental support of Reform and Conservative rabbis and congregations as compared with the Orthodox.
- The lack of civil marriage and divorce in the state.
- The government's legislative and rhetorical attacks on human rights NGOs.
- The state's systemic second-class treatment of non-Jewish Israeli citizens and the ill-treatment of African political asylum seekers.

These policies effectively give a green light for the government to continue doing what it does while at the same time providing an excuse not to address the many challenges that compromise the state's liberal Jewish and democratic values.

Our Israeli Reform Movement leaders are telling us that they need Diaspora Reform Jews not only to help them build our Israeli Reform Movement, but to support them as they address these greater challenges to Israeli democracy, human rights, and the Jewish character of the state. To assist them and be more able partners in this next stage of Zionist and Israeli history, Diaspora Reform Jews need to educate themselves far more deeply and broadly than they do currently about Israel's history, government, policies, people, and competing interests and narratives. They ought to visit Israel more frequently, learn to speak Hebrew, develop friendships with Israeli Reform and Progressive Jews, and learn what it means for Israeli Arabs to live as second-class Israeli citizens and for non-Israeli Palestinian residents to live under occupation in East Jerusalem and the West Bank. All of us ought to strive to understand the competing Jewish and Palestinian narratives, to support efforts to achieve a truly shared society, and to promote publicly Israel as both the nation-state of the Jewish people and a democratic state supporting the rights of all its citizens.

After all is said and done, our primary purpose as Diaspora Reform Zionists vis-à-vis Israel and its citizens ought to be to support what we believe to be in Israel's best long-term security, democratic, and Jewish interests; align ourselves with those in Israel who support those interests; and become partners with our Israeli brothers and sisters in this next era of Jewish and Zionist history. That is what it means to be Progressive Reform Zionists and lovers of the people and State of Israel.

NOTES

1. *We Are There: The Urgent and the Important*, Jewish Agency for Israel 2014 Financial Report, p. 2, http://www.jewishagency.org/sites/default/files/ JA_1678_FinancialReport2014_SinglePages_JS_R8.pdf.

2. Cited by Stuart Schoffman in "Bialik on the Lecture Circuit," *Havruta: A Journal of Jewish Conversation* (Summer 2011): 65.

3. Tal Becker, "Beyond Survival: Jewish Values and Aspirational Zionism," *Havruta: A Journal of Jewish Conversation* (Summer 2011): 56–63.

4. Interview by Kingsley Martin, editor of the *New Statesman*, January 1939.

Where Do We Go from Here?
One Liberal Zionist's Vision for the Future

RABBI LAWRENCE A. ENGLANDER

ONE COMMON MESSAGE emerges from the chapters of this volume: there are many ways to be a Liberal Zionist—which also means that it is not easy. Rabbi Stanley M. Davids and I are trying to see your faces as you sit around our imaginary discussion table with this book in hand. Some of you may be rabbis, educators, Federation executives, or other Jewish community leaders who are reluctant to speak up from fear of causing even more dissension within an already fragmented community. Some of you may be philanthropists or fundraisers who resent the naysayers and who want to get everyone on the same page. Some of you are university academics or students who are besieged daily by anti-Israel propagandists—and who are deeply concerned, since you agree in part with what they are saying. Some of you may be Israelis living either at home or abroad, worrying what will become of your country. Some of you may simply be concerned but confused. Some of you are not at all convinced that you should care. If I have failed to mention your presence at the table, please feel free to identify yourself and speak up.

The authors of our symposium, who join us at this virtual table, have identified several of the dilemmas we face in our relationship to the State of Israel. How do we overcome our frustration with the contrast between the ideals of Israel's founders and the harsh reality of broken or unfulfilled promises? How can we steer beyond the inertia of cynicism and expediency to address the pressing concerns of racism, ultra-nationalist messianism, and economic and social inequality? How might we exert some influence in forwarding the peace process? And as we ponder these questions, we need to determine whether there is a unique role for Progressive *Religious* Zionism.[1]

If it is any consolation, Jewish history has witnessed such disappointment before. The covenant at Sinai was the Jewish people's earlier "declaration" to build a society worthy of the Divine Presence to dwell within. However, few were the times that any generation came close to that ideal, and even those times did not last long. When Elijah, for example, defied the corrupt King Ahab and assembled the people for a showdown on Mount Carmel, he uttered a prayer meant primarily for his human audience: "The people of Israel have forsaken Your covenant, thrown down Your altars, and killed Your prophets with the sword" (I Kings 19:14). For the biblical prophets, the people's survival was not to be assumed; it had to be deserved.

Taking up this theme in our own era, Dr. Eugene B. Borowitz identified a similar dissonance between the ideal and the real with regard to the State of Israel:

> The State of Israel came into being on [a] surge of particularism and since its existence has so continually been threatened, one might reasonably feel that it fulfills its role as a Jewish state merely by keeping our people alive. That continues to be all many Israelis and some Diaspora Jews feel ought to be asked of it. Many other Israelis and much of world Jewry, though agreeing on the necessity of Jewish survival, also press our corollary Covenant commitment to high humane standards.[2]

Since covenant has been a persistent theme throughout Jewish history, it is an approach that offers a fertile range of possibilities in our current discussion. Just as the political Zionism of Herzl and the cultural Zionism of Achad HaAm resonated in their own time, a new expression of "Covenantal Zionism" may give us a framework to face our current challenges. However, a twenty-first-century covenant must have a different foundation than its biblical predecessor. First of all, whereas the covenant of Sinai evinced a common response and a unified set of behaviors from our ancestors, covenantal Zionism must enable us to wrestle with a host of questions that result in a variety of responses. Second, whereas the covenant of

Sinai embraced the people as a *collective*, our contemporary culture views the autonomous *individual* as primary when it comes to entering into agreements. Therefore, covenantal Zionism must allow for personal choice. It can best do so by offering several gates of entry into the covenant, among which a person may choose one, many, or all.[3] In what follows, I shall try to identify some gates of this multiple partnership.

Covenant between Present and Past

For many Jews on their first visit to Israel, what binds them most to the Land are the archaeological sites that bring Jewish history to life and the street signs that bear the names of the Zionist pioneers whose labors brought about the State of Israel. The land roots us in our past. For myself, I still remember the lines of Psalm 122 that I recited each Shabbat as a rabbinical student in the sanctuary of Hebrew Union College in Jerusalem, just meters away from the Old City walls:

> Our feet are standing inside your gates, O Jerusalem:
> Jerusalem built up, a city knit together, to which tribes
> would make pilgrimage . . .
> to praise the name of the Eternal.
> There the thrones of judgment stood, the thrones of the
> house of David.
> Pray for the well-being of Jerusalem.
> May those who love you be at peace.

Even now, when I revisit that sacred space, I still get a lump in my throat as I say those words. This historical relationship with Israel is, for many of us, the core of our Zionism. Yet how do we apply this primal, visceral response to our current relationship with the State of Israel? Covenantal Zionism, while grounded in the past, must also address the present. It is my hope that the following "gates" may lead us there.

Covenant between the Diaspora and Israel

This gate leads to a closer relationship between Israeli and Diaspora liberally minded Jews. A few of our authors, such as Joshua Weinberg, have pointed out that historically North American Zionism has stressed support for Israel from afar, leaving *aliyah* further down the agenda. Contemporary Progressive Religious Zionists, they argue, must begin to take Israel more seriously, either by greater encouragement of *aliyah* or by arranging extended visits to Israel. I suggest, however, that *aliyah* need not be an all-or-nothing proposition. Rabbi Gilah Dror of Mercaz, the global Conservative Zionist organization, draws a comparison with Maimonides's ladder of *tzedakah* and suggests that the mitzvah of *aliyah* may be fulfilled on different levels.[4] The highest level is to come to live in Israel. Going further down the ladder, but still perceived as mitzvah, is to make frequent visits to Israel, to form deep and lasting friendships with Israeli citizens, to support Israel spiritually and financially from abroad, to educate oneself about Israel and Zionism. Rabbi Dror concludes that, perceived in this way, *aliyah* "is a mitzvah that calls to each other and every one of us to give what they can toward building the People and the Land in our time."

Whichever rung we happen to be standing on, we must find a way to build alliances with our progressive communities around the world, to share each other's Zionist perspectives, and to work in concert to support the State of Israel. In doing so, we need to identify those organizations and individuals in Israel who are working to promote our common democratic and pluralistic ideals. Within the Reform Movement, we are blessed to have the Israel Religious Action Centre (IRAC), which toils daily toward these ideals. Many other NGOs[5] work with Israelis to help build a civil society, and they, too, are worthy of our support. The more involved we become in shaping Israel's future, we may also come to understand that the ladder of *aliyah* is a dynamic one: it is important not only to mount this ladder, but also to keep on climbing.

In the meantime, from our homes *chutz laaretz* (outside of Israel), Progressive Religious Zionists in the Diaspora are called upon to play an essential political role. Many liberal Israelis, especially those in the Reform Movement, have said to me, "We are a minority here in Israel, and that status is not likely to change soon. The only way we will be heard by our government is if your voice is added to ours. We need your support to advocate not only for religious pluralism, but also for the values of social justice and peace that our movement espouses." I add to this a word of caution: For those of us who do not live in Israel, we must take our cue from those who do. We must form a strong alliance with like-minded Israelis and be ready to respond to their call. We also need to keep in mind that liberal Israelis who belong to organizations such as the Israel Movement for Reform and Progressive Judaism represent a wide ideological spectrum; it is therefore up to their leadership to set the agenda when it comes to the political arena.

Beyond political action, there is yet another way in which Diaspora Jews can forge a closer connection with Israel, and that is by delving into the rich culture that Israel has produced in its less than seventy years of existence. The scholarship that is emerging from Israeli academe enriches our understanding of Jewish history and thought. In the arts, Israeli musicians, writers, and visual artists are producing material that richly reflects contemporary Israeli identity—much of which has no direct relation to Jewish religious expression. It is not uncommon to notice snatches from Israeli music, poetry, art, and literature in our Diaspora prayer books, synagogue bulletins, and many other media. In this way, Israeli and Diaspora cultures may cross-fertilize each other and lead to a stronger bond between us.

Covenant between the Generations of K'lal Yisrael

Some authors have called our attention to a growing generation gap in our understanding of the Zionist narrative. This is especially evident on university and college campuses, as Rabbi Leah Cohen's essay attests. Jesse Paikin has pointed out that many arguments develop due to a lack of common language. Different meanings are often assigned to the same word; different interpretations are derived from the same historical event. By entering this gate, covenanters must agree to widen the scope of their discourse to include honest, if sometimes painful, listening to each other and to live with a degree of ambiguity in finding a way to ensure Israel's welfare.

Covenant between the People and the Land

Alon Tal remarks that in the early years of the state, Israel was a "land with a political conscience." This generation needs to find a middle ground between the old collectivist ideology and contemporary rampant individualism in order to preserve the environment for future generations. In doing so, we must also ensure that the resources of the land are distributed equitably among all sectors of the population, Jewish and non-Jewish—another aspect of the political conscience.

Covenant between Jews and Palestinian Arabs

This gate opens to a barrage of unresolved questions. If Jews and Palestinian Arabs are to covenant to an open dialogue, how will we learn to understand each other's claim to the same land? As Jews, how do we balance the two consequences of the 1967 war: the liberation of Jerusalem and the beginning of the Occupation? How do the events of the 1948 war affect both Jewish and Palestinian Arab attitudes to these questions?

Most challenging of all: how does each people take serious responsibility for pursuing the path of peace? Amos Oz has cautioned that a peace agreement will not be a joyful celebration but rather something akin to a divorce, "a painful compromise . . . a route paved with shattered dreams and broken illusions and injured hopes and blown-up slogans from the past on both sides."[6] This presents a challenge to both Diaspora and Israeli Jews: how do we teach and speak about Israel and the Middle East in a way that enables us to go beyond the defensive crisis narrative toward a more open understanding of the other? And if this cultural shift leaves us less certain and more ambivalent—even vulnerable—how do we still assert with confidence our own historical claim to the land?

Covenant between the Jewish People and Nations of the World
A few of our authors have cited the Israel Declaration of Independence to show how the State of Israel was founded on a unique blend of Jewish prophetic values and Western democratic principles, so that it

> will foster the development of the country for the benefit of all its inhabitants; it will be based on freedom, justice, and peace as envisaged by the prophets of Israel; it will ensure complete equality of social and political rights to all its inhabitants irrespective of religion, race, or sex; it will guarantee freedom of religion, conscience, language, education, and culture; it will safeguard the Holy Places of all religions; and it will be faithful to the principles of the Charter of the United Nations.

The possibility of Jewish self-rule in the modern era gave us the hope that Israel would truly become a "light to the nations" (Isaiah 42:6, 49:6) to represent Jewish ethical values to the world. In this regard, the State of Israel is accountable not only to its own inhabitants, not only to the Jewish Diaspora, but also to the global forum of nations. Part of our role as covenantal Zionists is to insist that Israel abide by international law.

Covenant between Jews and God
This gate is one of the most difficult, because it involves wrestling with our theology as well as with our Zionism. For example, what role—if any—do we perceive God to be playing in the establishment and preservation of the State of Israel? Rabbi Dalia Marx has cited the traditional prayer for the state, printed in many progressive siddurim, which characterizes Israel as *reishit tz'michat g'ulateinu*, "the beginning of the flowering of our redemption." This presupposes a God who intervenes in history on behalf of the Jewish people. Yet Palestinian Arabs generally regard Israel's 1948 War of Independence as the Nakba—the disaster. How do they regard the answer to *their* prayers?

Other Jewish thinkers, such as Yeshayahu Leibowitz, perceive no role for God at all in the affairs of the state. "Zionism," he claims,

> is the expression of our being fed up with being ruled by *Goyim*.
> ... Zionism as an aspiration to political-national independence
> is a legitimate Jewish aspiration, and the state is dear to us as its
> fulfillment. But it must not be given a religious aura. Only what
> is done for the sake of Heaven has religious significance. The
> category of holiness is inapplicable to the state.[7]

What, then, are we to pray for? How will our prayers reflect the values that we espouse and motivate us to pursue them? It seems to me that a great deal more attention must be paid to this aspect of our liturgy.

Conclusion: Obligations of Covenantal Zionism
In the Sinai covenant, the Jewish people fulfill their partnership through the performance of mitzvot. I believe this term applies also to covenantal Zionism. However we may define mitzvah—and multiple options are available to progressive Jews[8]—the term implies *obligation*. In our Zionist covenant of many gates, this obligation may be to God, to Israelis, to the Jewish people, or to the values of Jewish tradition. Each individual will decide which Zionist mitzvot obligate him or her and how to actualize them. Some may be performed willingly, and others reluctantly due to misgivings as to where the truth lies or what consequences may ensue. Each person will also decide where these mitzvot fall within their own scale of priorities. Nevertheless, one option that covenantal Zionism does *not* offer is for us to choose no mitzvah, to turn our backs on Israel and detach ourselves from the debates that swirl around us. In the process, I believe we shall also discover that the safeguards to democracy that we fight for in our Diaspora communities are the same ones that liberal Israelis beckon us to support. Our work as covenantal Zionists can serve to put these safeguards in place on both fronts.

We are looking around the table again to ask how you are reacting to our virtual discussion. Did you react favorably to some of the arguments, even some different from your own, or are you even more uncomfortable? Do you acknowledge why there is such a diversity of opinion, or do you wish to ask some participants to leave the room? Do you feel that you have been excluded from this discussion altogether; are you looking for a welcome place around the table? Or are you still simply confused? It is clear by now that there is no single set of answers, either within this volume or beyond it, to the many challenges we face as Zionists. It is also clear that if we exclude from our dialogue those who are committed to the survival of Israel as a Jewish and democratic state, but whose approach to achieving this end differs dramatically from our own, then we are making a tragic mistake.

I humbly suggest that covenantal Zionism does present us with a single obligation, a mitzvah for each of us to perform. Simply put: *Thou shalt engage each other.* By engaging in frank discussion around this table and others, we open ourselves to the opportunity to learn from each other, even from those with whom we passionately disagree. By engaging, we allow for the possibility of new insights and responses to emerge. And besides, the stakes are simply too high for us to walk away from the table.

I share the opinion of many Progressive Religious Zionists that we are currently engaged in nothing less than a battle for Israel's soul. Several years from now, as we attempt to gauge what progress Israel has made since today, will we be able to say that we played some role in moving Israel closer toward our hopes for her? For me, although this battle is time-consuming, frustrating, and often depressing, it is more meritorious to continue the fight than to abandon the battlefield. For me, this is my Zionist prayer:

אוֹר חָדָשׁ עַל צִיּוֹן תָּאִיר וְנִזְכֶּה כֻלָּנוּ מְהֵרָה לְאוֹרוֹ.
בָּרוּךְ אַתָּה יי יוֹצֵר הַמְּאוֹרוֹת.

Cause a new light to dawn upon Zion, and may we be worthy to bask in its splendor. Praised are You, Adonai, who enables us to seek enlightenment.

NOTES

1. The reader is again reminded that although "Reform Zionism" is most frequently used in North America, "Liberal Zionism" and "Progressive Zionism" are utilized elsewhere in the Diaspora. In this volume, we use these terms interchangeably.

2. Eugene B. Borowitz, *Renewing the Covenant* (Philadelphia: Jewish Publication Society, 1991), 233.

3. Choosing none is also an option, which will be discussed below.

4. "Rabbi Gilah Dror's Speech for Aliyah Program," Mercaz Olami, http://mercaz.masortiolami.org/rabbi-gilah-drors-speech-aliyah-program/.

5. Some examples are the New Israel Fund, Association for Civil Rights in Israel, Hand in Hand Schools, Shatil, and Bizchut. This list is by no means exhaustive.

6. Amos Oz, "Between Right and Right," in *How to Cure a Fanatic* (Princeton, NJ: Princeton University Press, 2002), 8–9.

7. Yeshayahu Leibowitz, *Judaism, Human Values and the Jewish State* (Cambridge, MA: Harvard University Press, 1992), 116–18. Leibowitz expressed this view as an Orthodox Jew.

8. See, e.g., Peter Knobel, ed., *Navigating the Journey* (New York: CCAR, 2017), especially the section "What Is Mitzvah?" xx ff.

APPENDIX

CCAR Statements on Israel

CCAR Platforms: 1885–1999

CCAR Resolution: Expression of Love and Support
for the State of Israel and Its People, 2015

1885

"The Pittsburgh Platform"

1885 PITTSBURGH CONFERENCE

CONVENING *at the call of Kaufmann Kohler of New York, Reform rabbis from around the United States met from November 16 through November 19, 1885 with Isaac Mayer Wise presiding. The meeting was declared the continuation of the Philadelphia Conference of 1869, which was the continuation of the German Conference of 1841 to 1846. The rabbis adopted the following seminal text:*

1. We recognize in every religion an attempt to grasp the Infinite, and in every mode, source or book of revelation held sacred in any religious system the consciousness of the indwelling of God in man. We hold that Judaism presents the highest conception of the God-idea as taught in our Holy Scriptures and developed and spiritualized by the Jewish teachers, in accordance with the moral and philosophical progress of their respective ages. We maintain that Judaism preserved and defended midst continual struggles and trials and under enforced isolation, this God-idea as the central religious truth for the human race.

2. We recognize in the Bible the record of the consecration of the Jewish people to its mission as the priest of the one God, and value it as the most potent instrument of religious and moral instruction. We hold that the modern discoveries of scientific researches in the domain of nature and history are not antagonistic to the doctrines of Judaism, the Bible reflecting the primitive ideas of its own age, and at times clothing its conception of divine Providence and Justice dealing with men in miraculous narratives.

3. We recognize in the Mosaic legislation a system of training the

Jewish people for its mission during its national life in Palestine, and today we accept as binding only its moral laws, and maintain only such ceremonies as elevate and sanctify our lives, but reject all such as are not adapted to the views and habits of modern civilization.

4. We hold that all such Mosaic and rabbinical laws as regulate diet, priestly purity, and dress originated in ages and under the influence of ideas entirely foreign to our present mental and spiritual state. They fail to impress the modern Jew with a spirit of priestly holiness; their observance in our days is apt rather to obstruct than to further modern spiritual elevation.

5. We recognize, in the modern era of universal culture of heart and intellect, the approaching of the realization of Israel's great Messianic hope for the establishment of the kingdom of truth, justice, and peace among all men. We consider ourselves no longer a nation, but a religious community, and therefore expect neither a return to Palestine, nor a sacrificial worship under the sons of Aaron, nor the restoration of any of the laws concerning the Jewish state.

6. We recognize in Judaism a progressive religion, ever striving to be in accord with the postulates of reason. We are convinced of the utmost necessity of preserving the historical identity with our great past. Christianity and Islam, being daughter religions of Judaism, we appreciate their providential mission, to aid in the spreading of monotheistic and moral truth. We acknowledge that the spirit of broad humanity of our age is our ally in the fulfillment of our mission, and therefore we extend the hand of fellowship to all who cooperate with us in the establishment of the reign of truth and righteousness among men.

7. We reassert the doctrine of Judaism that the soul is immortal, grounding the belief on the divine nature of human spirit, which forever finds bliss in righteousness and misery in wickedness. We reject as ideas not rooted in Judaism, the beliefs both in bodily resurrection and in Gehenna and Eden (Hell and Paradise) as abodes for everlasting punishment and reward.

8. In full accordance with the spirit of the Mosaic legislation, which strives to regulate the relations between rich and poor, we deem it our duty to participate in the great task of modern times, to solve, on the basis of justice and righteousness, the problems presented by the contrasts and evils of the present organization of society.

1937

"The Columbus Platform"

The Guiding Principles of Reform Judaism

IN VIEW of the changes that have taken place in the modern world and the consequent need of stating anew the teachings of Reform Judaism, the Central Conference of American Rabbis makes the following declaration of principles. It presents them not as a fixed creed but as a guide for the progressive elements of Jewry.

A. Judaism and its Foundations

1. *Nature of Judaism.* Judaism is the historical religious experience of the Jewish people. Though growing out of Jewish life, its message is universal, aiming at the union and perfection of mankind under the sovereignty of God. Reform Judaism recognizes the principle of progressive development in religion and consciously applies this principle to spiritual as well as to cultural and social life. Judaism welcomes all truth, whether written in the pages of scripture or deciphered from the records of nature. The new discoveries of science, while replacing the older scientific views underlying our sacred literature, do not conflict with the essential spirit of religion as manifested in the consecration of man's will, heart and mind to the service of God and of humanity.

2. *God.* The heart of Judaism and its chief contribution to religion is the doctrine of the One, living God, who rules the world through law and love. In Him all existence has its creative source and mankind its ideal of conduct. Though transcending time and space, He is the indwelling Presence of the world. We worship Him as the Lord of the universe and as our merciful Father.

3. *Man.* Judaism affirms that man is created in the Divine image. His spirit is immortal. He is an active co-worker with God. As a child

of God, he is endowed with moral freedom and is charged with the responsibility of overcoming evil and striving after ideal ends.

4. *Torah.* God reveals Himself not only in the majesty, beauty and orderliness of nature, but also in the vision and moral striving of the human spirit. Revelation is a continuous process, confined to no one group and to no one age. Yet the people of Israel, through its prophets and sages, achieved unique insight in the realm of religious truth. The Torah, both written and oral, enshrines Israel's ever-growing consciousness of God and of the moral law. It preserves the historical precedents, sanctions and norms of Jewish life, and seeks to mould it in the patterns of goodness and of holiness. Being products of historical processes, certain of its laws have lost their binding force with the passing of the conditions that called them forth. But as a depository of permanent spiritual ideals, the Torah remains the dynamic source of the life of Israel. Each age has the obligation to adapt the teachings of the Torah to its basic needs in consonance with the genius of Judaism.

5. *Israel.* Judaism is the soul of which Israel is the body. Living in all parts of the world, Israel has been held together by the ties of a common history, and above all, by the heritage of faith. Though we recognize in the group loyalty of Jews who have become estranged from our religious tradition, a bond which still unites them with us, we maintain that it is by its religion and for its religion that the Jewish people has lived. The non-Jew who accepts our faith is welcomed as a full member of the Jewish community. In all lands where our people live, they assume and seek to share loyally the full duties and responsibilities of citizenship and to create seats of Jewish knowledge and religion. In the rehabilitation of Palestine, the land hallowed by memories and hopes, we behold the promise of renewed life for many of our brethren. We affirm the obligation of all Jewry to aid in its upbuilding as a Jewish homeland by endeavoring to make it not only a haven of refuge for the oppressed but also a center of Jewish culture and spiritual life. Throughout the ages it has been Israel's mission to witness to the Divine in the face of every form of paganism and materialism. We regard it as

our historic task to cooperate with all men in the establishment of the kingdom of God, of universal brotherhood, Justice, truth and peace on earth. This is our Messianic goal.

B. Ethics

6. *Ethics and Religion.* In Judaism religion and morality blend into an indissoluble unity. Seeking God means to strive after holiness, righteousness and goodness. The love of God is incomplete without the love of one's fellowmen. Judaism emphasizes the kinship of the human race, the sanctity and worth of human life and personality and the right of the individual to freedom and to the pursuit of his chosen vocation. justice to all, irrespective of race, sect or class, is the inalienable right and the inescapable obligation of all. The state and organized government exist in order to further these ends.

7. *Social justice.* Judaism seeks the attainment of a just society by the application of its teachings to the economic order, to industry and commerce, and to national and international affairs. It aims at the elimination of man-made misery and suffering, of poverty and degradation, of tyranny and slavery, of social inequality and prejudice, of ill-will and strife. It advocates the promotion of harmonious relations between warring classes on the basis of equity and justice, and the creation of conditions under which human personality may flourish. It pleads for the safeguarding of childhood against exploitation. It champions the cause of all who work and of their right to an adequate standard of living, as prior to the rights of property. Judaism emphasizes the duty of charity, and strives for a social order which will protect men against the material disabilities of old age, sickness and unemployment.

8. *Peace.* Judaism, from the days of the prophets, has proclaimed to mankind the ideal of universal peace. The spiritual and physical disarmament of all nations has been one of its essential teachings. It abhors all violence and relies upon moral education, love and sympathy to secure human progress. It regards justice as the foundation of the well-being of nations and the condition of enduring

peace. It urges organized international action for disarmament, collective security and world peace.

C. Religious Practice

9. *The Religious Life.* Jewish life is marked by consecration to these ideals of Judaism. It calls for faithful participation in the life of the Jewish community as it finds expression in home, synagogue and school and in all other agencies that enrich Jewish life and promote its welfare. The Home has been and must continue to be a stronghold of Jewish life, hallowed by the spirit of love and reverence, by moral discipline and religious observance and worship. The Synagogue is the oldest and most democratic institution in Jewish life. It is the prime communal agency by which Judaism is fostered and preserved. It links the Jews of each community and unites them with all Israel. The perpetuation of Judaism as a living force depends upon religious knowledge and upon the Education of each new generation in our rich cultural and spiritual heritage.

Prayer is the voice of religion, the language of faith and aspiration. It directs man's heart and mind Godward, voices the needs and hopes of the community and reaches out after goals which invest life with supreme value. To deepen the spiritual life of our people, we must cultivate the traditional habit of communion with God through prayer in both home and synagogue.

Judaism as a way of life requires in addition to its moral and spiritual demands, the preservation of the Sabbath, festivals and Holy Days, the retention and development of such customs, symbols and ceremonies as possess inspirational value, the cultivation of distinctive forms of religious art and music and the use of Hebrew, together with the vernacular, in our worship and instruction.

These timeless aims and ideals of our faith we present anew to a confused and troubled world. We call upon our fellow Jews to rededicate themselves to them, and, in harmony with all men, hopefully and courageously to continue Israel's eternal quest after God and His kingdom.

1976

Reform Judaism: A Centenary Perspective

ADOPTED IN SAN FRANCISCO

T HE CENTRAL CONFERENCE OF AMERICAN RABBIS has on special occasions described the spiritual state of Reform Judaism. The centenaries of the founding of the Union of American Hebrew Congregations and the Hebrew Union College–Jewish Institute of Religion seem an appropriate time for another such effort. We therefore record our sense of the unity of our movement today.

One Hundred Years: What We Have Taught

We celebrate the role of Reform Judaism in North America, the growth of our movement on this free ground, the great contributions of our membership to the dreams and achievements of this society. We also feel great satisfaction at how much of our pioneering conception of Judaism has been accepted by the Household of Israel. It now seems self-evident to most Jews: that our tradition should interact with modern culture; that its forms ought to reflect a contemporary esthetic; that its scholarship needs to be conducted by modern, critical methods; and that change has been and must continue to be a fundamental reality in Jewish life. Moreover, though some still disagree, substantial numbers have also accepted our teachings: that the ethics of universalism implicit in traditional Judaism must be an explicit part of our Jewish duty; that women have full rights to practice Judaism; and that Jewish obligation begins with the informed will of every individual. Most modern Jews, within their various religious movements, are embracing Reform Jewish perspectives. We see this past century as having confirmed the essential wisdom of our movement.

One Hundred Years: What We Have Learned

Obviously, much else has changed in the past century. We continue
to probe the extraordinary events of the past generation, seeking
to understand their meaning and to incorporate their significance
in our lives. The Holocaust shattered our easy optimism about humanity and its inevitable progress. The State of Israel, through its
many accomplishments, raised our sense of the Jews as a people to
new heights of aspiration and devotion. The widespread threats to
freedom, the problems inherent in the explosion of new knowledge
and of ever more powerful technologies, and the spiritual emptiness
of much of Western culture have taught us to be less dependent on
the values of our society and to reassert what remains perenially
valid in Judaism's teaching. We have learned that the survival of
the Jewish people is of highest priority and that in carrying out our
Jewish responsibilities we help move humanity toward its messianic
fulfillment.

Diversity Within Unity, the Hallmark of Reform

Reform Jews respond to change in various ways according to the
Reform principle of the autonomy of the individual. However, Reform Judaism does more than tolerate diversity; it engenders it. In
our uncertain historical situation we must expect to have far greater
diversity than previous generations knew. How we shall live with
diversity without stifling dissent and without paralyzing our ability
to take positive action will test our character and our principles. We
stand open to any position thoughtfully and conscientiously advocated in the spirit of Reform Jewish belief. While we may differ in
our interpretation and application of the ideas enunciated here, we
accept such differences as precious and see in them Judaism's best
hope for confronting whatever the future holds for us. Yet in all our
diversity we perceive a certain unity and we shall not allow our differences in some particulars to obscure what binds us together.

1. *God*— The affirmation of God has always been essential to our
    people's will to survive. In our struggle through the centuries to

preserve our faith we have experienced and conceived of God in many ways. The trials of our own time and the challenges of modern culture have made steady belief and clear understanding difficult for some. Nevertheless, we ground our lives, personally and communally, on God's reality and remain open to new experiences and conceptions of the Divine. Amid the mystery we call life, we affirm that human beings, created in God's image, share in God's eternality despite the mystery we call death.

2. *The People Israel*— The Jewish people and Judaism defy precise definition because both are in the process of becoming. Jews, by birth or conversion, constitute an uncommon union of faith and peoplehood. Born as Hebrews in the ancient Near East, we are bound together like all ethnic groups by language, land, history, culture, and institutions. But the people of Israel is unique because of its involvement with God and its resulting perception of the human condition. Throughout our long history our people has been inseparable from its religion with its messianic hope that humanity will be redeemed.

3. *Torah*— Torah results from the relationship between God and the Jewish people. The records of our earliest confrontations are uniquely important to us. Lawgivers and prophets, historians and poets gave us a heritage whose study is a religious imperative and whose practice is our chief means to holiness. Rabbis and teachers, philosophers and mystics, gifted Jews in every age amplified the Torah tradition. For millennia, the creation of Torah has not ceased and Jewish creativity in our time is adding to the chain of tradition.

4. *Our Religious Obligations:* Religious Practice— Judaism emphasizes action rather than creed as the primary expression of a religious life, the means by which we strive to achieve universal justice and peace. Reform Judaism shares this emphasis on duty and obligation. Our founders stressed that the Jew's ethical responsibilities, personal and social, are enjoined by God. The past century has taught us that the claims made upon us may begin with our ethical obligations but they extend to many other aspects of Jewish

living, including: creating a Jewish home centered on family devotion: lifelong study; private prayer and public worship; daily religious observance; keeping the Sabbath and the holy days: celebrating the major events of life; involvement with the synagogues and community; and other activities which promote the survival of the Jewish people and enhance its existence. Within each area of Jewish observance Reform Jews are called upon to confront the claims of Jewish tradition, however differently perceived, and to exercise their individual autonomy, choosing and creating on the basis of commitment and knowledge.

5. *Our Obligations:* The State of Israel and the Diaspora— We are privileged to live in an extraordinary time, one in which a third Jewish commonwealth has been established in our people's ancient homeland. We are bound to that land and to the newly reborn State of Israel by innumerable religious and ethnic ties. We have been enriched by its culture and ennobled by its indomitable spirit. We see it providing unique opportunities for Jewish self-expression. We have both a stake and a responsibility in building the State of Israel, assuring its security, and defining its Jewish character. We encourage *aliyah* for those who wish to find maximum personal fulfillment in the cause of Zion. We demand that Reform Judaism be unconditionally legitimized in the State of Israel.

At the same time that we consider the State of Israel vital to the welfare of Judaism everywhere, we reaffirm the mandate of our tradition to create strong Jewish communities wherever we live. A genuine Jewish life is possible in any land, each community developing its own particular character and determining its Jewish responsibilities. The foundation of Jewish community life is the synagogue. It leads us beyond itself to cooperate with other Jews, to share their concerns, and to assume leadership in communal affairs. We are therefore committed to the full democratization of the Jewish community and to its hallowing in terms of Jewish values.

The State of Israel and the Diaspora, in fruitful dialogue, can show how a people transcends nationalism even as it affirms it, thereby setting an example for humanity which remains largely concerned with dangerously parochial goals.

6. *Our Obligations:* Survival and Service— Early Reform Jews, newly admitted to general society and seeing in this the evidence of a growing universalism, regularly spoke of Jewish purpose in terms of Jewry's service to humanity. In recent years we have become freshly conscious of the virtues of pluralism and the values of particularism. The Jewish people in its unique way of life validates its own worth while working toward the fulfillment of its messianic expectations.

Until the recent past our obligations to the Jewish people and to all humanity seemed congruent. At times now these two imperatives appear to conflict. We know of no simple way to resolve such tensions. We must, however, confront them without abandoning either of our commitments. A universal concern for humanity unaccompanied by a devotion to our particular people is self-destructive; a passion for our people without involvement in humankind contradicts what the prophets have meant to us. Judaism calls us simultaneously to universal and particular obligations.

Hope: Our Jewish Obligation

Previous generations of Reform Jews had unbound confidence in humanity's potential for good. We have lived through terrible tragedy and been compelled to reappropriate our tradition's realism about the human capacity for evil. Yet our people has always refused to despair. The survivors of the Holocaust, being granted life, seized it, nurtured it, and, rising above catastrophe, showed humankind that the human spirit is indomitable. The State of Israel, established and maintained by the Jewish will to live, demonstrates what a united people can accomplish in history. The existence of the Jew is an argument against despair; Jewish survival is warrant for human hope.

We remain God's witness that history is not meaningless. We affirm that with God's help people are not powerless to affect their destiny. We dedicate ourselves, as did the generations of Jews who went before us, to work and wait for that day when "They shall not hurt or destroy in all My holy mountain for the earth shall be full of the knowledge of the Lord as the waters cover the sea."

1997

"*The Miami Platform*"

REFORM JUDAISM AND ZIONISM: A CENTENARY PLATFORM

Preamble

IN RECOGNITION of the centenary of the first World Zionist Congress (August 29, 1897), the Central Conference of American Rabbis hereby issues its first platform dedicated exclusively to the relationship between Reform Judaism and Zionism.

In 1885 the framers of the Pittsburgh Platform of Reform Judaism declared that they no longer expected Jews to return to a national homeland in Palestine. The Platform's authors proclaimed: "We consider ourselves no longer a nation, but a religious community, and, therefore, expect neither a return to Palestine . . . nor the restoration of any of the laws concerning the Jewish state."

By 1937 the CCAR had reversed its stand on Jewish peoplehood, and declared in its "Columbus Platform" that "Judaism is the soul of which Israel [the people] is the body." The document further states: "We affirm the obligation of all Jewry to aid in its [Palestine's] up-building as a Jewish homeland by endeavoring to make it not only a haven of refuge for the oppressed but also a center of Jewish culture and spiritual life." This affirmation of Jewish peoplehood was accompanied by a reaffirmation of Reform Judaism's universal message: "We regard it as our historic task to cooperate with all men in the establishment of the kingdom of God, of universal brotherhood, justice, truth and peace on earth. This is our Messianic goal."

The CCAR returned again to the question of Zionism in 1976, asserting in its "Centenary Perspective": "We are bound to . . . the newly reborn State of Israel by innumerable religious and ethnic ties. . . . We have both a stake and a responsibility in building the State of Israel, assuring its security and defining its Jewish character." The

"Centenary Perspective" also affirmed the legitimacy of the Diaspora and the historic universalism of Reform Judaism: "The State of Israel and the Diaspora, in fruitful dialogue, can show how a people transcends nationalism even as it affirms it, thereby setting an example for humanity, which remains largely concerned with dangerously parochial goals." Here again, the CCAR embraced Zionism as a means of fulfilling its universal vision and its opposition to narrow nationalism.

A century after Theodor Herzl called for the creation of a modern Jewish state and nearly fifty years since the State of Israel joined the family of modern nations, the fundamental issues addressed in the previous CCAR pronouncements continue to challenge us, making this a fitting time to re-examine and redefine the ideological and spiritual bonds that connect *Am Yisrael* [the People of Israel] to *Eretz Yisrael* [the Land of Israel] and to *Medinat Yisrael* [the State of Israel]. The CCAR affirms through this Platform those principles which will guide Reform Judaism into the 21st century.

I. Judaism: A Religion and a People

The restoration of *Am Yisrael* to its ancestral homeland after nearly two thousand years of statelessness and powerlessness represents an historic triumph of the Jewish people, providing a physical refuge, the possibility of religious and cultural renewal on its own soil, and the realization of God's promise to Abraham: "to your offspring I assign this land." From that distant moment until today, the intense love between *Am Yisrael* and *Eretz Yisrael* has not subsided.

We believe that the eternal covenant established at Sinai ordained a unique religious purpose for *Am Yisrael*. *Medinat Yisrael*, the Jewish State, is therefore unlike all other states. Its obligation is to strive towards the attainment of the Jewish people's highest moral ideals to be a *mamlechet kohanim* [a kingdom of priests], a *goy kadosh* [a holy people], and *l'or goyim* [a light unto the nations].

II. From Degradation to Sovereignty

During two millennia of dispersion and persecution, *Am Yisrael* never abandoned hope for the rebirth of a national home in *Eretz Yisrael*. The Shoah [Holocaust] intensified our resolve to affirm life and pursue the Zionist dream of a return to *Eretz Yisrael*. Even as we mourned for the loss of one-third of our people, we witnessed the miraculous rebirth of *Medinat Yisrael*, the Jewish people's supreme creation in our age.

Centuries of Jewish persecution, culminating in the Shoah, demonstrated the risks of powerlessness. We, therefore, affirm *Am Yisrael*'s reassertion of national sovereignty, but we urge that it be used to create the kind of society in which full civil, human, and religious rights exist for all its citizens. Ultimately, *Medinat Yisrael* will be judged not on its military might but on its character.

While we view *Eretz Yisrael* as sacred, the sanctity of Jewish life takes precedence over the sanctity of Jewish land.

III. Our Relationship to the State of Israel

Even as *Medinat Yisrael* serves uniquely as the spiritual and cultural focal point of world Jewry, Israeli and Diaspora Jewry are interdependent, responsible for one another, and partners in the shaping of Jewish destiny. Each *kehilla* [Jewish community], though autonomous and self-regulating, shares responsibility for the fate of Jews everywhere. By deepening the social, spiritual, and intellectual relationship among the *kehillot* worldwide, we can revitalize Judaism both in Israel and the Diaspora.

IV. Our Obligations to Israel

To help promote the security of *Medinat Yisrael* and ensure the welfare of its citizens, we pledge continued political support and financial assistance.

Recognizing that knowledge of Hebrew is indispensable both in the study of Judaism and in fostering solidarity between Israeli and Diaspora Jews, we commit ourselves to intensifying Hebrew instruction in all Reform institutions. Hebrew, the language of our sacred texts and prayers, is a symbol of the revitalization of *Am Yisrael*.

To enhance appreciation of Jewish peoplehood and promote a deeper understanding of Israel, we resolve to implement educational programs and religious practices that reflect and reinforce the bond between Reform Judaism and Zionism.

To deepen awareness of Israel and strengthen Jewish identity, we call upon all Reform Jews, adults and youths, to study in, and make regular visits to, Israel.

While affirming the authenticity and necessity of a creative and vibrant Diaspora Jewry, we encourage *aliyah* [immigration] to Israel in pursuance of the precept of *yishuv Eretz Yisrael* [settling the Land of Israel]. While Jews can live Torah-centered lives in the Diaspora, only in *Medinat Yisrael* do they bear the primary responsibility for the governance of society, and thus may realize the full potential of their individual and communal religious strivings.

Confident that Reform Judaism's synthesis of tradition and modernity and its historic commitment to *tikkun olam* [repairing the world], can make a unique and positive contribution to the Jewish state, we resolve to intensify our efforts to inform and educate Israelis about the values of Reform Judaism. We call upon Reform Jews everywhere to dedicate their energies and resources to the strengthening of an indigenous Progressive Judaism in *Medinat Yisrael*.

V. Israel's Obligations to the Diaspora

Medinat Yisrael exists not only for the benefit of its citizens but also to defend the physical security and spiritual integrity of the Jewish people. Realizing that *Am Yisrael* consists of a coalition of different, sometimes conflicting, religious interpretations, the Jewish people will be best served when *Medinat Yisrael* is constituted as a pluralistic, democratic society. Therefore we seek a Jewish state in which no religious interpretation of Judaism takes legal precedence over another.

VI. Redemption

We believe that the renewal and perpetuation of Jewish national life in *Eretz Yisrael* is a necessary condition for the realization of the physical and spiritual redemption of the Jewish people and of all humanity. While that day of redemption remains but a distant yearning, we express the fervent hope that *Medinat Yisrael*, living in peace with its neighbors, will hasten the redemption of *Am Yisrael*, and the fulfillment of our messianic dream of universal peace under the sovereignty of God.

The achievements of modern Zionism in the creation of the State of Israel, in reviving the Hebrew language, in absorbing millions of immigrants, in transforming desolate wastes into blooming forests and fields, in generating a thriving new economy and society, are an unparalleled triumph of the Jewish spirit.

We stand firm in our love of Zion. We resolve to work for the day when waves of Jewish pride and confidence will infuse every Jewish heart, in fulfillment of the promise: When God restores the fortunes of Zion we shall be like dreamers. Our mouths will fill with laughter and our tongues with songs of joy. Then shall they say among the nations God has done great things for them.

Submitted by CCAR Tripartite Zionist Platform Committee:
Rabbi Ammiel Hirsch, Chair

CCAR Representatives:
Rabbi Stanley Davids
Rabbi Dow Marmur
Rabbi Sheldon Zimmerman

UAHC Representatives:
Constance Kreshtool
Norman Schwartz
Rabbi Eric Yoffie

HUC-JIR Representatives:
Dr. Susan Einbinder
Rabbi Ezra Spicehandler
Rabbi Gary Zola
Dr. Michael Meyer, alternate

Additional Representatives:
Dr. Leon Jick
Rabbi Norman Patz

The Committee gratefully acknowledges the significant contributions of:
Aron Hirt-Manheimer, Drafter and Editor
Rabbi Harvey Fields, Drafter

1999

A Statement of Principles
for Reform Judaism

ADOPTED AT THE MAY 1999 PITTSBURGH CONVENTION

Preamble

ON THREE OCCASIONS during the last century and a half, the Reform rabbinate has adopted comprehensive statements to help guide the thought and practice of our movement. In 1885, fifteen rabbis issued the Pittsburgh Platform, a set of guidelines that defined Reform Judaism for the next fifty years. A revised statement of principles, the Columbus Platform, was adopted by the Central Conference of American Rabbis in 1937. A third set of rabbinic guidelines, the Centenary Perspective, appeared in 1976 on the occasion of the centenary of the Union of American Hebrew Congregations and the Hebrew Union College–Jewish Institute of Religion. Today, when so many individuals are striving for religious meaning, moral purpose and a sense of community, we believe it is our obligation as rabbis once again to state a set of principles that define Reform Judaism in our own time.

Throughout our history, we Jews have remained firmly rooted in Jewish tradition, even as we have learned much from our encounters with other cultures. The great contribution of Reform Judaism is that it has enabled the Jewish people to introduce innovation while preserving tradition, to embrace diversity while asserting commonality, to affirm beliefs without rejecting those who doubt, and to bring faith to sacred texts without sacrificing critical scholarship.

This "Statement of Principles" affirms the central tenets of Judaism—God, Torah and Israel—even as it acknowledges the diversity of Reform Jewish beliefs and practices. It also invites all Reform Jews to engage in a dialogue with the sources of our tradition, responding out of our knowledge, our experience and our faith. Thus we hope to transform our lives through קְדוּשָׁה (*kedushah*), holiness.

God

We affirm the reality and oneness of God, even as we may differ in our understanding of the Divine presence.

We affirm that the Jewish people is bound to God by an eternal בְּרִית (*b'rit*), covenant, as reflected in our varied understandings of Creation, Revelation and Redemption.

We affirm that every human being is created בְּצֶלֶם אֱלֹהִים (*b'tzelem Elohim*), in the image of God, and that therefore every human life is sacred.

We regard with reverence all of God's creation and recognize our human responsibility for its preservation and protection.

We encounter God's presence in moments of awe and wonder, in acts of justice and compassion, in loving relationships and in the experiences of everyday life.

We respond to God daily: through public and private prayer, through study and through the performance of other מִצְווֹת (*mitzvot*), sacred obligations—בֵּן אָדָם לַמָּקוֹם (*bein adam la Makom*), to God, and בֵּן אָדָם לַחֲבֵרוֹ (*bein adam la-chaveiro*), to other human beings.

We strive for a faith that fortifies us through the vicissitudes of our lives—illness and healing, transgression and repentance, bereavement and consolation, despair and hope.

We continue to have faith that, in spite of the unspeakable evils committed against our people and the sufferings endured by others, the partnership of God and humanity will ultimately prevail.

We trust in our tradition's promise that, although God created us as finite beings, the spirit within us is eternal.

In all these ways and more, God gives meaning and purpose to our lives.

Torah

We affirm that Torah is the foundation of Jewish life.

We cherish the truths revealed in Torah, God's ongoing revelation to our people and the record of our people's ongoing relationship with God.

We affirm that Torah is a manifestation of עוֹלָם אַהֲבַת (*ahavat olam*), God's eternal love for the Jewish people and for all humanity.

We affirm the importance of studying Hebrew, the language of Torah and Jewish liturgy, that we may draw closer to our people's sacred texts.

We are called by Torah to lifelong study in the home, in the synagogue and in every place where Jews gather to learn and teach. Through Torah study we are called to מִצְווֹת (*mitzvot*), the means by which we make our lives holy.

We are committed to the ongoing study of the whole array of מִצְווֹת (*mitzvot*) and to the fulfillment of those that address us as individuals and as a community. Some of these מִצְווֹת (*mitzvot*), sacred obligations, have long been observed by Reform Jews; others, both ancient and modern, demand renewed attention as the result of the unique context of our own times.

We bring Torah into the world when we seek to sanctify the times and places of our lives through regular home and congregational observance. Shabbat calls us to bring the highest moral values to our daily labor and to culminate the workweek with קְדוּשָׁה (*kedushah*), holiness, מְנוּחָה (*menuchah*), rest and עֹנֶג (*oneg*), joy. The High Holy Days call us to account for our deeds. The Festivals enable us to celebrate with joy our people's religious journey in the context of the changing seasons. The days of remembrance remind us of the tragedies and the triumphs that have shaped our people's historical experience both in ancient and modern times. And we mark the milestones of our personal journeys with traditional and creative rites that reveal the holiness in each stage of life.

We bring Torah into the world when we strive to fulfill the highest ethical mandates in our relationships with others and with all of God's creation. Partners with God in עוֹלָם תִּקּוּן (*tikkun olam*), repairing the world, we are called to help bring nearer the messianic age. We seek dialogue and joint action with people of other faiths in the hope that together we can bring peace, freedom and justice to our world. We are obligated to pursue צֶדֶק (*tzedek*), justice and righteousness, and to narrow the gap between the affluent and the poor, to act against discrimination and oppression, to pursue peace, to welcome the stranger, to protect the earth's biodiversity and natural resources, and to redeem those in physical, economic and spiritual bondage. In so doing, we reaffirm social action and social justice as a central prophetic focus of traditional Reform Jewish belief and practice. We affirm the מִצְוָה (*mitzvah*) of צְדָקָה (*tzedakah*), setting aside portions of our earnings and our time to provide for those in need. These acts bring us closer to fulfilling the prophetic call to translate the words of Torah into the works of our hands.

In all these ways and more, Torah gives meaning and purpose to our lives.

Israel

We are Israel, a people aspiring to holiness, singled out through our ancient covenant and our unique history among the nations to be witnesses to God's presence. We are linked by that covenant and that history to all Jews in every age and place.

We are committed to the מִצְוָה (*mitzvah*) of אַהֲבַת יִשְׂרָאֵל (*ahavat Yisrael*), love for the Jewish people, and to כְּלַל יִשְׂרָאֵל (*k'lal Yisrael*), the entirety of the community of Israel. Recognizing that כֹּל יִשְׂרָאֵל עֲרֵבִים זֶה בָּזֶה (*kol Yisrael arevim zeh ba-zeh*), all Jews are responsible for one another, we reach out to all Jews across ideological and geographical boundaries.

We embrace religious and cultural pluralism as an expression of the vitality of Jewish communal life in Israel and the Diaspora.

We pledge to fulfill Reform Judaism's historic commitment to the complete equality of women and men in Jewish life.

We are an inclusive community, opening doors to Jewish life to people of all ages, to varied kinds of families, to all regardless of their sexual orientation, to גֵרִים (*gerim*), those who have converted to Judaism, and to all individuals and families, including the intermarried, who strive to create a Jewish home.

We believe that we must not only open doors for those ready to enter our faith, but also to actively encourage those who are seeking a spiritual home to find it in Judaism.

We are committed to strengthening the people Israel by supporting individuals and families in the creation of homes rich in Jewish learning and observance.

We are committed to strengthening the people Israel by making the synagogue central to Jewish communal life, so that it may elevate the spiritual, intellectual and cultural quality of our lives.

We are committed to מְדִינַת יִשְׂרָאֵל (*Medinat Yisrael*), the State of Israel, and rejoice in its accomplishments. We affirm the unique qualities of living in אֶרֶץ יִשְׂרָאֵל (*Eretz Yisrael*), the land of Israel, and encourage עֲלִיָּה (*aliyah*), immigration to Israel.

We are committed to a vision of the State of Israel that promotes full civil, human and religious rights for all its inhabitants and that strives for a lasting peace between Israel and its neighbors.

We are committed to promoting and strengthening Progressive Judaism in Israel, which will enrich the spiritual life of the Jewish state and its people.

We affirm that both Israeli and Diaspora Jewry should remain vibrant and interdependent communities. As we urge Jews who reside outside Israel to learn Hebrew as a living language and to make periodic visits to Israel in order to study and to deepen their relationship to the Land and its people, so do we affirm that Israeli Jews have much to learn from the religious life of Diaspora Jewish communities.

We are committed to furthering Progressive Judaism throughout the world as a meaningful religious way of life for the Jewish people.

In all these ways and more, Israel gives meaning and purpose to our lives.

בָּרוּךְ שֶׁאָמַר וְהָיָה הָעוֹלָם.
(*Baruch she-amar ve-haya ha-olam*).
Praised be the One through whose word all things came to be.
May our words find expression in holy actions.
May they raise us up to a life of meaning devoted to God's service
And to the redemption of our world.

CCAR RESOLUTION: *Expression of Love and Support for the State of Israel and Its People*

Reform Rabbis' Enduring Commitment to the State of Israel

THE CENTRAL CONFERENCE OF AMERICAN RABBIS has a long history of support for the State of Israel.[1] As bearers of Torah, we Reform rabbis hold sacred the Land of Israel and its people. Our fullest, most formal expression of these core values was the 1997 CCAR Platform on Reform Judaism and Zionism, adopted by the plenary in Miami, which we hereby reaffirm.

The modern State of Israel, as expressed in Israel's Declaration of Independence, is the means to the fulfillment of the age-old Jewish dream to return to the land; to develop it for the benefit of all its inhabitants; to affirm the principles of freedom, justice and peace as envisaged by the prophets of Israel; to establish complete equality of social and political rights for all its inhabitants irrespective of religion, race or sex; to preserve freedom of religion, conscience, language, education and culture; and to safeguard all Holy Places for all religions.

The Central Conference of American Rabbis gathers each seventh year for our annual convention in the nation-state of the Jewish people as a deep expression of more than 2,300 CCAR members' love for, support of, commonality with, and dedication to the Zionist project.

The Reform rabbinate worldwide celebrates the modern State of Israel, its vibrancy and creativity in all areas of human endeavor, and it embraces as partners with the people of Israel the many challenges and opportunities to build a modern Jewish and democratic society. We Reform rabbis of the CCAR are grateful that Israel represents a safe haven for Jews from around the world. With a rising tide of anti-Semitism in many countries, we value Israel's commitment, as stated in its Declaration of Independence, to "be open for Jewish immigration and for the ingathering of the Exiles."

The CCAR supports the growing Israeli Reform Movement and partners with our Israeli sister organizations, institutions and programs—MARAM; Israel Council of Reform Rabbis; IMPJ, the Israel Movement for Reform and Progressive Judaism, its vibrant congregations, communities, and programs; IRAC, the Israel Religious Action Center; HUC–JIR, the Jerusalem Campus of Hebrew Union College–Jewish Institute of Religion; the Leo Baeck School in Haifa and the Yozma-Tali School in Modi'in; dozens of Reform-sponsored Tali schools and Ganim; two Reform Kibbutzim: Yahel and Lotan; an active pre-army program and the Noar Telem Reform youth movement; and dozens of other efforts to spread Reform and Progressive Judaism, democracy, pluralism, and religious diversity in the state.[2] The CCAR values its role as a founding partner of ARZA, the Association of Reform Zionists of America; and our involvement worldwide in ARZENU, the international Reform Zionist federation. We value ARZA's and ARZENU's leading role representing the Reform Movement in Israel's National Institutions (World Zionist Organization, Jewish Agency for Israel, Keren Kayemet L'Yisrael).

Further, we share in ARZA's work in encouraging and instilling active progressive Zionism within our congregations and communities, and providing significant financial resources to our partner institutions in Israel.[3]

CCAR rabbis cherish our role as a partner with the Women of the Wall.[4]

CCAR rabbis bring thousands of Reform Jews, of all ages, annually to visit Israel[5] in synagogue groups. We support the many programs offered by the Union for Reform Judaism, through NFTY-in-Israel[6] and *Taglit*-Birthright Israel.[7]

We Affirm

The CCAR affirms that our love and support for the State of Israel are unconditional. When we disagree with specific government policies and pronouncements, we do so according to tradition's principle of מחלוקת לשם שמים (*machloket l'sheim shamayim*, disagreement for the sake of Heaven), and the words of the prophet Isaiah (62:1), "For Zion's sake I will not hold my peace, and for Jerusalem's sake I will not rest, until her righteousness goes forth like radiance..."

The CCAR calls upon the State of Israel, as both a Jewish and democratic state, to recognize all mainstream expressions of Judaism, and the rabbis that serve them, on an equal basis.[8] We insist that all Jewish holy places in Israel be accessible to women and men, with options for those who wish to worship together and for those who wish to worship separately.[9]

The CCAR affirms its commitment to expanding civil liberties in Israel for all citizens of the State, including but not limited to equal rights for both men and women, equality for all LGBT persons living under Israeli sovereignty, and civil liberties not afforded to most of the inhabitants of the wider region.

The CCAR supports the institution of civil marriage and divorce[10] for all marriages, including same-gender marriage. We believe that the continued control by the Chief Rabbinate in determining and judging the personal status of any individual Jew or group of Jews undermines Israel's democracy, as well as its Jewish nature.

The CCAR affirms that Israel must continue to seek every opportunity to live in peace with its neighbors despite the immense challenges.

Throughout its history, Israel has been beset by enemies. Israel has extended a hand of peace to it neighbors over the years, successfully concluding peace agreements with both Egypt and Jordan. However, other nations and non-state actors, notably Iran and the terrorist organizations it supports, including Hamas and Hezbollah, remain committed to Israel's destruction. Other terrorist organizations, such as ISIS, also seek Israel's demise. We remain unwaveringly committed to Israel's security. The CCAR takes seriously the government of Iran's long-standing intention to acquire nuclear weaponry, with the desire and capacity to direct that destructive force upon Israel. We of the CCAR emphasize the need for the on-going monitoring of Iranian compliance with the agreement it made in 2015 with the P5 +1 nations.[11] Many of Israel's leaders across the political spectrum have expressed their willingness to relinquish territory for the sake of peace.[12] We of the CCAR encourage the same spirit of compromise among Israel's leaders today.

We deplore Palestinian intransigence, incitement, terror, and internal divisions, as well as an unwillingness of many Palestinians to accept the legitimacy of Israel as the nation-state of the Jewish people. These actions impact negatively on the peace process with Israel. We condemn all incitement to violence by the Palestinian Authority and Hamas.

The CCAR rejects the Boycott, Divestment and Sanctions Movement, the primary motivation of which is the delegitimization of Israel as the nation state of the Jewish people.

We are saddened that some Israeli policies have had a negative impact on the daily lives of non-combatant West Bank Palestinian residents. We firmly believe that the expansion of West Bank Settlements is detrimental to the peace process.[13]

Only through direct negotiations can Israel and the Palestinians end their conflict and fulfill both people's legitimate national aspirations. We of the CCAR encourage Israel and the Palestinians to resume direct peace talks immediately, supported by trusted international partners, with the end goal being a two-state solution to the conflict in which the Jewish State of Israel and the State of Palestine will live peaceably side by side.

We of the CCAR are united in the belief that military force will not resolve the Israeli-Palestinian conflict. Nevertheless, Israel has the right and moral obligation to protect the safety and security of its people. We support the Government of Israel in its war against terrorism and in its efforts to stop those who execute, support and encourage it. We reject the simplistic moral equation that would draw a parallel between the actions of Palestinian terrorists who target innocent civilians and the generally measured responses of Israel's defense forces that target Palestinian terrorists. We affirm

Israel's principle of טוהר הנשק (*tohar haneshek*, purity of arms) that calls upon all IDF soldiers to employ reasonable restraint in order to protect human life.[14]

Peaceful coexistence between Israel, the Palestinians, and the Arab states, based on justice and mutual recognition, is a political and moral necessity that will preserve both Israel's Jewish character and democracy. No final resolution to the Middle East conflict can be achieved until each side recognizes the justice and moral claims of the other for national independence and freedom.

Our Call to Action

Therefore, we rabbis of the CCAR:

Pray for the fulfillment of the prophetic vision: "Nation shall not lift up sword against nation; neither shall they learn war anymore" (Isaiah 2:4);

Condemn all incitement to violence and terrorist acts[15] by the Palestinian Authority and Hamas, Hezbollah, ISIS and Iran;

Call upon Israeli leaders to reiterate, clearly and consistently, that Israel accepts Palestinian national rights even as it demands that the Palestinians recognize Israel's right to exist in peace and security as the nation-state of the Jewish People;[16]

Hold that Palestinian right to political self-determination must not be achieved at the expense of Israel's right to exist as a Jewish democratic state with a Jewish majority;

Believe that a Palestinian State can only be established through direct negotiations between Palestinian and Israeli leaders;[17]

Call upon Palestinian leaders to discontinue unilateral actions intended to isolate Israel in international forums and circumvent the negotiating process and, instead, accept Israel's invitation to return to the bargaining table promptly and without preconditions;

Believe that while all parties share responsibility to address the tragedy of Palestinian refugees, the return of Palestinian refugees to Israel should be limited to a symbolic number that would allow Israel to maintain safely its Jewish majority and democracy, recognizing the individual and collective rights of all minority groups.

Urge the government of Israel to work with credible, willing Palestinian leaders and other interested parties within and beyond the Arab world towards a political solution to the Israeli-Palestinian conflict;[18]

Reaffirm Israel's and the Palestinian Authority's obligation to abide by the Oslo Accord;

Call upon Israel's security forces in the West Bank to do everything reasonably possible to respect and defend the human rights, dignity and property of the Palestinian population;

Call upon Israel to stop building and expanding settlements across the "Green Line" in the occupied territories, except in areas clearly marked for Israel in any future political agreement;[19]

Believe that the future border between Israel and the future state of Palestine should be based on the 1967 borders with mutually agreeable land swaps;

Hold that any future negotiated settlement should include in the State of Israel the Old City of Jerusalem and all Jewish neighborhoods of Jerusalem, with access for all peoples to their holy sites;[20]

Call upon Israel to eschew all collective punishment,[21] including demolition of the homes of terrorists' families;

Call upon Israel to recognize the residency rights of Palestinians who live in the Jerusalem Municipality or any other territory occupied and/or annexed by Israel since June, 1967;

Agree with Israel's President Reuven Rivlin that all citizens of the State of Israel are entitled to full and equal civil, political, economic, and educational rights and privileges.

Oppose any Israeli law that would attenuate the equality of its Arab citizens.

Call upon Israel's leaders to suppress vigorously all extremist and violent actions and provocations that have characterized a segment of Jewish-Israeli society in recent years;

Call on rabbis of all streams to be seekers and pursuers of peace by rejecting teachings which elevate the dignity and rights of Jews over those of non-Jews;[22]

Call upon Palestinian Authority President Mahmoud Abbas and the
Palestinian leadership to end its incitement to violence.[23] Furthermore, we call upon secular and religious leaders among the
Palestinian people to reject their teachings which denigrate the
dignity and rights of Jews;

Encourage and support grassroots programs that bring Israelis and
Palestinians together to understand one another. We support the
many NGO exchanges, businesses and academic friendships that
currently exist between Palestinian and Israelis and urge the recognized governments of Israel and the Palestinian Authority to
strengthen and support those ties as well;

Commend organizations, including IMPJ and MARAM, who confront vicious terrorist attacks on Palestinian lives and property.

Express pride that the Central Conference of American Rabbis is
among those who affirm that Israel is the Jewish homeland and
central to our religious and national life, and who work toward
a stronger, more secure, safer, and ever-more just Israel living in
harmony with its neighbors.

We of the CCAR pray for the peace of Jerusalem: *"May those who love
you find serenity. May there be peace within your ramparts, calm in your
citadels. For the sake of my kin and my friends, I pray for your well-being;
for the sake of the house of the Eternal our God, I seek your good." (Psalm
122:6–8)*

Notes

1. See, for example, the *Columbus Platform*, 1937; CCAR resolution, "Israel,"
   1976; CCAR resolution, "Supporting the State of Israel," 1979; CCAR
   resolution, "Israel," 1980; CCAR resolution, "Support for Israel," 1990;
   the CCAR's "Resolution on Peace in Israel," 2001; the CCAR Statement,
   "Where We Stand on Israel," 2002; and the CCAR resolution, "Engagement with Israel," 2005.

2. Support for Reform institutions in Israel and ARZA is clearly expressed in
   the CCAR resolution, "Support for Israel," 1990; in the CCAR resolution,
   "Religious Freedom in Israel," 1998; in "Resolution on Progressive Judaism
   in the State of Israel," 2002; in the CCAR resolution, "Engagement with
   Israel," 2005; and in "CCAR Resolution Calling Upon the Government of

Israel to Recognize Rabbi Miri Gold and to Cease Discrimination against Non-Orthodox Jews," 2009.

3. Ibid.

4. The CCAR was an early supporter of the Women of the Wall, as evidenced in its resolution, "The Women of the Wall," 1990.

5. The CCAR previously emphasized the importance of visiting Israel. See, for example, "Israel IV," 1987; and "Encouraging Pilgrimage to Israel among Reform Jews," 2005.

6. The CCAR particularly supported URJ (then UAHC) summer programs in Israel in its resolution, "Israel Experiences," 1982.

7. The CCAR noted the importance of Kesher Birthright, the Union for Reform Judaism's Birthright Israel program, in its resolution, "Support for Reform Jewish College Students," 2005.

8. The CCAR has previously called for equality for all Jewish religious streams in Israel, notably in a CCAR resolution, "Religious Pluralism in Israel," 1994; and in a CCAR resolution, "Religious Freedom in Israel," 1998; and in "CCAR Resolution Calling Upon the Government of Israel to Recognize Rabbi Miri Gold and to Cease Discrimination against Non-Orthodox Jews," 2009.

9. "The Women of the Wall," 1990.

10. The CCAR advocated for "full and equal rights to all of Israel's citizens in matters of marriage and divorce," in its resolution, "Non-Orthodox Marriage and Divorce in Israel," 2006.

11. "Reform Movement Response to Iran Deal: Address Important Concerns, Focus on the Day After," 2015. See also the CCAR resolution, "The Threat from Iran," 2016.

12. We would cite in particular Prime Minister Menachem Begin, z"l, who sacrificed the Sinai Peninsula as part of the Camp David Accords that established a peace treaty with Egypt; Prime Minister Yitzchak Rabin, z"l, and former Prime Minister and past President Shimon Peres, who advocated —and, in the case of Peres, continues to advocate—for the Oslo Accords, which established a framework of territorial compromise to achieve two states for two peoples; former Prime Minister Ehud Barak, who agreed to significant territorial compromise in exchange for a proposed final peace agreement with the Palestinians at Camp David in 2002; Prime Minister Ariel Sharon, z"l, who abandoned Israeli control over the Gaza Strip; and former Prime Minister Ehud Olmert, who proposed territorial compromise in exchange for peace; among others. The CCAR supported efforts of this nature, and particular the Oslo process, in "Where We Stand on Israel," 2002.

13. The CCAR has taken this position multiple times in the past. Specifically, the 1980 resolution, "Israel," included these words "[T]he Central Conference of American Rabbis . . . calls upon the Israeli government to freeze the establishing of new settlements in the West Bank (Judea and Samaria) and Gaza Strip." The CCAR "Resolution on Peace in Israel," 2001, called "upon the government of Israel to adopt a policy of neither building nor expanding settlements in the West Bank and Gaza." That position was reaffirmed in the CCAR resolution, "Gaza and the West Bank," 2006.

14. The points, and in many ways, the words, of this paragraph are found in the section "Israel's Right to Self-Defense," in the CCAR's statement, "Where We Stand on Israel," 2002.

15. CCAR resolutions have previously called for the end to violence, for example, in resolutions on "Israel" in 1978 and 1980; and in the CCAR's "Resolution on Peace in Israel," 2001.

16. See "Mutual Recognition" in the CCAR statement, "Where We Stand on Israel," 2002.

17. CCAR resolutions have previously called for such negotiations, for example, in a resolution on "Israel," 1980; and in the CCAR resolution, "Gaza and the West Bank," 2006.

18. Ibid.

19. See footnote 12.

20. With respect to holy sites, see "CCAR Resolution on the Temple Mount," 2015.

21. The CCAR called on Israel to "refrain from acts of collective punishment" in its "Resolution on Peace in Israel," 2001.

22. The CCAR has stressed the equality of Jews and non-Jews in Israel in the past—for example, in "Resolution on Social Justice in Israel," 2001.

23. See footnote 14.

For Further Reading

Aaron, David. "The First Loose Plank: On the Rejection of Reason in the Pittsburgh Principles of 1999." *CCAR Journal* (Fall 2001): 87–116.

Alpher, Yossi. *No End of Conflict*. Lanham, MD: Rowman & Littlefield, 2016.

Arendt, Hannah. *The Jewish Writings*. Edited by Jerome Kohn and Ron H. Feldman. New York: Schocken Books, 2017.

Beinart, Peter. *The Crisis of Zionism*. New York: Times Books, 2012.

Berger, Shalom. "A Year of Study in an Israeli Yeshiva Program: Before and After." Doctoral dissertation, Yeshiva University, January 1997.

Buber, Martin. *A Land of Two Peoples*. New ed. Edited by P. Mendes-Flohr. Chicago: Chicago University Press, 2005.

———. *On Zion: The History of an Idea*. New York: Schocken Books, 1973.

Deutsch, Kenneth L., and Walter Nicgorski. *Leo Strauss: Political Philosopher and Jewish Thinker*. Lanham, MD: Rowman & Littlefield, 1993.

Elad, Gidon. *Light in the Arava? Yahel—Dialogue and a Joint Undertaking between the Kibbutz Movement and the Reform Movement*. Aravah Valley: Tzell HaTamar, 2008.

Ernst, Renan. "What Is a Nation?" Translated by Martin Thom. Chapter 2 in *Nation and Narration*, edited by Homi K. Bhabha, 8–22. London: Routledge, 1882 (1990).

Feingold, Henry L. *American Jewish Political Culture and the Liberal Persuasion*. Syracuse, NY: Syracuse University Press, 2013.

Gellner, Ernest. *Nations and Nationalism*. Ithaca, NY: Cornell University Press, 1983.

Gordon, Adi. *Toward Nationalism's End: An Intellectual Biography of Hans Kohn*. Hanover, NH: Brandeis University Press, 2017.

Gorenberg, Gershom. *The Accidental Empire: Israel and the Birth of the Settlements, 1967–1977*. New York: Henry Holt, 2006.

———. *The Unmaking of Israel*. New York: HarperCollins, 2011.

Hertzberg, Arthur, ed. *The Zionist Idea*. Philadelphia: Jewish Publication Society, 1997; originally published 1959.

Hoffman, Adina. *My Happiness Bears No Relation to Happiness*. New Haven, CT: Yale University Press, 2009.

Hutchinson, John. *The Dynamics of Cultural Nationalism: The Gaelic Revival and the Creation of the Irish Nation State*. London: Allen & Unwin, 1987.

Kaplan, Mordecai Menahem. *Judaism as a Civilization: Toward a Reconstruction of American-Jewish Life*. New York: Schocken Books, 1967.

Kashua, Sayed. *Native Dispatches from an Israeli-Palestinian Life*. New York: Grove Press, 2016.

Khalidi, Rashid. *Palestinian Identity: The Construction of Modern National Consciousness*. New York: Columbia University Press, 2009.

Klein Halevy, Yossi. *Like Dreamers*. New York: HarperCollins, 2013.

Knobel, Peter. "A New Light Upon Zion? The Liturgy of Reform Judaism and Reform Zionism." *CCAR Journal: The Reform Jewish Quarterly* 54, no. 2 (Spring 2007): 69–83.

Kushner, Tony. *Wrestling with Zion: Progressive Jewish-American Responses to the Israeli-Palestinian Conflict*. New York: Grove Press, 2003.

Leibowitz, Yeshayahu. *Yahadut, Am Yehudi, U-Medinat Yisrael*. Jerusalem: Schocken, 1975.

Leibowitz, Yeshayahu, Eliezer Goldman, and Yoram Navon. *Judaism, Human Values, and the Jewish State*. Cambridge, MA: Harvard University Press, 1997.

Liebman, Charles S., and Eliezer Don-Yihya. *Civil Religion in Israel: Traditional Judaism and Political Culture in the Jewish State*. Berkeley: University of California Press, 1983.

Lorberbaum, Menchem. "Making Space for Leviathan: On Hobbes' Political Theology." *Hebraic Political Studies* 2 (2007): 78–100.

Magid, Shaul. *American Post-Judaism: Identity and Renewal in a Postethnic Society.* Religion in North America. Bloomington: Indiana University Press, 2013.

Maimonides, Moses. *The Code of Maimonides.* New Haven, CT: Yale University Press, 1949.

Mendes-Flohr, Paul, and Jehuda Reinharz, eds. *The Jew in the Modern World: A Documentary History.* 3rd ed. Oxford: Oxford University Press, 2010.

Miles, William F. S. *Zion in the Desert: American Jews in Israel's Reform Kibbutzim.* Albany: State University of New York Press, 2008.

Morris, Benny. *Righteous Victims: A History of the Zionist-Arab Conflict, 1881–2001.* New York: Vintage Books, 2001.

Norton, Bonny. *Identity and Language Learning: Extending the Conversation.* Bristol: Multilingual Matters, 2013.

Nusseibeh, Sari. *Once Upon a Country: A Palestinian Life.* New York: Farrar, Straus and Giroux, 2008.

Oz, Amos, and Fania Oz-Salzberger. *Jews and Words.* New Haven, CT: Yale University Press, 2014.

Pianko, Noam. *Zionism & The Roads Not Taken: Rawidowicz, Kaplan, Kohn.* Bloomington: Indiana University Press, 2010.

"Progressive Religious Zionism: An Ongoing Dialogue." *CCAR Journal* (Fall 2011).

Raider, Mark. *The Emergence of American Zionism.* New York: New York University Press, 1998.

Rawidowicz, Simon. *State of Israel, Diaspora, and Jewish Continuity: Essays on the "Ever Dying People."* Hanover, NH: University Press of New England, 1998.

Raz-Krakotzkin, Amnon. *Exil et souveraineté: judaïsme, sionisme et pensée binationale.* Paris: Fabrique éditions, 2007.

Rechnitzer, Haim O. "Haim Guri and Rabbi David Buzaglo: A Theo-Political Meeting Place of Zionist Sabra Poetry and Jewish Liturgy." *Journal for the Study of Sephardic and Mizrahi Jewry* 2, no. 1 (Summer 2008): 37–62.

———. "Judaism and the Idea of the Law: Leo Strauss and Yeshayahu Leibowitz' Philosophical and Ideological Interpretation of

Maimonides." *Hebrew Union College Annual* 79 (2008): 165–91.

———. "Redemptive Theology in the Thought of Yeshayahu Leibowitz." *Israel Studies* 13, no. 3 (Fall 2008): 137–59.

———. "Tell Me What Your Questions Are and I Will Tell You Who You Are: Some Reflections on 'The Proposed Taxonomy for a Twenty-First-Century Theology of Reform Zionism' by S. M. Davids." *CCAR Journal* (Summer 2008): 104–9.

Reinharz, Shulamit, and Mark A. Raider, eds. *American Jewish Women and the Zionist Enterprise.* Waltham, MA: Brandeis University Press, 2005.

Rotenstreich, Nathan. *Zionism: Past and Present.* Albany: State University of New York Press, 2007.

Sarna, Jonathan D. *American Judaism: A History.* New Haven, CT: Yale University Press, 2004.

Sasson, Theodore. *The New American Zionism.* New York: New York University Press, 2014.

Schweid, Eliezer, Hava Tirosh-Samuelson, Aaron W. Hughes, and Leonard Levin. *The Responsibility of Jewish Philosophy.* Library of Contemporary Jewish Philosophy 1. Leiden: Brill 2013.

Segev, Tom. *1967: Israel, the War, and the Year That Transformed the Middle East.* New York: Metropolitan Books, 2007.

Shapira, Anita. *Israel: A History.* Waltham, MA: Brandeis University Press, 2012.

Shavit, Ari. *My Promised Land: The Triumph and Tragedy of Israel.* New York: Spiegel and Grau, 2013.

Staub, Michael E. *Torn as the Roots: The Crisis of Jewish Liberalism in Postwar America.* New York: Columbia University Press, 2002.

Steiner, George. *Our Homeland, the Text.* Saratoga Springs, NY: Skidmore College, 1985.

Strack, Hermann L., and Gunter Stemberger. *Introduction to the Talmud and Midrash.* Minneapolis: Fortress Press, 1992.

Strauss, Leo, and Kenneth Hart Green. *Jewish Philosophy and the Crisis of Modernity: Essays and Lectures in Modern Jewish Thought.* SUNY Series in the Jewish Writings of Leo Strauss. Albany: State University of New York Press, 1997.

Waxman, Dov. *Trouble in the Tribe: The American Jewish Conflict over Israel*. Princeton, NJ: Princeton University Press, 2016.

Wolfe, Alan. *At Home in Exile*. Boston: Beacon Press, 2014.

Contributor Biographies

Rabbi Stanley M. Davids is a Phi Beta Kappa graduate of Case Western Reserve University and was ordained by Hebrew Union College–Jewish Institute of Religion in 1965. Following his service as a chaplain in the U.S. Army, he served as senior rabbi in congregations in Massachusetts, New York, and Georgia before retiring in 2004 as rabbi emeritus of Temple Emanu-El of Atlanta. He was chair of the CCAR Israel Committee, honorary life chair of the Israel Bonds Rabbinic Cabinet, a life member of NFTY, international president of Alpha Epsilon Pi fraternity, and past national president of ARZA, the Association of Reform Zionists of America. Following his *aliyah* in 2004, he served for many years both as a member of the Board of Governors of the Jewish Agency and as a member of the Executive of the World Zionist Organization. He currently is a member of the Board of Overseers of HUC-JIR's Los Angeles campus. Resa and Rabbi Davids have three children and eight grandchildren.

Rabbi Lawrence A. Englander is immediate past chair of ARZENU Olami, the international Reform Zionist organization. In this capacity he also served on the Executive of the Jewish Agency and the Extended Executive of the World Zionist Organization. He is currently a Board member of ARZA Canada. He is rabbi emeritus of Solel Congregation of Mississauga, Ontario, and adjunct rabbi of Temple Sinai in Toronto. He is former editor of the *CCAR Journal: The Reform Jewish Quarterly*.

* * *

Rabbi David Ariel-Joel is a senior rabbi at The Temple in Louisville, Kentucky. He served as executive director for the Israel Movement for Progressive Judaism (the Reform Movement in Israel), rabbi of Har-El Congregation in Jerusalem, director for the Progressive Beit Midrash, and executive director and educational director of

Hamdat, the Association for the Freedom of Science, Religion, and Culture in Israel. A founding member of Kibbutz Lotan, the second Reform kibbutz in Israel, Rabbi Ariel-Joel has dual American and Israeli citizenship. He served in the Israel Defense Forces and in the Israeli army reserves for twenty-three years. He has coedited three books: *Baruch She'assani Isha* (Praised be the One Who Made Me a Woman), about the women in Judaism from biblical times to the present; *The War of Gog and Magog: The Jewish Messianic Idea*; and *Who Is a Jew in Our Times?* He is a graduate of Hebrew Union College–Jewish Institute of Religion in Jerusalem, where he received his MA in Jewish studies and was ordained in 1994. He received an MA in Jewish philosophy from the Hebrew University of Jerusalem in 1993.

Rabbi Charley Baginsky is the director of Strategy and Partnerships for Liberal Judaism, and as part of this role she oversees the Israel Desk for the Alliance of Progressive Judaism. She studied theology, first at Cambridge and then King's College London. She spent several years working in Israel, which included a period at Leo Baeck in Haifa, where she also studied at Haifa University. She was ordained as a rabbi from Leo Baeck College and served as a congregational rabbi for ten years. She has three children, Joshua, Eliana, and Cassia.

Joshua S. Block is CEO and president of The Israel Project (TIP), a non-partisan educational organization that informs press, policymakers and the public about Israel and the Middle East. A foreign policy and political strategist involved in national politics and policymaking for over twenty years, Block got his start on Capitol Hill with Sen. Ted Kennedy, subsequently working on numerous Democratic House, Senate, and Presidential campaigns, and serving as an appointee to the Clinton administration at the U.S. State Department's U.S. Agency for International Development. The *Forward* named Block one of America's fifty most influential Jews, and *Foreign Policy* magazine to its Twitterati 100 list of the most influential foreign policy experts on Twitter (@JoshBlockDC). The proud father of four Reform Jews and son of Rabbi Richard and Susan Block, he and his wife Kim live with their beautiful Jewish babies outside Washington D.C.

Rabbi Danny Burkeman is the senior rabbi at Temple Shir Tikva in Wayland, Massachusetts. Previously he served as the associate rabbi at The Community Synagogue in Port Washington, New York, and The West London Synagogue in England. He has served on the board of the World Union for Progressive Judaism and is a former Vice Chairman of Arzenu, serving as a delegate at three World Zionist Congresses. He is married to Micol and is father to Gabby and Benny.

Max Chaiken is currently studying toward rabbinic ordination at the Hebrew Union College–Jewish Institute of Religion in Los Angeles. He serves as the student rabbi of Congregation Kol Ami in West Hollywood, California, and previously served as the student rabbi at Congregation Etz Chaim in Merced, California. Originally from Teaneck, New Jersey, Max is a proud alumnus of the URJ Camp Harlam and the URJ Kutz Camp. He studied on an Israel gap-year program prior to beginning his BA in economics and public policy at Brown University. He is a passionate songleader and composer and spent several years teaching and working in Jewish communities around Greater Boston.

Rabbi Leah Cohen, DMin, served as the executive director and senior Jewish chaplain at Joseph Slifka Center for Jewish Life at Yale. She has over thirty years of rabbinic and executive management experience. In her current position, she enjoys working with students in the formation of their Jewish identity through programs, counseling, travel, study, worship, and relationship. Rabbi Cohen has served as a congregational rabbi, hospital chaplain, camp rabbi, and police chaplain. Ordained from Hebrew Union College–Jewish Institute of Religion, Cincinnati campus in 2000, she received her DMin from the New York campus in 2015. Prior to her rabbinic career, she worked in corporate healthcare for more than a decade in Asia and the United States. She has a master's degree in international management and a BA in international studies and has lived and traveled extensively abroad. A member of the CCAR Board of Trustees, fellow in the Shalom Hartman Institute Fellowship for Campus Professionals, and participant in the Rabbinic Leadership Program of the Institute of Jewish Spirituality, Rabbi Cohen is a passionate student and teacher of Jewish life.

Rabbi Neal Gold is the director of content and programming for ARZA, the Association of Reform Zionists of America. He was ordained as a rabbi from Hebrew Union College–Jewish Institute of Religion in 1997 and is currently pursuing graduate work in Near Eastern and Jewish studies at Brandeis University. A committed teacher, counselor, and social activist, for over eighteen years he has served congregations in New Jersey and Massachusetts. He was a delegate for ARZENU, the international Reform Jewish movement, at the Thirty-Seventh World Zionist Congress in Jerusalem in October 2016.

Rabbi Lisa D. Grant, PhD is professor of Jewish education at Hebrew Union College–Jewish Institute of Religion. Her research and teaching interests focus on adult Jewish learning, Jewish leadership development, and the place of Israel in American Jewish life. She has written numerous articles, book chapters, and curriculum guides and coauthored (with Ezra Kopelowitz) *Israel Education Matters: A 21st Century Paradigm for Jewish Education* (2012). She has coedited (along with Helena Miller and Alex Pomson) *International Handbook of Jewish Education* (2011) and (with Diane T. Schuster, Meredith Woocher, and Steven M. Cohen) *A Journey of Heart and Mind: Transformative Jewish Learning in Adulthood* (2004). She was ordained by HUC-JIR in 2017.

Dr. Joshua Holo is associate professor of Jewish history and dean of the Jack H. Skirball Campus of the Hebrew Union College–Jewish

Institute of Religion in Los Angeles. He served as director of the Louchheim School of Judaic Studies from 2006 to 2010. Dr. Holo's publications focus on medieval Jews of the Mediterranean, particularly in the Christian realm. His book *Byzantine Jewry in the Mediterranean Economy* was published in 2009.

Rabbi Michael Marmur, PhD is the Jack, Joseph and Morton Mandel Provost of the Hebrew Union College–Jewish Institute of Religion. He is the author of *Abraham Joshua Heschel and the Sources of Wonder* (2016). Originally from England, he has lived in Israel since 1984.

Rabbi Dalia Marx, PhD is a professor of liturgy and midrash at the Jerusalem campus of Hebrew Union College–Jewish Institute of Religion and teaches in various academic institutions in Israel and Europe. Marx, tenth generation in Jerusalem, earned her doctorate at the Hebrew University and her rabbinic ordination at HUC-JIR in Jerusalem and Cincinnati. She is involved in various research projects and is active in promoting liberal Judaism in Israel. Marx writes for academic and popular journals and publications, and has published several books. She is currently serving as the co-editor of the new IMPJ siddur.

Jesse Paikin is a rabbinical student at Hebrew Union College-Jewish Institute of Religion in New York City, where he received his MA in Hebrew literature, and has worked as rabbinic fellow at the New Israel Fund and at the 14th Street Y. He is a graduate of Toronto's York University, where he received a degree in religious studies, philosophy, and theatre. He has also studied at New York University, Yeshivat Hadar, and the National Theatre School of Canada. A 2016 Kevah Teaching Fellow, he has worked as a Jewish educator throughout North America, Europe, and Israel, with particular devotion to European Jewish history and Israel education among adolescents and young adults. Among other things, Jesse is a voracious music listener, a vegetarian, and a runner. He blogs regularly at jessepaikin. wordpress.com.

Rabbi Dr. Haim O. Rechnitzer is associate professor of Modern Jewish Thought at the Hebrew Union College–Jewish Institute of Religion and a poet. He earned his doctorate from the department of Jewish Thought at the Hebrew University of Jerusalem, and his rabbinic ordination from HUC-JIR (Jerusalem). Rechnitzer's research is dedicated to themes of political theology, theological trends in Hebrew poetry, Israeli theology, and Jewish education. In his poetry Rechnitzer explores the manifold manifestations of "Exile" and theological themes such as the possibility of communication with the Divine, sacred time, the Land of Israel, the Garden of Eden, and Second Naïveté. His recent books are *Prophecy and the Perfect Political Order: The Political Theology of Leo Strauss* (Jerusalem, 2012), *Songs of the Third Exile* (Jerusalem, 2014), and *Shibolet (Vortex)* (Jerusalem, 2015).

Liya Rechtman is a member of the Board of Trustees of the Association of Reform Zionists of America (ARZA), the American Zionist Movement, and a member of the All That's Left Collective. A graduate of Amherst College, she is currently a dual-degree candidate for a master's of theological studies at Harvard Divinity School and a master's of law and diplomacy at the Tufts University Fletcher School. In addition to her academic work, she is a freelance journalist and has published pieces in *Lilith*, *Washington Jewish Week*, *JewSchool*, the *Energy Collective*, and the *Interfaith Observer*. Previously, she was a Dorot Fellow, a legislative assistant at the Religious Action Center of Reform Judaism, and the manager of the Coalition on the Environment and Jewish Life.

Eric Rosenstein is a rabbinical and education student at the Hebrew Union College–Jewish Institute of Religion in Los Angeles. He currently serves as an education intern at Leo Baeck Temple in Los Angeles and served Temple Ner Ami in Camarillo, California, as their student rabbi. In addition to his rabbinical studies, Eric is a songleader and has served as a cantorial soloist in his native Los Angeles and in Harrisburg, Pennsylvania. He came to his Zionism during his time lived in Jerusalem during an undergraduate semester abroad, through his rabbinical studies in Israel, and through the enduring friendships with many of the Israeli *sh'lichim* who spent summers at camp. He lives in Los Angeles with his wife and baby daughter.

Rabbi John L. Rosove is senior rabbi of Temple Israel of Hollywood, Los Angeles, since 1988. He was ordained by the Hebrew Union College–Jewish Institute of Religion, New York, in 1979. He serves as the national chair of the Association of Reform Zionists of America (ARZA). He has a seat on the Conference of Presidents of Major American Jewish Organizations, the Board of Governors of the Jewish Agency for Israel, the Vaad HaPoel of the World Zionist Organization, the American Zionist Movement, and the Executive Committee of ARZENU (the international Reform Zionist Organization). Rabbi Rosove was the 2002 recipient of the World Union for Progressive Judaism International Humanitarian Award and has received special commendation from the State of Israel Bonds. In 2013 he was honored by J Street at its Fifth Anniversary Celebration in Los Angeles. He is the author of *Why Judaism Matters: Letters of a Liberal Rabbi to His Children and the Millennial Generation*, to be published in the fall of 2017, and writes a regular blog for the *Los Angeles Jewish Journal*. Rabbi Rosove and his wife, Barbara, are the parents of two sons, Daniel and David.

Rabbi Rachel Sabath Beit-Halachmi, PhD serves the Hebrew Union College–Jewish Institute of Religion as President's Scholar and the National Director of Recruitment and Admissions. Prior to this appointment, Rabbi Sabath served as vice president of the Shalom Hartman Institute in Jerusalem. Ordained at HUC-JIR in New York, Rabbi Sabath also earned a PhD in Jewish philosophy from the Jewish Theological Seminary. Rabbi Sabath wrote a monthly column in *The Jerusalem Post* and writes regularly for *The Times of Israel*, *The Huffington Post*, and other publications. She co-authored two books and published numerous articles including "Radically

Free and Radically Claimed" in *Jewish Theology in Our Time*. Rabbi Sabath also teaches and mentors students of HUC-JIR and speaks throughout North America on leadership, Israel, gender, and theology. She is currently writing a book on the future of Jewish peoplehood.

Rabbi Noa Sattath is the director of the Israel Religious Action Center (IRAC), the social justice arm of the Reform Movement in Israel. She is charged with leading the staff of the organization, developing and implementing social change strategies in the fields of separation of religion and state, women's rights, and the struggle against racism. Prior to her work in IRAC, Rabbi Sattath was the executive director of the Jerusalem Open House, the LGBT community center in Jerusalem. She was also the executive director of MEET a nonprofit organization that uses technology to create a common language between Israeli and Palestinian young leaders. Prior to her work in civil society, she worked as a leader in the Israeli software industry. She is a graduate of the Hebrew University and Gratz College and was ordained by the Hebrew Union College–Jewish Institute of Religion in 2014. She is a member of Congregation Kol Haneshama in Jerusalem.

Yoav Schaefer is a recent graduate of Harvard University, where he studied political and social theory and modern European intellectual history. His undergraduate thesis, which explored the political thought of several prominent Weimar Jewish intellectuals, was awarded the Hoopes Prize for outstanding scholarly work and research. Yoav currently studies Jewish philosophy at Tel Aviv University and is a 2017–2018 Dorot Fellow.

Professor Alon Tal, PhD is presently chair of the Department of Public Policy at Tel Aviv University. Dr. Tal was the founding director of Adam Teva V'din, the Israel Union for Environmental Defense, from 1990 to 1997, a leading public interest law group. Subsequently, he was chairman of Life and Environment, an umbrella group for eighty environmental organizations in Israel, from 1998 to 2003. Dr. Tal also founded the Arava Institute for Environmental Studies, a graduate studies center for Israeli, Jordanian, and Palestinian students.

Rabbi David Z. Vaisberg is spiritual leader of Temple Emanu-El in Edison, New Jersey. He was ordained from Hebrew Union College–Jewish Institute of Religion's New York campus in 2012 as a Mandel Fellow, with an additional MA in religious education. He has an Honours BA in psychology from York University in Toronto, Ontario. He edited *Thank You My Teacher, Thank You My Friend: Festschrift in Honour of Rabbi Lawrence A. Englander* (2014) and wrote *A Study of Sefer Yezirah and Its Commentators* (2012) and *Keep It Together, Keep It Real: A Curriculum of Holistic Healthy Living for Teenage Jews* (2010).

Rabbi Joshua Weinberg has been president of ARZA, the Association of Reform Zionists of America, since 2013. After receiving his BA from the University of Wisconsin, engaging in the NFTY-EIE program, and studying at the Hebrew University, Rabbi Weinberg came to Israel on *aliyah* in 2003. He began teaching as a Jewish history faculty member on the EIE program. He subsequently served in the Israel Defense Forces (IDF) spokesperson's unit and studied for an MA at the Hebrew University in Jewish education. He was ordained from the Hebrew Union College–Jewish Institute of Religion Israeli Rabbinic Program in Jerusalem and is currently living in New York. Rabbi Weinberg has taught and lectured widely throughout Israel, the United States, and Europe. He currently serves as a mentor for the iCenter's iFellows mentoring program. He is also a reserve officer in the IDF spokesperson's unit and has hiked the Israel-trail. He is passionate about Israel and reimagining Zionism, and his mission is to strengthen the connection between the Reform Movement and the Jewish state. He is married to Mara Sheftel Getz, and they have three daughters, Noa, Ella, and Mia.